Gustavus Hines

Oregon and its Institutions

Comprising a full history of the Willamette University, the first established on the

Pacific Coast

Gustavus Hines

Oregon and its Institutions
Comprising a full history of the Willamette University, the first established on the Pacific Coast

ISBN/EAN: 9783337018696

Printed in Europe, USA, Canada, Australia, Japan

OREGON AND ITS INSTITUTIONS;

COMPRISING A

Full History of the Willamette University,

THE FIRST ESTABLISHED ON THE PACIFIC COAST.

By Rev. GUSTAVUS HINES.

WITH FOUR ENGRAVINGS.

REV. GUSTAVUS HINES.

INTRODUCTION.

THE *home* of the author of the following pages is within
the limits of the country which he has attempted to
describe. A native of the great state of New York, a
visitor to every continent on the globe, an admirer of
ten thousand beautiful localities in the numerous countries which have come under his observation, he would
not exchange his humble sunset *home* in the delightful
valley of the Willamette River, near the blue and placid
waters of the great Pacific Ocean, either for mansions
of wealth in the crowded city, or for any other spot
which he has ever seen upon the surface of this green
earth.

Twenty-eight years ago he became a voluntary exile
to that far-off land. From that period he has felt that
he had an identity of interests with the country of his
adoption, and for twenty-one years he has lived and
labored and traveled within its bounds, and claims to
be thoroughly posted upon all those subjects to which,
with all due deference, he would invite the attention of
the reading public.

Conscious of his want of power to array his work
in that fascinating drapery necessary to charm the
reader at once into an unqualified approval, he would
endeavor to conciliate him into a purpose to peruse the

volume by assuring him that, in whatever it may be deficient as to ornate qualities, its truthfulness and reliability are not to be called in question.

In the excitement of the times the public, especially in the Eastern and Middle States, seem almost to have lost sight of Oregon, and one of the primary objects which the author has in view is again to awaken an interest in the community generally, and in the Christian Churches particularly, in relation to that distant and feeble member of this great family of states.

The history of the Willamette University, which has been traced in this volume, cannot fail deeply to enlist the reader's sympathies in behalf of an infant people struggling in their weakness and poverty to lay the foundations of a Christian civilization in the future Pacific empire; and the author hopes the reader will come to the conclusion that an institution commenced and carried forward under the embarrassments that have pressed upon this one, is worthy of all confidence, and should be sustained by every necessary means.

And now, reader, you need just the information which this book can give you with regard to Oregon and Washington Territory. Read it; though an unpretending book, the instructions conveyed will be more valuable than volumes of fiction.

GUSTAVUS HINES.

NEW YORK, *January* 10, 1868.

CONTENTS.

Illustrations.

OREGON AND ITS INSTITUTIONS.

CHAPTER I.

GENERAL DESCRIPTION OF THE COUNTRY.

THE State of Oregon and Washington Territory are mainly embraced within that portion of the great western slope of the North American Continent drained and watered by the Columbia River and its numerous tributaries. There are, however, in the northern part of Washington Territory a few small rivers, watering valleys more or less extensive, which take their rise in the cascade range of mountains, and empty directly into the Pacific Ocean; and there are also a few valleys, watered by independent rivers, in the southern part of the State of Oregon; but by far the greater part of both Oregon and Washington Territory is comprehended in the great valley of the Columbia.

In the general description of this country, therefore, it will be necessary to embrace both of these political divisions in the same account. Oregon and Washington Territory comprehend a vast extent of country, and lie within the following boundary. Commencing at the northwest corner of said territory, consider the north line as extending along the center of the Strait of Juan de Fuca eastward, the distance of one hundred and twenty-five miles; thence northward till it strikes the forty-ninth parallel of north latitude; thence due east along said parallel the distance of five hundred and fifty miles, dividing Washington Territory from British Columbia, to the summit of the Rocky Mountains; and on the east, the line extends along the summit of the Rocky Mountains from the forty-ninth to the forty-second degree of north latitude; and on the south, the line runs along on the forty-second parallel, and near the summit of the Sisku Mountains, and separating Oregon from California, to the Pacific Ocean; and on the west, the Pacific Ocean is the boundary from Cape Mendocino northward, to the mouth of the Strait of Juan de Fuca, the place of beginning. These limits embrace Idaho, the "gem of the mountains," which has been taken off from the southeastern part of what was at first Washington Territory, and lies directly east of the state of Oregon.

The northern line, separating this country from British Columbia is a very unnatural one, and greatly to the disadvantage of the United States. Any one in casting his eye over a correct map of the country west of the Rocky Mountains will discover at one glance that a much more appropriate division than the one which has been established between the two countries would have been a line extending from Puget's Sound northeastwardly along the summit of the high lands which separate the waters of the Columbia River from those of Frazer's River to the Rocky Mountains, so as to embrace in Oregon and Washington Territory all the country drained by the Columbia River. This would have given a natural boundary to the country on all sides, while the forty-ninth parallel is a very unnatural one, because it cuts the great valley of the Columbia, leaving the upper part of the valley in the British dominions, and the lower part in the United States, thus putting asunder that which the God of nature has joined together.

The extent of the area embraced in the boundary which we have traced will measure four hundred thousand square miles: sufficient for a mighty empire. It will be perceived that we do not take into consideration the magnificent state of California, which alone contains one hundred and sixty thousand square miles, our object being simply a clear and reliable description of that portion of our vast sunset domains lying north of California and south of British Columbia. This country has six hundred and fifty miles of coast on the Pacific Ocean, the Strait of Juan de Fuca, and Puget's Sound.

The coast itself deserves particular notice. The shores of the Strait of Fuca are mainly composed of beaches of sand and stones overhung by sandy and rocky cliffs; and from these the land ascends gradually to the foot of the mountains, which rise abruptly to a great height within a few miles of the ocean. The shores along the Pacific are nearly straight from north to south, varying but a few degrees; but in other respects, characterized by great variety. In some places the coast is abrupt, and iron-bound ; in others, it is composed of low sand beaches, which, from appearances, seem to have been widening, either by an accumulation of sand for untold ages, or, according to another theory, by the gradual receding of the ocean from the shore. In many places, along this extended coast, this accumulation of sand has resulted in the formation of undulating plains, which extend back some miles from the ocean, and finally become covered with a dense growth of various grasses, weeds, and shrubbery. A particular description of every part of the coast possessing these characteristics would extend these remarks to an undue length; and, therefore, as an illustration of this peculiarity of the Pacific coast, attention is invited to a somewhat minute account of the Clatsop Plains.

These plains lie on the south side of the mouth of the Columbia River, back of that point of land known by the name of Cape Adams. They constitute that low tract of country which lies in the form of a triangle, one of whose sides is washed by the waves of the Pacific, and the other by those of Youngs' Bay; while its base rests against the range of mountains extending back from Tilamook Head, and its point, or apex, is washed by the south channel of the Columbia River. The height of this triangle, or the distance from Cape Adams back to the mountains, is about twenty-five miles, while the mean width is probably not more than four miles. The plains themselves, or that portion of this triangle not covered with timber, is about twenty miles long, and from one to two and a half broad, the whole tract containing about seventy or eighty square miles. These plains lie directly on, and open beautifully to, the Pacific Ocean, and command a fine view of all the ships that pass over the bar of the Columbia. The beautiful sand beach, extending their entire length, forms at low water a firm and commodious road. Between these open plains and Youngs' Bay is a tract of timbered land, comprising about twice as much as the plains, but similar in every other respect, except the dense forest of fir, spruce, pine, cedar, hemlock, and alder, by which it is shaded. It is only necessary for one to walk across the isthmus from Youngs' Bay to the Pacific, to be convinced that this entire tract, and all others of a similar character on the coast, have been formed by the vast quantities of sands and vegetable substances which have been conveyed from time immemorial by the Columbia River to the ocean, and deposited by the ceaseless action of the tide. The evidences of this are, first, the fact that the soil of the plains is of the same alluvial character that appears on the banks of the river above. Secondly, from the several ridges or undulations, which curve precisely with the shores of the ocean, and all of which appear to have successively formed the boundary of the great deep. And, thirdly, from the fact that shells and other marine substances are found deeply embedded in the sands, thus deposited in a state of perfect petrifaction. Indeed, there is little doubt but that all this tract of land, which now lies but a few feet above the level of the ocean, was once entirely submerged, and by the causes referred to has been redeemed from the ocean bed, and constituted a delightful place for the residence of man.

The foundation of the soil of these plains is sand, and in many places this sand is bare; but even here, where the winds admit of vegetation taking root, its growth shows clearly that this sand is far from being destitute of vegetative properties. Generally, however, the surface of this land is composed of a black mold, which is from six to ten inches deep, and which, doubtless, has been formed by the constant decay of various kinds of vegetation, which here grow in abundance. This black mold, with a portion of the sand beneath, forms a rich and productive soil, which, from its proximity to the ocean, and perhaps from the nature of the soil itself, is not so well adapted to wheat, but produces peas, oats, potatoes, turnips, and, indeed, all kinds of vegetables in great abundance. In connection with these dry plains are extensive tracts of tide land, which are covered with an immense growth of grass and at low water are accessible to stock, so that cattle, horses, and hogs thrive in this region as well as in any part of the country.

Along the extended coast of this country there are many scores, and it would not be varying far from the truth to say hundreds, of miles of land similar in nature to the Clatsop Plains above described. On the weather beach north of the mouth of the Columbia, in Washington Territory, and on the Oregon coast at the mouth of Tilamook, Salmon River, Alsea, Silets, Umpqua, Coose, and Coquille Rivers, and at various other points, are to be found tracts of the same kind of land extending back from the shore from one to perhaps five miles, in some places bare of timber, and covered with grass and sallal bushes, and in others with an immense growth of the forest trees which characterize the Pacific coast. There are also many miles of coast both in Washington Territory and Oregon which are rock bound, where the mountains extend to the water's edge, and with their overhanging cliffs frown down upon the ever rolling surges of the Pacific a bold defiance.

There are other portions of this coast different from any that we have described. The land rises above the alluvial deposits already mentioned, and extends back from the ocean in the form of plains, level or inclined, and covered with magnificent forests of fir, spruce, cedar, and hemlock, and varying in width from one to many miles. This portion of the country is considered valuable at present, mostly on account of its lumbering facilities; but the time will come, doubtless, when the timber will be consumed, and the land, now so wild and forbidding, will be cultivated, and teem with a settled population. The appearance of the coast in approaching it from the ocean is indeed rough and forbidding, but on traversing it from Puget's Sound to Cape Mendocino one becomes impressed from personal observation with the facilities which it offers for extended settlements and improvements, and its natural commercial advantages. The harbors or places of refuge for vessels along the coast of Oregon and Washington Territory are not very numerous, and, if we except a few, are not of the first quality. Puget's Sound, with its numerous arms and inlets stretching far inland, constitutes one of the finest harbors in the known world, and it is sufficiently commodious to accommodate all the navies in existence. There is nothing to bar the way of vessels of the largest class to the safest possible anchorages anywhere in this most beautiful body of water that can be found in any land. At some future day, when railroads shall have been constructed everywhere, Puget's Sound will doubtless constitute the port of entry for the northwest coast. At present, however, the most important harbor is that formed by the Columbia River, as it forms the grand entrepot to the most valuable portions of the State of Oregon, as also to much of Washington Territory. This harbor, though difficult of access in the winter season, when the prevailing winds on the coast are from the south and east, may at other seasons be safely entered by vessels drawing not more than eighteen feet. The mouth of this harbor is blockaded by a sand bar, which renders the navigation difficult and dangerous. The channel across this bar, which was formerly used, took a sweep around close under Cape Disappointment, and thence in a southerly direction about three miles, where it united with a south channel, and thus the two channels becoming one, their course across the last and most formidable bar of the Columbia, was southwest by west. At present, however, the channel runs not far from Cape Adams in a southwest direction, the old north channel being filled up and entirely forsaken.

From Cape Adams, on the south of the mouth of the Columbia, and from the shore around and a little to the west of Cape Disappointment on the north side, are two immense sand bars, which, converging toward each other, meet at the distance of about four miles from each cape, and form that fearful obstacle to the navigation of these waters, the bar of the Columbia. The channel across this bar is five fathoms deep, and a half of a mile wide. When the wind is strong from the south and west, as it generally is in the winter season, the waves of the Pacific Ocean and the rushing torrents of the Columbia River meet upon this with the most terrific violence, producing a line of breakers often extending from one cape to the other, and calculated, from their frightful appearance, to appall even the heart of the storm-beaten sailor. Formerly vessels were often detained at this bar for many days together to wait for an opportunity to cross; but now, by the aid of steam-tugs and skillful pilots, the bar is navigated without much detention, and with very little danger.

While describing the harbors along the coast it will be proper to mention a number of others of less note, some of which are beginning to attract attention. Bulfinch's Harbor, discovered by Captain Robert Gray, of Boston, in 1792, is situated forty miles north of the mouth of the Columbia, and by some improvements may be constituted a safe anchorage. Port Discovery, situated near the southeast angle of the Strait of Fuca, is pronounced perfectly safe, and convenient for ships of any size. It is defended from the violence of the ocean storm by Protection Island. Tilamook Bay, some fifty miles south of Cape Adams, is accessible to small craft, and forms an entrepot to a delightful and fertile little valley, which opens beautifully to the Pacific Ocean. At the mouth of the Umpqua River, one hundred miles south of Tilamook Bay, there is a tolerable harbor for small craft, and the channel across the bar will admit of the entrance of vessels drawing eight or ten feet.

The Bay of Yaquina, midway between Tilamook and Umpqua, is now being visited by small vessels, and something of a trade has already been established between it and other portions of the coast. It is easy of access, and will probably one day constitute the port of entry for Benton County, and perhaps some other portions of the Willamette Valley. It is attracting considerable attention, and already improving settlements are springing up on and near the shores of the bay.

Twenty miles south of the Umpqua River you come to Coose Bay, which constitutes a fine harbor for vessels which do not require more than ten or twelve feet of water. This bay is a most beautiful body of water, and extends up into the country forty or fifty miles; and on its shores are already established several extensive lumber manufactories, and quite a trade is carried on between it and San Francisco. This bay is important for various reasons. It not only affords facilities for the exportation of untold quantities of the finest lumber, but is also the channel of entrance to an extensive country watered by the Coose and Coquille rivers and their tributaries, which is destined in the future to contain a very heavy population.

2

CHAPTER II.

THE CAPES AND COAST RANGE OF MOUNTAINS.

THERE are but few capes along this extended coast, and none that project far into the ocean. The principal are Cape Blanco, Cape Hancock, Cape Mendocino, Cape Adams, and Cape Flattery. Cape Blanco is a high point of land extending into the ocean between the Rogue and Umpqua Rivers, and nearly under the forty-third parallel of north latitude. Cape Adams is a low sandy point, the terminus of Clatsop Plains, and on the south side of the mouth of the Columbia River. Cape Hancock is a high point of land on the north side of the Columbia, and, though three miles inside of the dreaded bar of that river, holds a very prominent place on all our maps and charts, as from its peculiar location, and the appearance of the majestic fir trees which adorn its summit, but more especially from the fact that every night from its rounded top

> "The blaze of the lighthouse looks lovely ashore,
> Like a star in the midst of the ocean,"

it forms an unerring guide to the storm-beaten sailor who is desirous of seeking shelter in the quiet and peaceful waters of Baker's Bay. Cape Flattery is a high point of land marking the terminus of Washington Territory on the south side of the mouth of the Strait of Juan de Fuca. Though there are other points along the coast called capes, these are all that are worthy of particular mention.

There are no islands of importance along this coast, if you except those situated in the Strait of Fuca and Puget's Sound. Of those in this region Whidby's Island is by far the most valuable. This island forms a county in Washington Territory, and contains a population of four hundred souls. It is beautiful and fertile, and one of the most delightful and healthy localities imaginable.

Having traced the boundary, and given the dimensions, and described to some extent the character of the immediate coast of this magnificent country, we now proceed to examine it in its more general character. The first thing to which attention is directed is its remarkable topography. A just description of the surface of this country—one to the life—so that a person never having been in the country would be able to form a correct idea of it from reading, would probably be impossible; an approximation toward the reality is all that we propose to furnish. The face of this country is indeed most wonderfully diversified; and presents to the eye of the lover of nature every variety of scenery, from the most awfully grand and sublime to the most beautiful and picturesque in nature. Almost everything in relation to the country is upon a grand scale. The mountains are grand, the valleys are grand, the forests are grand, the rivers are grand, and the hills are little mountains.

In Washington Territory, extending back from Puget's Sound for many miles, the country is level and beautiful, a considerable portion of it prairie land, and the remainder covered with magnificent forests; but on approaching the coast on a vessel at the mouth of the Columbia River ridges of high lands appear on either hand as far as the eye can reach, and the more elevated points serve as land-marks to guide the mariner into a haven of safety. These ridges, which constitute the first land which rises above the surface of the water to one approach-ing the coast from sea, are parts of that range of mountains known as the Coast Range. This range of mountains extends from near Cape Flattery, in Washington Territory, all along the coast to the Columbia River, and thence the whole extent of the State of Oregon to the line of California. It is pierced by all the rivers that flow directly into the Pacific, and hence the outlines of the range appear very broken. At points the waves of the Pacific Ocean dash impotently against their rocky base; but generally along the coast they commence their grad-ual rise from one to five miles from the shore, and continue to rise in the same manner until they attain their highest elevation, which is from four to six thousand feet. They cover a surface from the Pacific back into the interior of from thirty to forty miles in width. A great portion of this extent, however, is comprised in the numerous valleys and depressions in the mountains, more or less extensive, and through which meander the limped brook and rivulet, where the deer and the elk slake their thirst, and in whose waters in their season glisten the silvery sides of the rich and luscious salmon. It will be seen by a slight arithmetical calculation that this mountain range comprehends about fifteen or twenty thousand square miles; but it must not be supposed that this vast extent of country, larger than some of the states of our Union, is a barren waste, for really, in the valleys and on the mountain sides, and even upon the tops of the highest mountains, the soil is good. Some of the higher elevations in this range are worthy of particular note.

The most remarkable in the vicinity of the Columbia River is one called by the Indians Swallalahoost, concerning which they have a singular tradition. One of their great and mighty chiefs a long time ago. according to the tradition, after having accomplished the most wonderful exploits in behalf of his people, was finally killed by his enemies; but after death he assumed the form of a monstrous eagle, and, taking wing, flew to the top of this mountain, and there became the creator of the lightning and the thunder. From this tradition, as well as from the appearance of the mountain, it is supposed by some that it might probably have once been an active volcano. Commodore Wilkes, on his exploring visit to the country in 1842, gave it the name of " Saddle Mountain," from the resemblance of its top to the shape of a saddle.

Some ten miles to the southwest of the city of Corvallis, so named from the fact that it occupies the center, or heart of the valley, rises the rounded summit of the most graceful and beautiful mountain belonging to the Coast Range, and known by the name of "Mary's Peak." A very trifling circumstance gave name to this mountain.

There is a small river which empties into the Willamette River near the city of Corvallis. This river in an early day had to be forded by travelers in passing through the country. It happened that in connection with one of the earliest parties that traveled through to California was an Indian woman by the name of Mary, who was the wife of a white man. When the company reached this river, Mary was riding a very stuborn and willful mule, which she found it quite difficult to manage. The mule, it seems, was very unwilling to go into the stream; but at length, by whipping and scolding, and belaboring in various ways, he became excited, and rushed into the stream with great violence, where the water was so deep that donkey, Mary, and all went under, and had to strive hard for life. After struggling some time in the water, poor Mary and her mule were brought safe to shore. Subsequently, when the company had occasion to refer to this locality from this catastrophe, they invariably called the river "Mary's River," and this name was soon adopted throughout the whole country. Now Mary's River takes its rise in the Coast Range of mountains, and some of its principal branches are from the reservoirs of Mary's Peak. Thus the name of the river issuing from this mountain was very naturally transferred to the mountain itself. Mary's Peak is perhaps the highest point in the Coast Range, and overlooks a vast extent of country; and the writer that will attempt to portray the scenery that presents itself to the astonished vision of one standing upon its summit has more confidence in his powers of delineation than the author of this sketch has in his own. The reader who has not the privilege of visiting the bald top of this beautiful mountain, and gaze upon the scenery for himself, must be satisfied to know that it absolutely beggars description. The summit of this mountain is becoming quite a resort for pleasure seekers, and admirers of the romantic and sublime in nature, and there is a tolerable bridle path to it. On the top, inclining a little to the south and east, is a section of a mile square or more of excellent prairie land, covered late in the season with a luxuriant growth of grass. Snow remains upon the summit generally until the middle of June, and it is often an excellent place to manufacture ice-cream on the Fourth of July. Immediately on the disappearance of the snow the summit assumes a beautiful green; but whether white-capped, or crowned with verdure, it ever presents itself as an object of interest to every lover of fine scenery. The cultivable character of a great portion of the land of this mountain region, in connection with the fact that great portions of the country are covered with an immense growth of excellent timber, would be of itself sufficient to stamp it with great value; but discoveries have been made recently which show clearly that vast mineral treasures also lie embedded in the midst of these mountains.

For some years past gold has been found in paying

quantities in various parts of this range, especially on the Coquille, and on the lower part, and at the mouth of Rogue River. This has led many to suppose, with good reason, that it in all probability will be found in many other parts of the range. Besides this, silver, copper, iron, and coal have been found, most of them in considerable quantities. Coal especially has been discovered of late in the vicinity of Coose Bay in inexhaustible quantities, and mining is already carried on in the coal beds with considerable success. Indeed, there can be no question that the Coast Range of mountains, which has hitherto been considered as a great objection to our country, will, when properly understood and developed, and its eligible parts shall be occupied, as doubtless they will be, by an industrious population, become a source of immense wealth to the different states with which they are connected, and, perhaps, render them even more valuable than they would be if the mountains were not there.

CHAPTER III.

THE LOWER VALLEYS AND THE CASCADE MOUNTAINS.

HAVING left the coast, and passed over this range of mountains, you descend on the north side of the Columbia into the valley of the Cowilitz, and on the south into that of the Willamette River; and in the southern part of the state of Oregon, you come down into the valleys watered by the Umpqua and Rogue Rivers and their numerous tributaries.

The Cowilitz valley forms an important part of the agricultural portion of Washington Territory. It is about fifty miles long, and varies in breadth from ten to twenty miles. It is watered by a river of the same name, which flows down from one of the magnificent glaciers of the Cascade Range, known as St. Helen's. The river discharges itself into the Columbia some sixty miles above the mouth of that stream. This valley is one of the oldest settled valleys on the Pacific coast, attracting at an early day, by its great beauty and fertility, the attention of the members of the Hudson's Bay Company.

The Chehalis River, which discharges its waters into the Pacific Ocean through Shoal Water Bay, runs through another delightful portion of Washington Territory, fertilizing a valley of many miles in length. It is already occupied by an industrious and thriving population.

The valley of White River, in the northern part of the Territory, is also an interesting and valuable locality. Besides these there are also many other valleys and plains in various parts of the Territory, which together render this portion of the Pacific coast not only beautiful and interesting, but valuable as a place of settlement.

The Willamette Valley, in the state of Oregon, is by far the most extensive and important valley on the northwest Pacific coast. This valley lies between the Coast Range of mountains on the west, and the Cascade Range on the east. On the south it is separated from the Umpqua Valley by the Callapooia Mountains, and northward it extends to the Columbia River. In round numbers it is one hundred and fifty miles long, and fifty broad. This boundary embraces the foot hills extending down from the mountains on either side of the valley, and the small valleys watered by the numerous tributaries of the main river. This calculation, which is a careful one, gives the valley seven thousand five hundred square miles. This, reduced to acres, would show that the Willamette Valley contains four million eight hundred thousand acres of land. Suppose that five acres of land were sufficient to support one person, the Willamette Valley, at that rate alone, would support a population of one million of people. But, to a correct understanding of the valley, especially to those who have never been delighted with surveying its unrivaled scenery, it will be necessary to give it a more particular description.. The Willamette River, by which, with its numerous tributaries, the valley is watered, takes its rise in two ranges of mountains, the Coast Range on the west, and Cascade Range on the east side of the valley, and after meandering the distance of two hundred miles or more from its source, its main course being nearly due north, and reaching to within three miles of the Columbia River, it then divides into two branches, the upper branch entering the Columbia six miles below the city of Vancouver, and ninety miles from the mouth of that river, and the lower branch, which is the Multnomah of Lewis and Clark, eighteen miles further down. As the lower branch takes quite a swing inland, there is quite an island between the branches, formerly called Wapatoo, from an edible root found growing in abundance upon it. This island is about five miles broad and twenty long, and of great fertility. It is now called "Sauvies' Island." And now, commencing at the northern extremity on the Columbia River, we will take a more particular survey of the Willamette Valley, and as we advance up the river we will note everything of interest in relation to the stream itself, and the country through which it flows, so that the reader shall be able to form a correct idea of this most desirable portion of the countries washed by the Pacific Ocean.

The waters of the Willamette flow in about equal proportions into the Columbia River through the two channels already mentioned, and both channels will admit of the passage of steamboats of a large size. At the confluence of the lower channel with the Columbia, on the left hand shore, and commanding a fine view of both rivers, stands the town of Saint Helens. This town occupies a beautiful locality, on an elevated plain above all danger from inundation, and in the future developments of the country is destined to take a leading position among the rival towns of the state. The plains, at the lower end of which stands St. Helens, extends some ten miles up the Multnomah branch of the Willamette, and vary in width from one to four miles. They are called the Scappoose Plains, and they are separated from the Tuality Plains by an elevated spur of the Coast Range called the Scappoose Mountains, which are twelve miles across, and over which there is now a good mountain road.

On the opposite side of this branch lies Wapato Island, already mentioned, most of which is low land, and subject to overflows by the Columbia River. It is quite densely populated, as there are many points of land so high that it is thought safe to erect dwellings upon them.

Having ascended the Multnomah branch twenty miles, we are now at the point where the river divides, and within three miles of the mouth of the upper branch. Here, on the eastern side of the Willamette, and extending to the Columbia, the land is low, and subject to annual overflows. From the amazing fertility of this land, and the abundance of grass which grows after the overflow passes away, and continues fresh during the rest of the year, even after many other portions of the country are literally dried up, it is considered as possessing equal value with many other kinds which are sought after with much more avidity. On leaving the bottom lands in our progress up the river on the eastern side we come to a more elevated tract of a very different quality. It rises to some hundred feet, more or less, above the waters of the river, and then extends off in a somewhat level plain, the distance of twelve or fifteen miles, to another river known as Quicksand, or Sandy, which empties also into the Columbia. This tract, which lies on the opposite side of the river from the city of Portland, and extends southward ten miles to the Clackamas, and eastward to the Cascade Mountains, comprehends an excellent variety of soil, but it is mainly covered with a heavy fir and cedar forest. Powell's Valley, which is a very fertile depression, is situated in this tract. It is variegated with elevations, some of which pious people have honored with distinguished names. Here is Mount Zion, and here also is Mount Pisgah.

On the west bank of the Willamette River, and thirty miles from the lower mouth, and twelve from the upper mouth of the river, is the city of Portland, the present commercial emporium of the state of Oregon. This city will be described particularly in connection with the counties. The bottom upon which the city is located is narrow, it being but one mile from the water's edge to the foot of the range of hills lying back of the city. These hills continue for a few miles to the west of the city, and then settling away in gentle undulations, finally lower down into what are called the Tuality Plains. This region between Portland and the plains, though covered with heavy timber, is found by cultivation to be rich and productive.

Eight miles above the city of Portland, on the same side of the river, is the little town called Oswego, which has been struggling for notoriety in various ways, and which seems likely now to realize its wishes, in the fact that it has, on account of the discovery of rich iron ore in the vicinity, become the locality of the " Oregon Iron Works." These works, which are owned by some of the wealthiest men in the state, have recently been put in operation, and are capable of turning out twelve tons of iron per day. The ore used is taken from the hills from one quarter of a mile to two miles distant from the works, and yields from fifty-five to ninety per cent. of iron. The company has in its employment from eighty to one hundred men as miners, coal-burners, heavers, teamsters, and artisans at the works. The iron produced is said by competent judges to be equal in quality to any made in any part of the United States. It is very soft and fine in grain, and, it is said, might be worked off into castings for machinery as run from the furnace. This establishment is very properly regarded as an important adjunct to the wealth of the country, and especially to this particular locality.

Passing up the river from Oswego four miles, we

reach a point opposite Oregon City, where once stood a rival city by the name of Linn. The rocks, however, upon which Linn was built were too low for the safety of the city, and consequently have been swept clean by the swelling floods of the Willamette River.

Two miles above this we reach the Tuality River, which flows into the Willamette from the west. This river rises in the Coast Range of mountains in numerous streamlets which water the fertile and extended plains which, after the name of the river, are called the Tuality Plains. These streamlets, flowing into each other twenty miles from the Willamette, constitute a fine little river of great importance to this portion of the country, as it can easily be made navigable for boats far into the plains, while the branches above the junction thirty and forty miles from the Willamette River may be advantageously used for the purpose of driving different kinds of machinery. The Tuality Plains, from their importance, demand a more particular notice. They exist in a circular form, somewhat irregular on the rim of the circle; the diameter of the circle, embracing the flat timbered lands around the borders, being about twenty-five miles. From the top of one of the elevations commanding a view of these plains they present the appearance of a vast natural amphitheater, whose walls are mountains, and whose dome is the azure blue. These plains are beautiful and fertile; in some places undulating, in others level. This area embraces one of the most thickly settled portions of the Willamette Valley. It comprises in beautiful proportions both prairie and wood land, and from its advantageous position, extending as it does to within a few miles of the Willamette River, and connected with Portland by good roads, constitutes one of the most valuable portions of the country.

We will now return to the eastern side of the Willamette, and take some observations there. Twenty-four miles above the upper mouth of the Willamette, and twelve above Portland, comes dancing down the rocks from the eastward the Clackamas River. This river rises in the Cascade Mountains, its principal waters being supplied by the reservoirs of Mount Hood. It passes through a country variegated by hills and valleys, plains and rising grounds. Portions of the country watered by this stream are superior as to richness of soil, and other portions not so good. The river runs the distance of some seventy-five miles from its source to where it mingles its waters with those of the Willamette. Two miles above this river, near the falls of the Willamette, we reach a very pleasantly located town known as Oregon City. At this place the Willamette River rushes over a precipice of rocks thirty feet perpendicular. This is a most beautiful cataract, and the hydraulic privileges which it affords are almost boundless. A woolen factory built of brick, presenting a noble and most substantial appearance, running six sets of machinery, and employing one hundred and fifty hands; a paper mill, a foundery, and extensive flouring mills, together with other manufacturing establishments, have already given to this city the soubriquet of the " Lowell of Oregon."

Continuing up the river on the eastern bank the distance of ten miles above Oregon City, we come to the Molalla and Pudding rivers, which unite their waters just before flowing into the Willamette. These rivers also rise in the Cascade Mountains. They both water beautiful and extensive plains in their serpentine course to the Willamette. Fifteen miles above the Pudding River, on the western shore of the Willamette, we come to Yamhill River, which rises in the Coast Range of mountains, and after meandering for more than fifty miles in a northeastwardly direction, through one of the most beautiful and fertile portions of the valley, collecting together the numerous tributaries which water the extended plains through which they flow, it rushes down a ledge of rocks a few feet, forming a beautiful cascade, and then hastens to mingle its waters with the main river of the valley.

Again moving camp, and continuing up the valley, and passing a number of small branches on each side, we at length reach a point twenty-two miles above the Yamhill, and seventy miles by water from the Columbia River, where the city of Salem, the capital of the state of Oregon, is located. Here a small stream, which is called Mill Creek, flows into the Willamette in two channels, one mile apart. Between and extending beyond these two branches of Mill Creek, is the site of the city of Salem, a description of which will be found in connection with

Marion County. The valley at this point embracing the foot hills, is about sixty miles wide, and the river is in the center. Westward from Salem, on the opposite side of the river, is a very beautiful and fertile range of prairie hills, rendered more attractive by the groves of oak and fir with which their brows are adorned. These, commencing near the river, extend for several miles, and then lower away into a beautiful valley beyond; passing over which we find ourselves in a hilly, undulating country, which extends several miles further before we reach the unsettled slopes of the Coast Range, which tower up in the background of the picture, and cast their shadows against the western sky. Southward of Salem, and on the same side of the river, is another range of hills called the Salem Hills. These commence directly on the south borders of the city, and rise gradually and gracefully until they attain to a height of several hundred feet above the level of the surrounding country, and then roll away in irregular rounded swells for twelve miles, and finally sink and lose themselves in the plains which border the Santiam River.

Southeastward from Salem is the Mill Creek bottom, extending nearly forty miles in that direction, and varying from one to five miles in width. Some portions of this bottom are gravelly and unproductive, the soil having been washed away by successive floods. The greater part of it, however, is very beautiful and fertile.

East and northeastwardly from Salem for a few miles

the country is level; and beyond this we reach another range of hills, which, after the name of the gentleman who, attracted by their unrivaled beauty and fertility, first located himself among them are called the " Waldo Hills."   These are separated from the Salem Hills by the Mill Creek bottom, their nearest approach to Salem being about five miles from that place.   From this point they gradually rise to the height of two or three hundred feet, and then roll off in regular rounded swells for some twenty-five or thirty miles to the east and north, each successive swell rising a little higher than the former, until they tower into the majesty and grandeur of the Cascade Range, whose dark ridges and snowy pinnacles mark the line of the eastern horizon.   Standing upon the top of one of the elevations near the city of Salem, and casting one glance around the horizon encircling that interesting locality, we will, before proceeding on our tour of observation up the valley, feast our eyes upon the beauty and grandeur of the scenery around us.

It is the first of June, and Flora has robed the hills and valleys around with a dress reflecting all the colors of the rainbow.   The trees and shrubbery are clothed with verdure, and innumerable birds of beautiful plumage are chirping and singing in the branches.   The ground is reddened with the luscious strawberry, springing spontaneously and abundantly from the soil.   There is not a cloud to darken the heavens, and the air is as clear as an Italian sky. Now, lifting our eyes above and beyond the front ground of the picture, and looking directly northward, an object of great beauty meets our gaze, and we can distinctly trace its outlines against the azure sky. What is it? I exclaimed, when first its mellow brightness formed its image on my eye. It is Mount St. Helen's, the most regular in its form, and the most beautiful in appearance, of all the snow-capped mountains of the western slope. Being smooth and conical in its form, and lifting its hoary head fifteen thousand feet above the level of the sea, the eye can gaze upon it without weariness from innumerable points more than one hundred and fifty miles from its base. A little to the right of this stands Mount Ranier, another of nature's grand sentinels, whose snows have never been marked by human feet. Still further to the right is Mount Baker, standing at a greater distance, yet equally visible. These, and Mount Elias, which we cannot quite discern from where we stand, are all on the north side of the Columbia River. Now, turning a little further, and facing to the northeast, the grand and majestic form of Old Hood rises up before us, clad in the terrible beauty which covers him as with a garment of light. This celebrated mountain stands in the midst of the Cascade Range, some fifty miles south of the Columbia River, and in the state of Oregon. It is necessary to a proper appreciation of the country on both sides of the Columbia River, that this stupendous range, of which Mount Hood is the most prominent point, should be properly understood. To give a correct idea of this astonishing pile of basalt and snow, and the range with which it stands connected, I here append what has excited an interest even in the literary circles of Great Britain :

AN ASCENT OF MOUNT HOOD.

BY REV. H. K. HINES.

" The Cascade Range of mountains is a northward continuation of the *Sierra Nevada* of California, and cuts the State of Oregon and Territory of Washington from south to north, at a distance of one hundred miles from the Pacific Ocean. The range springs up to an average altitude of eight or ten thousand feet, while at intervals of many miles more aspiring summits, from five to ten thousand feet higher, luminous with the sheen of everlasting snow, dome the ever-green roofing of the mountains. The highest of these is Mount Hood. It stands about fifty miles south of where the Columbia has plowed its way through the Cascade, and nearly in the center of the range from east to west.

" Here is a range of mountains eighty miles in width, and all that distance so broken, rugged, and wild as to be entirely irrecoverable to the uses of civilized man. But few of these wild gorges have ever been marked by the heel of the explorer. An occasional hunter has sometimes strayed into these fastnesses in pursuit of the elk or bear; or a miner, with pick, shovel, and pan, has followed some stream near to its icy fountain ; but nearly all these mountains have over them the mystery of an unpathed solitude. For thirteen years I had looked with wonder and desire toward the summit of Mount Hood. The desire to visit it, to stand upon it, to commune with nature and with God amid the wild sublimities of its gorges and glaciers, grew upon me till my spirit seemed ever asking for the intense delight.

" In September, 1864, in company with three gentlemen of Vancouver, Washington Territory, I first attempted to scale that hoary pinnacle. On reaching an altitude about eight hundred feet below the summit, as we stood gazing on the magnificent panorama spread around and below us, a dense cloud came sweeping against the north side of the mountain, and drifting rapidly over it, instantly enveloped us in its folds. The air changed suddenly to a fierce cold ; the winds howled around the side of the mountain and shrieked away in doleful cadences below ; the driving snow filled the air so entirely that a cliff of rocks three hundred feet high, standing not more than fifty feet from us, was entirely invisible. To go up, or to go down, was for the time, alike impossible. We could only stand on that chill altitude stoutly braving the beating of the blast. Frost and ice gathered on our hair and beards and clothes, till we looked like four ice kings shaking winter from our grizzly locks. The snow was swept by the fierce winds in waves and drifts in every direction. One of my companions was chilled nearly to insensibility ; but we yet struggled against the tempest for hours, unwilling to be defeated in our purpose to reach the summit of the mountain. We stood seventeen thousand feet above the ebb and flow of the sea, before the very throne of the storm king, and were witnesses of the sweep of his tempest, as few mortals had ever been before us. There was sublimity in the thought, and it inspired us to daring; but the tempest was too strong for us, and we at length reluctantly yielded to its imperious power. Subsequently I was glad of the disappointment, as it gave me occasion again to visit the mountain; and having seen it clad in garments of cloud and storm, I could better appreciate it when robed in the gorgeous drapery of summer brightness. Of this second ascent I will now tell.

"On the morning of the twenty-fourth day of July, 1866, in company with three gentlemen of the city of Portland, Oregon, I set out with heart and hope, full of determination to stand upon that summit if mortal energy and determination could reach it. Our place of rendezvous was at the house of a Canadian by the name of Revnue, who, fourteen years before, had erected a cabin at the place where the emigrant road leaves the mountains and enters the valley of the Willamette. Our way here entered the mountains in the gorge, through which flows a dashing river three hundred feet wide, which rises from beneath the glaciers of Mount Hood. Up this stream we traveled for thirty miles, when, leaving the gorge, the way makes a *detour* to the right to gain the summit ridge. Here is the celebrated 'Laurel Hill.' For three or four miles the ascent is continuous, and in many places very steep and difficult. The top of Laurel Hill is the general summit of the range, which is perhaps ten miles in width, and has the general character of a marsh or swamp. There is here a dense and grand growth of fir, cedar, sugar-pine, and kindred evergreens, with an almost impenetrable undergrowth of laurel. There is an inexpressible sense of loneliness in these deep solitudes. Struggling rays of sunlight only here and there find way through the dense foliage, and then fall cold and white upon the damp ground. Passing over this level we crossed several bold, clear streams, dashing across our way from the direction of Mount Hood over beds of scoriaceous sand, which had been borne down from that vast pile of volcanic material, now only five or six miles away. We now found an old Indian trail leading in the direction of the mountain, and, after a ride of an hour and a half upon it, came out into an opening of scattered trees, which sweeps around the south side of the mountain. It was five o'clock when we emerged from the forest, and stood for the time appalled, confronting the body of rocks and snow which springs up from the average altitude of the mountains and enters into wedlock with the bending ether. The bewildering greatness without inspired an unutterable awe within. Selecting a place for our camp on a beautiful grassy ridge between one of the main affluents of the Des Chutes and the Clackamas Rivers, and which really constitute the dividing ridge, we erected a booth of boughs, gathered fuel for a large fire during the night, and gave ourselves up to hours of contemplation of the strange scene around, above, and beneath us.

"The evening now came on, creeping noiselessly

over the mountains, and shedding a strange, weird, and melancholy splendor over the scene. The moon was at its full, the sky clear as crystal, and the moon-beams seemed to troop in columns along the glittering acclivities of the glaciers. Mount Hood seemed taller, grander, and more glorious than before. Often, during the march of that night over the hills, I arose from my blankets, walked to a point a few rods away, and contemplated with something of awe and much of reverence the divinely-illumined picture. Those who study Mount Hood only in the studio of the artist, before such paint and brush caricatures as Bierstadt's, know nothing of its real grandeur, its overwhelming greatness. Men praise the artist who, on canvas, can make some slight imitation of such a scene; why will they not adore the Maker whose power and skill builds and paints the grand originals?

"At seven o'clock of Thursday, having provided ourselves with staves seven feet in length, and taken such refreshments as we should need on the mountain, we were ready for the ascent. For the first mile and a half the way was easy, over a bed of volcanic rock, decayed, and intermixed with ashes. Huge rocks stood here and there, and two or three stunted junipers and a few varieties of mosses were all the vegetation.

" We now reached the foot of a broad field of snow which sweeps around the south side of the mountain for several miles in length, and extending upward to the immediate summit of the mountain, perhaps four miles. Two miles of this snow field is smooth, and only in places so steep as to render the footsteps uncertain. Near its upper edge the deep gorges, from which flow affluents of the Des Chutes on the right, and Sandy on the left, approach each other, cutting down to the very foundations of the mountain. The waters are rushing from beneath the glaciers, which, at the upper extremity, were rent and broken into fissures and caverns of unknown depth.

"The present summit of the mountain is evidently what was long since the northern rim of an immense crater, which could not have been less than three miles in diameter. Its southern wall has fallen completely away, and the crater itself is filled with rock and ashes, overlaid with the accumulated snows of ages, through the rents and chasms of which now escape smoke, steam, and gases from the pent-up fires below. The fires are yet so near that many of the rocks which project upward through these icy depths are so hot that the naked hand cannot be held upon them. Just at the southwest foot of the circular wall now constituting the summit, and at a distance of about two thousand feet from its extreme height, is now the main opening of the crater. From this a column of smoke and steam is continually issuing, at times rising and floating away on the wind, at other times rolling heavily down the mountain. Into this crater I descended as far as it was possible without ropes, or till the descent was prevented by a perpendicular wall of ice sixty or seventy feet high, which rested below on a bed of broken rock and ashes so hot as immediately to convert the water which dripped continually from the icy roof one hundred feet above into steam. The air was hot and stifling; but I did so desire to gather some ashes and rocks from the bottom of the crater that if ropes had been at hand I should certainly have ventured down.

"At this point the real peril of the ascent begins. It leads out and up the inner wall of what was once the crater, and near a thousand feet of it is at an angle of sixty degrees. This ascent is up an ice field, the upper limit of a great glacier, which is crashing and grinding its slow journey down the mountain far to the right. About seven hundred feet from the summit a *crevasse* from five to fifty feet in width, and of unknown depth, cuts clear across the glacier from wall to wall. There is no evading it. The summit cannot be reached without crossing it. There is no other pathway. Steadily and deliberately poising myself on my staff, I sprang over the *crevasse* at the most favorable place I could select, landing safe on the declivity two or three feet above it, and then with my staff assisted the others to cross. The last movement of fifteen feet had considerably changed the prospect of the ascent. We were thrown by it directly below a wall of rock and ice five hundred feet high, down which masses, detached by the sun, were plunging with fearful velocity. To avoid them it was necessary to skirt the *crevasse* on the upper side for a distance, and then turn diagonally up the remaining steep. It was only seven hundred feet high, but it was two hours' sinewy tug to climb it.

The hot sun blazed against the wall of ice within two feet of our faces, the perspiration streamed from our foreheads, our breath was labored and difficult, yet the weary steps of inches were multiplied till, on nearing the summit, the weariness seemed to vanish, an ecstatic excitement thrilled along every nerve, and with feelings and shouts of triumph we bounded upon the pinnacle of the highest mountain in North America.

" The summit was reached at about the center of the circular wall which constitutes the extreme altitude, and where it had so sharp an edge that it was impossible to stand erect upon it. Its northern face is an escarpment several thousand feet high. Here we could only lie down on the southern slope, and holding firmly to the rocks, look down the awful depth. A few rods to the west was a point forty or fifty feet higher, to the summit of which we crawled, and there discovered that forty rods eastward was a point still higher, the highest of the mountains. We crawled back along the sharp escarpment, and in a few minutes stood erect on the highest pinnacle. This was found to be seventeen thousand six hundred and forty feet high ; the thermometer, by a very careful observation, standing at one hundred and eighty degrees, where the water boiled about forty feet below the summit. This gives thirty-two degrees of depression, which, at the usual estimate of five hundred and fifty feet to the degree, gives the astonishing altitude indicated above.

" The scene around us was indescribable. We

were favored with one of the clearest, brightest days of summer, and in this latitude and on this coast objects are plainly visible at an almost incredible distance. It would be impossible to convey to the reader an adequate impression of the scene, yet a few general observations may be taken. The first is the Cascade Range itself. From south to north, from Diamond Peak to Rainier, a distance of not less than four hundred miles, the whole mountain line is under the eye. Within that distance are Mounts Saint Helens, Baker, Jefferson, the Three Sisters, making, with Mount Hood, nine snowy mountains. Eastward the Blue Mountains are in distinct view for at least four hundred miles in length, and lying between us and them are the broad plains of the Des Chutes, John Day's, and Umatilla Rivers, one hundred and fifty miles in width. On the west the piny crests of the Coast Range cut clear against the sky, with the Willamette Valley sleeping in quiet beauty at their feet. The broad silver belt of the Columbia winds gracefully through the evergreen valley toward the ocean, which we see blending with the horizon through the broad vista at the mouth of the river. Within these wide limits is every variety of mountain and valley, lake and prairie, bold, battling precipices, and gracefully rounded summits, blending and melting away into each other, forming a whole of unutterable magnificence. The descent to the great *crevasse*, though much more rapidly accomplished, was perhaps quite as perilous as the ascent. We were now approaching the gorge, and a single misstep might precipitate us into unfathomed depths. Less than half an hour was sufficient to retrace the weary climbing of three hours, and, standing for a moment on the upper edge of the chasm, we bounded over it where it was about eight feet in width. The impetus of the leap sent us plunging down the icy steep below.

"In two hours from the summit we reached our camp. At dark we began to pay the price of our pleasure. The glare of the sun on the ice had burned our faces and dazzled our eyes till they were so painful that not one of the party slept a moment during the night. I kept over my eyes and face a cloth wetted with ice-water all night, and in the morning was able to see; but two of the party were as blind as rocks for forty-eight hours. But we were well compensated for all our toil and pain. And now, as often as thought recurs to the moment when I stood upon that awful height, and the same awe of the infinite God who settest fast the mountains, being girded with power, comes over my soul, I praise him that he gave me strength to stand where his power speaks with words few mortals ever hear, and the reverent worshipings of mountains and solitudes seem flowing up to his throne."

From this magnificent picture, in which we have seen blended in beautiful harmony extended valleys and fertile plains, dotted here and there with numerous signs of civilization, lines of forest, rising grounds, lofty hills, towering mountains, majestic glaciers, meandering streams, and flowing rivers, we will turn our faces southward, and there, as clearly as from the top of Mount Hood, the shimmering summit of Jefferson greets the eye, and, looking a little further still, the Three Sisters, clad in their robes of unsullied whiteness, stand out in bold relief, as if to add a finish to the glorious panorama which we have been contemplating. We have as yet gone round but half the circle, and we have time only to glance at the other half, where the Coast Range draws its lines against the western sky, and then leave this point of observation, and proceed up the valley with our explorations. Six miles above the city of Salem comes flowing down into the Willamette from the west a stream called La Creole, which can also boast of its privileges for milling operations, and of watering a splendid portion of the country. Fifteen miles above this is the Luckimute, a fine stream, bordered on each side by fertile plains. Three miles further on is Soap Creek, which can also boast of its advantages. These all rise in the Coast Range, and, running eastward from thirty to fifty miles crosswise of the valley, hasten to mingle their waters with those of the Willamette. Fifteen miles above Salem, on the east side of the Willamette, the Santiam comes dancing down its channel as clear as the crystal drop that oozes from the pines, whose forms are reflected from its limped waters. This is a very considerable stream, and flows through an excellent portion of the country. The springs of the Cascade Mountains supply its several branches, and from the extent of the country watered, and the driving power which it affords, it is not second to any of the tributaries of the Willamette. Eight miles above the Santiam we come to the point where the flourishing city of Albany is located, at the mouth of the Callapooia River. This stream, rising far up in the Cascades, and flowing across the eastern half of the valley diagonally, fertilizes and beautifies a large portion of the county of Linn. Above this a few miles is another stream, appropriately named Muddy, from the appearance of its dark, turbid waters. Its principal value consists in its affording an abundance of stock water in the dry season. Above this some twenty miles the M'Kenzie fork of the Willamette comes booming out of a gorge in the Cascade Mountains, and from this we will pass over to the westward side, and cross Grand Prairie, beautiful in the extreme, and at its further border we find a very interesting stream bearing the euphonious name of "Long Tom."

This stream rises in numerous rivulets which issue from the Coast Range, and, watering a large extent of country, unite, and, running northward at the base of the foot hills of the Coast Range, discharge their waters into the Willamette twelve miles above the city of Corvallis. We have now reached the upper or south end of the valley proper, and a collection of prairie and timbered hills, which are generally settled up, extend southward for twenty-five miles or more before they swell into the bolder and loftier outlines of the Callapooia Mountains, which form the southern boundary of the great Willamette Valley.

The Siuslaw is a small though independent valley, lying between the waters which flow into the Willamette River and those of the Umpqua. The upper part of this valley, some fifty miles from the ocean, though small, is rich and fertile, and capable of sustaining a much heavier population than have yet settled upon its limpid and health-giving waters. The river pierces the entire Coast Range, forming a valley of varied extent, and empties itself into the Pacific Ocean. Salmon enter this river, as also nearly all the streams that run into the ocean, in great abundance in their season, so that at times they literally fill the channel from bank to bank.

4

CHAPTER IV.

THE VALLEY OF THE GREAT COLUMBIA.

THE Columbia is the father of rivers on the great Pacific Slope, and into its capacious channel nearly all the waters of Oregon and Washington Territory discharge themselves. The river forms the dividing line between the state and territory, and in the advantages which it confers it equally belongs to both. With the exception of a few short portages by railroad, one at the Cascades of four miles, and one above Dalles City of ten miles in length, it is navigable for more than five hundred miles from its mouth. Draining more extent of country than any rivers upon the continent save the Mississippi and the Amazon, this majestic stream is supplied from the inexhaustible reservoirs of the Rocky Mountains, and, increasing in magnitude and power by an accumulation of unnumbered tributaries, it sweeps along in its resistless course, tearing away every obstacle, sapping the foundation of mountains, and hurling them down from their rocky heights, piercing the adamantine barriers that would impede its progress, or leaping down the fearful precipice into the deep chasm made by its own resistless power; now gliding smoothly and beautifully along near the surface, and now almost hiding itself thousands of feet below. Approaching the basaltic walls reared by the Cascade Range across its pathway, it gathers up its omnipotence, and lifting those mighty abutments from their foundations, bears them away upon its bosom and casts them into the depths below. Thus making itself a channel through every impediment, it comes gliding out from the gorges of the Cascades into the lower country a smooth, deep, broad, beautiful river, and enlarging as it goes until it widens to six miles across, it pours its immense volume of water into the bosom of the great Pacific between Cape Adams and Cape Hancock near the forty-sixth degree of north latitude.

To give a full description of the great valley of the Columbia with regard to its topography, climate, mining and agricultural resources, etc., would swell this work beyond our original design. Attention is invited, therefore, to only a few points. As to the surface of this portion of the country, it is as variegated and interesting as that already described. The same objects of beauty, sublimity, and grandeur, varying a little in their appearance in consequence of a change of the post of observation, are seen on every hand. Much of the land in the valleys, and on the hills and mountain sides, is similar to that already considered, if we except the bottom lands along the river. These, extending from Astoria to the Cascades, the distance of one hundred and thirty miles, are subject to an annual inundation in the month of June. Naturally rich and productive beyond description, when they overflow they seem to lose much of their value. There is, however, a redeeming consideration in reference to these bottom lands. They enjoy two spring seasons. Early in April the grass, which grows most luxuriantly upon them, shoots forth from the rich soil, and from that time until the period of the inundation affords an abundance of feed for the immense number of cattle that seek their living here. While the flood is on, these herds retreat to the highlands, and the water remains so long upon the grass that it dies, and is good for nothing. In July the water all recedes, the grass comes up afresh, and grows with great vigor and rapidity; the ground is soon covered with a heavy coating of nutritious herbage, the cattle and horses again rush to their favorite range, where during the rest of the year they revel with delight in the most luxuriant meadows. Back from the river, almost its entire length, the land rises rapidly, and generally abruptly, to the height of mountains, which leaves the impression that the Columbia Valley is very narrow; but it must be remembered that the valley proper comprehends all that vast extent of country drained by the numerous tributaries of the great river. Not only the largest portions of Washington Territory and the State of Oregon, but also of Idaho, Nevada, Montana, and British Columbia, are embraced within the circle of this magnificent valley. A comparison will enable us to form some just conception of the magnitude of its vast area. Massachusetts is considered a large state; but if you divide the country drained by the Columbia River into states of the size of Massachusetts, you will have at least two dozen such states, and land to spare. And what may be regarded as still more important, they would all be equal, if not superior, to the old state in climate, fertility of soil, and general resources and capabilities.

Through the Cascade Mountains, the distance of eighty miles, the valley of the Columbia is indeed narrow, consisting mainly of a tremendous gorge, which its own power has excavated through the entire range. In the midst of these mountains, however, in places, the valley widens out into bottoms which admit of settlement, and are all occupied by permanent and prosperous residents. It is at the center of this gorge through the mountains, where the Columbia pours her exhaustless flood down a ledge of rocks of some fifty feet fall in the distance of one half mile, that the beautiful cascades which give their name to the whole mountain range are formed. These cascades, in connection with the overhanging cliffs, and beetling summits towering high in the heavens on both sides, present an appearance of grandeur and sublimity not inferior to that of the famed Niagara above the great cataract. It is an astonishing fact that here, where the whole mighty torrent of the Columbia rushes down this ledge of rocks, the entire channel is not more than thirty rods wide. The Indians here have a tradition that less than a century ago the mountain was joined together over the river, which performed a subterraneous passage for some distance, with a slow current, and that their people used to pass up and down in their canoes without difficulty; but all at once the foundations of this mighty arch crumbled beneath its ponderous weight, and the whole mass came tumbling into the river, filling up the channel, and damming up the stream, and thus were formed the great cascades. There are evidences that this tradition has some foundation in truth. The river is wide and deep above the cascades, with little current, and from all appearances forests which were situated on its former banks have been overflown, as a vast number of stumps and trees, which have not yet wasted away, stand in the present bed of the stream. The cascades are fifty miles above the city of Vancouver, and one hundred and forty-five from the mouth of the Columbia. Forty miles above the cascades we reach what are called the Dalles of the Columbia, or Narrows, as the word signifies, where the river suddenly contracts and rushes through a mighty chasm in the rocks with fearful violence, tumbling, and boiling, and roaring in its passage, and ever and anon forming the most tremendous whirlpools. Here the country assumes altogether a different aspect. The hills are comparatively low, and, instead of being covered with timber, are verdant with grass from their base to their summit. The tributary valleys are small, but they are rich, and adapted to farming purposes. On the south side of the Columbia, in the state of Oregon, starting at Dalles City and proceeding upward, we may number the Three-Mile, the Nine-Mile, the Fifteen Mile, the Tigh Valley, the Des Chutes, the John Day, the

Umatilla, the Walla Walla; and beyond the Blue Mountains the Grand Round, the Burnt River, the Powder River, and the Malheur, with many others of greater or less extent, some of which will rank with the most beautiful and fertile portions of the Pacific slope, are all comprehended in the great valley of the Columbia, and though extending over hundreds of miles in all directions, are more or less occupied by permanent settlers, and made to contribute to the sustenance of their occupants, and of the mining population operating in the gulches and among the ledges found in the mountains near the heads of the streams.

In Washington Territory, across the river, north and east from the Dalles, the country is, if possible, still more interesting and valuable than the one we have just considered. Thousands and tens of thousands of acres of lands of the richest pasturage, and of good arable qualities, are to be found lying along the eastern base of the Cascade Mountains, and extending hundreds of miles to the line which separates Washington Territory from Idaho. In this region is the valley of the Klikitat, the Yakima, and Simcoe, the latter being the locality of the Yakima Indian reservation, which is under the agency of the Rev. James H. Wilbur. This portion of Washington Territory is capable of sustaining an immense population, and when the Indian title to the land shall be extinguished, which doubtless must be the case in the order of events in a very short time, these beautiful and fertile valleys, and these verdant and grassy hills, will become the theater of all the activities and the institutions belonging to civilization and Christianity.

The Yakima Valley of this region is very peculiar. The river rises in the Cascade Range, and runs eastwardly, nearly parallel with, and in an opposite direction from the Columbia, but finally works its way around into that river. Portions of this valley are fertile and beautiful, but it is now included in the Indian Reservation.

As it is not the purpose we have in view to trace the Columbia River through Idaho and British America to its source in the Rocky Mountains, or to give a description of the valleys watered by its numerous tributaries before entering Washington Territory and Oregon, we shall here close our sketch of this great artery of the western slope by giving a short history of the circumstances by which this great river received its name.

Up to the year 1788, only eighty years ago, it was not known by any civilized nation that the great Columbia had an existence on the face of the globe. The citizens of the United States appear to have taken no part in the discoveries on the northwest coast, and in the trade opened by such discoveries, previously to the year 1788. At that time a company of merchants from Boston sent two ships around Cape Horn, commanded respectively by Captain Robert Gray and Captain John Kendrick. The names of these vessels were the Columbia and Washington. These were the first American ships that visited the northwest coast. Both these vessels continued on the coast until the month of August, 1789, when it was determined between them that Captain Gray should take the command of the Columbia and proceed to China and the United States with all the furs which had been collected, and Hendrick should remain on the coast in the Washington. Gray accomplished this voyage in safety, and on the twenty-seventh day of September, 1790, again left Boston in the same ship for the Pacific, and some time in May, 1791, made land a little to the north of Cape Mendocino, near the forty-first degree of north latitude. While proceeding to the northward from this point Captain Gray discovered an opening in the shore of considerable width, in latitude forty-six degrees and sixteen minutes, from which issued a strong current which prevented his entrance. He continued off this opening for nine days, with an intention, if possible, to enter it; but from the strength of the current, and the appearance of the breakers across the opening, he was unable at this time to accomplish his object. Though convinced that he had discovered the mouth of a great river, without waiting longer for an opportunity to enter it he proceeded to the north, and in June arrived at Nootka Sound. From this point Gray continued his course north, and after making some important discoveries in the vicinity of Queen Charlotte's Island, returned to Clyoquot, near Nootka, where he continued during the winter. In the spring of 1792 the discoveries on the coast of Oregon were prosecuted both by the

English and Americans.   In the middle of April Captain Vancouver, an Englishman, arrived on the coast with two ships at his command, and commencing at Cape Mendocino, explored the whole extent of coast as he proceeded to the north, and passed the opening which Gray attempted to enter in latitude forty-six degrees sixteen minutes, without considering it as being worthy of his particular attention on account of the forbidding aspect which it presented. In his progress northward he says in his journal that "the coast was so minutely examined that the surf was constantly seen to break on its shores from the mast-head," and yet that he "saw no appearance of an opening in its shores which presented any certain prospect of affording shelter." On his way up the coast Vancouver fell in with the ship Columbia, Captain Gray, who had just left his wintering place at Clyoquot. In their interview Gray informed Vancouver that, the previous summer, he had been off the mouth of a river in latitude forty-six degrees ten minutes where the outset was so strong as to prevent his entering for nine days. In referring to this, Vancouver says that "this was probably the opening passed by us on the forenoon of the twenty-seventh, and was apparently inaccessible, *not from the current*, but from the breakers that extend across it." From this it appears that the English captain did not yet believe that such a river as was represented by Gray had any existence. Under this impression he proceeded on to the north, while Gray, to assure himself of the reality of his discovery of a great river, resolved, if it were possible, to enter it with his ship. While proceeding southward from Clyoquot he entered a harbor which he named after one of his principal owners, Bulfinch, now called with more propriety Gray's Harbor.

Passing on, he arrived on the eleventh of May, 1792, opposite the bay which, by a former Englishman by the name of Captain John Meares, who visited the coast early in 1788, was called Deception Bay, immediately south of Cape Hancock, and in latitude forty-six degrees ten minutes north. Though the breakers presented a formidable obstacle before them, and they did not know but that they were rushing to inevitable destruction, yet Captain Gray and his gallant comrades dashed bravely on, and discovering a narrow passage through the breakers, passed them in safety, and, as Gray had anticipated, found themselves in a large river of fresh water, up which they proceeded the distance of twenty miles. The natives, in their finely constructed canoes, flocked around the strangers, and manifested the utmost surprise at what they saw and heard. A traffic was opened with them, in which furs were received from the Indians in exchange for coarse goods; and after having continued in the river for eight days, making repairs, trading with the Indians, exploring the river, and taking observations of the surrounding country, Captain Gray again passed the breakers at the entrance, and put to sea through the dangerous and intricate channel, prepared to announce to the world the most important discovery that was ever made on the northwest coast. Before taking his departure Captain Gray bestowed the name of his vessel upon the majestic river which he had discovered, calling it the Columbia, a name which, in honor of the generous captain who bestowed it, and the gallant ship that first anchored in its waters, it should forever retain. It has been asserted by one very popular writer* that the existence of this river was long known before Gray or Vancouver visited it. Doubtless, it was known to the Indian tribes that roamed upon its banks. But if any white man ever saw it, he was not permitted to survive to tell of his discovery. From a thorough investigation of the whole question, it most clearly appears that Captain Robert Gray, of Boston, is entitled to the credit of being the original discoverer of this great river of the western slope; a river which, when viewed as the only convenient or practicable channel to and from one of the most extensive and fertile valleys on the American Continent, will bear comparison, in the natural advantages which it affords, with almost any river in the world.

* Washington Irving.

CHAPTER V.

THE COUNTIES OF OREGON.

THE state of Oregon is divided into twenty-two counties, and in describing them separately we will commence at the northwest corner of the state and present them in their regular order, so as to give a more distinct idea of their precise locality.

CLATSOP COUNTY.

This county is bounded north by the Columbia River, east by Columbia County, south by the county of Tilamook, and west by the Pacific Ocean. The topography of this county is wonderfully variegated. Within its limits are embraced the beautiful Clatsop Plains, already noticed in the general description of the country. This county is mainly covered with a heavy growth of fir, spruce, cedar, and hemlock timber, offering magnificent opportunities for lumbering purposes, though but little in that line is now done. The soil is of a good quality on the low lands, and, though some of the mountains are rocky and precipitous, yet generally the soil is good on the mountain sides, and even to the very tops of the mountains. We can only arrive at an approximation toward the precise area of the county, as its exact limits are not fully defined. It is not far from two thousand square miles.

The population is increasing, and taking the last census as the basis, it does not vary far from eight hundred. The number of voters at the last election was one hundred and seventy-nine. Acres of land under cultivation, seven hundred and sixty; value of assessable property in the county, two hundred and eighty thousand dollars. Astoria is the seat of justice. This town derived its name from the late John Jacob Astor, who established a trading post here as early as 1811. The town is beautifully and pleasantly located on the left or south bank of the Columbia River, ten miles above its mouth. It is ninety miles northwest from Portland, and by the way of the Willamette and Columbia Rivers it is one hundred and forty miles from Salem, the capital of the state. The town occupies a very salubrious and healthy locality, and at present it wears all the appearance of growing prosperity. The custom-house is located at this place, besides which the public buildings are a masonic hall, and a church. A public school is in successful operation, and the population generally are highly intelligent and refined. Astoria and Clatsop Plains, on the other side of Youngs' Bay, are becoming a frequent, as they are a very pleasant, resort for the people from the interior, especially during the warm part of the season. The fresh breezes from the bosom of the great Pacific are pleasant and exhilarating.

TILAMOOK COUNTY.

This county is bounded on the north by Clatsop, east by Washington, Yamhill, and Polk counties, south by Benton, and west by the Pacific Ocean. The general character of this county may be described by the terms rough and mountainous. It is large in extent, embracing not less than two thousand five hundred square miles. Its western limits are washed by the waters of the Pacific, and there are a number of points of interest along its coast. Tilamook Valley, on a river of the same name, is a beautiful and fertile valley, and opens to the ocean by the way of Tilamook Bay. The valley contains most of the population of the county at the present, though many other portions are susceptible of settlement. Tilamook Bay affords for the county a port of entry, and constitutes a safe harbor for small vessels.

The population of the county amounts to about three hundred persons. Lincoln is the county seat.

BENTON COUNTY.

This county is bounded on the north by Polk County and Tilamook, on the east by the Willamette River, which separates it from Linn County, on the south by Lane County, and on the west by the Pacific Ocean. This county contains an area of about one thousand seven hundred square miles. It is one of the most beautiful, fertile, and picturesque counties in Oregon. It embraces a very romantic section of the Coast Range of mountains; and near the center of this section, and rising above every other elevation for many miles around, stands the graceful form of Mary's Peak. The eastern portion of the county, lying on the Willamette River, is an extended prairie plain; the western, extending to the Pacific Ocean, is mountainous. The plains are rich and beautiful, and much of the land in the mountains is naturally very fertile, but covered with timber. The population of the county by the last census was three thousand and seventy-four. Number of voters at the last election, seven hundred and twenty-six. Assessable property, one million two hundred and ninety-three thousand and forty-seven dollars. Corvallis, a name signifying the center of the valley, is the county seat.

The public buildings are a court-house, a college, owned and conducted by the Methodist Church, South, and three churches, a Presbyterian, a Catholic, and a Methodist Episcopal. Here is published, by W. B. Carter, Esq., a sprightly and valuable newspaper called *The Gazette*. Corvallis is beautifully situated, just below the confluence of Mary's River with the Willamette River, and on the west bank of the latter stream. It forms the center of business for a splendid agricultural country, and is really among the flourishing towns of the state. The other points of special interest in the county are Monroe and the Belknap Settlement in the southern, Liberty and King's Valley in the central portion of the county, and Yaquina, Pioneer City, and Oysterville on Yaquina Bay. Benton County has received a wonderful impetus from the construction of a good wagon road, which has been recently opened from Corvallis to Yaquina Bay. This road has tended greatly to promote the advancement of Benton County in population, wealth, and importance.

LANE COUNTY.

This county is situated in the central part of the state, and is bounded north by Benton and Marion Counties, east by the Cascade Range of mountains, south by Douglas County, and west by the Pacific Ocean. It is about one hundred miles long from east to west, and thirty-five broad, containing three thousand five hundred square miles. The county is unsurpassed by any in the magnificence of its scenery, and it comprises one of the finest agricultural portions of the state. The population of the county by the last census is five thousand five hundred and twenty-seven. Number of voters in the last election, one thousand three hundred and eighteen; acres of land under cultivation, thirty thousand six hundred and eighty-three, about one seventieth part of the land embraced within the limits of the county. True, much of the unoccupied, uncultivated land is hilly and mountainous; yet vast portions in the smaller valleys, and on the foot hills of the Coast and Cascade Ranges of mountains, are eligible to settlement. The value of assessable property in the county is three million dollars.

Eugene City is the seat of justice for Lane County. It is situated seventy-five miles south of Salem, near the conjunction of the Coast Fork, the Middle Fork, and the M'Kenzie Fork of the Willamette River, and at the head of steamboat navigation. Eugene City is a place of growing importance, and from its central position in the midst of an agricultural country rivaling in excellence any other in the state, must become one of the finest inland cities in the country. A wagon road has been recently constructed, connecting this city with the valleys of De Chutes and John Day's River east of the Cascade Mountains. The road is quite practicable through the mountains, and already beginning to be much used.

The public buildings of Eugene City are a court-house, academy, one Episcopal church, one Catholic church, one Cumberland Presbyterian church, one Presbyterian church, Old School, one Baptist, and one Methodist Episcopal church. The population of the town is about one thousand five hundred, and is well supplied with public and private schools. Besides Eugene City there are many points of interest in other parts of the county which are worthy of notice.

Lancaster is a somewhat flourishing little town on the west bank of the Willamette River, sixteen miles below and north of Eugene City.

Franklin, Long Tom, Pleasant Hill, Willamette Forks, Cloverdale, Cottage Grove, and Siuslaw are all beautiful and pleasant localities.

Springfield, three miles above Eugene City, and

on the opposite side of the river, is a point of some importance from the facilities which it offers for milling operations.

DOUGLAS COUNTY.

This county is bounded north by the county of Lane, east by the Cascade Range, south by Josephine County, and west by the Pacific Ocean. It contains an area of not less than three thousand five hundred square miles, or what would be equal to two million two hundred and forty thousand acres of land. Of this, but twenty-one thousand four hundred and four acres are under cultivation. Douglas county contains a population of four thousand. The number of voters at the last election was eleven hundred and thirty-nine. The value of assessable property is one million three hundred and thirty-one thousand two hundred and eight dollars. The county of Douglas is, perhaps, the most wonderfully diversified of any portion of this most wonderful country. The main body of the county is comprised in the valley of the Umpqua River with its numerous tributaries. The level, or lower parts of the valley along the streams, are not extensive, though they are very beautiful and fertile. The whole valley, extending from the Callapooia Mountains south to the Cañon Mountains, and from the Coast Range east to the Cascade Range, comprises some fifteen hundred square miles. To a proper understanding of the nature of this valley it must be remembered that at least three fourths of this whole extent is composed of innumerable hills, many of which aspire to the dignity of young mountains, and that these are scattered promiscuously over the whole valley. This being the case, one in passing through the county is impressed with the idea that the Umpqua Valley is nowhere, or, rather, is no valley; whereas, if he will take the pains to place himself upon the top of some one of the highest of the elevations which abound in the valley, and cast his eye around him, he will not fail to see to the westward the Coast Range, to the eastward the Cascade Range, to the northward the Callapooia, and to the southward the Cañon Mountains, all towering far above the hills that immediately surround him, and distinctly marking the outlines of the grand, though uneven amphitheater known as the Umpqua Valley. This valley is finely watered by the numerous limpid rivulets, and rivers that come leaping down from the mountains by which it is environed, and which, with the salubriousness of the climate, render this one of the most healthy and delightful portions of the state.

Roseburg, situated on the direct road from Portland and Salem to Sacramento in California, and one hundred and fifty miles south of Salem, is the county seat. It is a sprightly little town containing a population of about five hundred. Its public buildings are a court-house, a public school-house, an Episcopal church, and a Methodist Episcopal church. The town stands upon a beautiful location at the confluence of the Deer Creek with the south fork of the Umpqua River, and is sustained by a good agricultural and stock-raising country.

Oakland, situated in the northern part of the county, and on the Callapooia Creek, is a fine growing town, and commands considerable trade from the country around. It is eighteen miles north of Roseburg, and one hundred and thirty-two miles south of Salem.

Wilbur is situated midway between Oakland and Roseburg. This place was selected in 1853 by Rev. James H. Wilbur for the site of an academy to meet the future demands of the country. This academy has since grown into a flourishing institution. A little town has sprung up at this point which derives most of its importance from the school. Here is a church building, which is owned by the Methodist Episcopal Church, South. The academy is in the hands of the Methodist Episcopal Church, and, doubtless, at some future day will become a college. Rev. T. F. Royal, A.M., has been for many years the efficient principal of this academy. The country around is fertile, and the scenery delightful.

Scottsburg, at the head of tidewater on the Umpqua River, and about twenty-five miles from the Pacific Ocean, is a place of some importance, as it forms an entrepot to the interior of the country.

Cañonville, situated in the southern part of the county at the mouth of the Great Cañon, is also an active and flourishing little town, sustained by a combination of agricultural and mining interests. Besides those already named, there are many other places within the limits of the county that, if space would permit, would be entitled to particular notice.

such as Yoncolla, the place of residence of the Applegates, Garden Bottom, Coles Valley, Lookingglass, Myrtle Creek, Cow Creek, Ten Mile, and Cammas Prairie. These, and many others, are all fine localities, and the last mentioned is one of the most beautiful little valleys that can be found on the Pacific Coast.

The water-courses of this county, which are numerous, from the rapidity with which they fall afford almost boundless facilities for manufacturing purposes, but are not yet being very extensively employed. Some lumber and flouring mills are in operation in various parts of the county, and measures are being taken to set in motion the spindles and looms requisite to convert into cloth the immense amount of wool that is annually clipped from the sheep that subsist upon the thousands of hills that checker this singular but interesting and promising county.

COOSE COUNTY.

This county is bounded on the north and east by Douglas County, on the south by Curry County, and on the west by the Pacific Ocean. The population, according to the last census, is one thousand and twenty-four. The number of voters at the last election was three hundred and thirteen. The land under cultivation does not exceed one thousand acres. The value of assessable property is two hundred thousand dollars.

Empire City is the county seat, and is situated on Coose Bay, about five miles from where the bay connects with the ocean, one hundred miles directly west from Roseburg in Douglas County, and two hundred and fifty miles southwest from Salem, the capital of the state. Empire City will, doubtless, become in time quite a town, though its growth has been very tardy. It occupies a beautiful site, that will admit of an indefinite expansion of the town whenever the abundant mineral, agricultural, and lumbering resources of the country back of it shall be fully opened and require an enlargement. The town contains a population of about one hundred and fifty. The principal objects of interest are an extensive lumber manufactory, and a very nice and commodious public school-house, newly built.

Coose Bay is but an enlargement of Coose River, and forms a safe and convenient harbor for vessels that are not of deep draught. The bay extends up into the country about forty miles, and upon its shores are erected a number of extensive mills for the manufacture of lumber. At North Bend, some ten miles above Empire City, is a fine establishment of this kind, owned and conducted by Captain Robert Simpson & Brother. Here also ship-building is carried forward to a considerable extent. Some eleven vessels of from two hundred to four hundred tons burden have already been launched, and others are in process of building. The Simpsons own a steam tug, which they employ in towing vessels out of and into the harbor; and in shipping lumber to San Francisco and other markets, they also use their own vessels. Many other vessels, however, visit the bay, and find cargoes at other establishments.

Randolph is in the southern part of the county, and important mainly as a mining town. There is also a settlement on Coose River, likewise on the Coquille. The Coose River and the Coquille River valleys are connected with the Umpqua Valley by two trails across the Coast Range of mountains. The valleys of Coose county are narrow and contracted, and generally covered with a dense growth of myrtle and maple timber. The soil of these valleys is good. The principal resources of this county are its lumber and mines. Of the latter, here are found gold, copper, iron, and coal; the last mentioned in abundance.

The population of the county has recently been strengthened by immigration, to facilitate which a wagon road is in process of being built through the Coast Range from Cammas Prairie in Douglas County to Coose River.

CURRY COUNTY.

This county is situated in the extreme southwestern corner of the state. It is bounded north by Coose County, east by Josephine, south by California, and west by the Pacific Ocean. It is a large county in extent, but rough and mountainous, and contains about two hundred inhabitants. The number of votes cast at the last election was one hundred and five. The value of the county consists principally in its timber and mineral resources. Copper leads have been discovered of great prospective value, and gold is found in various places. Farming is carried on to a very limited extent, there being but about four hundred acres of land under cultivation in the county. The value of assessable property is one hundred thousand dollars.

Ellensburg is the county seat. It is situated on the south bank of Rogue River, and is about three hundred and fifty miles southwest of Salem.

Port Orford is within this county, but is not a place of much importance.

JOSEPHINE COUNTY.

This county is in the extreme southern portion of Oregon, being bounded by Douglas County on the north, Jackson County on the east, the state of California on the south, and Curry County on the west. It embraces an area of about two thousand five hundred square miles, equal to one million five hundred thousand acres of land. Of this not more than four thousand acres are under cultivation. The value of assessable property is estimated at three hundred thousand dollars. The topography of this county is wonderfully variegated and interesting. It consists of a succession of beautiful valleys, separated by ranges of high hills which often rise to the dignity of mountains, and presenting, as one passes over the country, ever-varying scenery, mingling in one view the beautiful, romantic, and sublime, so that, though the ascending and descending may tax the physical energies, the mind is never weary in the contemplation of the picture.

The Cow Creek and the Grave Creek valleys are beautiful, and portions of them are fertile and under cultivation. The valley of Jump-off-Joe is beautiful, but fertile only in spots.

These valleys are in the northern part of the county. The Rogue River passes through the county from east to west, dividing it about in the center. That part of the Rogue River Valley embraced in Josephine County is of considerable extent, level, and in places very fertile, and under a good state of cultivation. In this county is also a considerable portion of the valley of Applegate Creek, a stream which, rising in the Siskin Mountains, and running northward, enters the Rogue River within Josephine County. A combination of mining and agricultural wealth renders this valley one of considerable importance. Gold mining is still carried on successfully in the valley; and, scattered along the stream, may be seen here and there a well-conducted and productive farm. The principal valley of the county, however, is one in the southern part, known by the name of Illinois Valley. A river of the same name, rising also in the Siskin Mountains, after meandering through this valley, finds its way to the Pacific Ocean through the channel of the Rogue River.

The Illinois Valley covers an area, embracing some of the foot hills, of about three hundred square miles. But little of this, however, is under cultivation. The main interests of the county are of a mining character, and these are immensely valuable. There are productive placer mines in various parts of the county. Sailor's Diggings, Waldo, Jump-off-Joe, and many other places, are producing more or less gold every year. Discoveries have been made of quartz ledges in various parts of the county; and at a place called Enterprise, in the upper end of the valley, a quartz mill has been put in operation with six stamps, and produces fair returns for the expenses incurred.

Kirbyville is the seat of justice of Josephine County, and constitutes the main center of trade for Illinois Valley. It is situated on the Illinois River, and occupies a very fine site, and will, doubtless, ultimately grow into quite a town. It derives considerable patronage from a public road leading from Crescent City to Jacksonville and Fort Klamath, in the interior; Crescent City, forming an entrepot for Curry, Josephine, and Jackson Counties. This road, though passing over high and rugged mountains, is very much used, as nearly all the goods shipped for Southern Oregon pass over it in four and six horse wagons. In fine, Josephine County, from a combination of mineral, agricultural, and pastoral resources, is destined to occupy a vastly higher position in the estimation of the people of other portions of the state than as yet it has attained.

JACKSON COUNTY.

A gentleman by the name of Jackson first prospected a little creek near where Jacksonville now stands, and found rich deposits of gold in the earth washed by the waters of the creek, and hence the name Jackson Creek, Jackson County, and Jacksonville.

The interesting and important portion of the state of Oregon embraced in Jackson County is situated in the southern part, and bounded as follows: north by Douglas County, east its limits are undefined, south by the state of California, and west by the county of Josephine. The population of the county at present is three thousand souls. The number of voters at the last election was one thousand two hundred and fifty-three. The number of acres of land under cultivation about fourteen thousand. The value of assessable property is one million two hundred and ninety-eight thousand four hundred and sixty-five dollars. This county is about eighty miles from the northern to the southern extremity, and one hundred or more east and west, covering an area of at least eight thousand square miles. The topography of the county, in its beauty and grandeur and variety, will not suffer when compared with any other county in the state. The Winter Range of mountains, which is but a continuance of the Cascade Range, appear on its eastern border, and passing through the county and dividing it into two equal parts as to extent of territory, is another broken part of the Cascade Range, of which Scott's Peak and the Three Brothers are the principal elevations. This last range forms the dividing ridge between the waters of Rogue River and those that flow into the Klamath River. In this eastern portion of Jackson County, comprehending the Klamath Lake country, and in the regions beyond, extending even to Nevada, are large extents of land, both hill and low land, beautiful and fertile, which will, doubtless, not many years hence, constitute delightful homes for thousands of intelligent citizens. In this region are found Alvord and Puebla valleys, Forest Creek, White Horse, and Willow Creek valleys. These are in the extreme southeastern portion of the state. West of these is a desert of some forty miles in extent, and on the west of this desert, and at the base of a mountain range, is a long and, in many places, narrow valley, with a chain of fresh-water lakes extending through it. It is north of Surprise Valley in California, and is divided from it by a low range of hills. In and around this valley are many inviting spots both for cultivation and raising stock.

The most important part of Jackson County, however, is that which is comprehended in the Rogue River Valley and its tributaries. This valley is surpassingly beautiful, and is surrounded with the most enchanting scenery. Snowy Butte, with its graceful outlines and conelike summit, casts its shadow against the eastern sky. The Siskiu Mountains lift their majestic summits on the southern border, as if to guard against invasion from that direction. The Table Rock, rising perpendicularly hundreds of feet, and spreading out upon its top a mile of broad flat surface, offers ample room for all the surrounding people to come to the "Table of Giants" and partake of their viands together. And a thousand other objects—mounds, hills, buttes, mountains, snow-peaks, rocky, jagged, smooth, round, and conical tops, with brooks, creeks, rivulets, cascades, etc., etc., all combine to make this region one of peculiar interest to every admirer of natural scenery. The county seat of Jackson County is Jacksonville, which is the largest and most flourishing town in the southern portion of Oregon. It is situated on the western borders of a beautiful plain, where two rich mining gulches, known as Jackson's Creek and Rich Gulch, come together, and at the base of the range of hills which divide the waters of Bear Creek from those of Applegate, and is ten miles south of Rogue River.

Jacksonville is a town of very considerable trade, and is sustained by a combination of mining and agricultural interests. It is situated about one hundred and twenty-five miles from Crescent City, on the Pacific Ocean, and receives all its merchandise from that point by the way of a wagon road which has been constructed over the Coast Range. This road has been considered in connection with Josephine County. Jacksonville is built in a very compact form, and contains many substantial fire-proof brick stores and hotels, with a variety of shops, saloons, groceries, livery stables, and manufactories, which, with a large number of fine private dwellings, standing in the backgrounds of delightful gardens, give the town an interesting and city-like appearance. The town is blessed with the presence of two churches, a Methodist Episcopal and Catholic. It has also a court-house, and has recently erected, in a most beautiful locality, an academical institution which will doubtless grow into a flourishing college. Here are published two weekly papers, the *Sentinel* and the *Review*, of course on each side of the great political questions of the day. In fine, Jacksonville possesses not only all the characteristics of cities of larger pretensions, but many of the elements of a continued and permanent prosperity. It is two hundred and fifty miles south of Salem, the capital of the state, and within twenty miles of the California line.

The valley immediately on Rogue River is not very wide, varying perhaps from one mile to three, and possibly in places it may widen out to five miles. The main body of what is called Rogue River Valley lies upon the tributaries of that stream. Bear Creek is one of these tributaries; and Jackson Creek, upon which Jacksonville is situated, is a tributary of Bear Creek. The Bear Creek Valley, or Stewart's Creek, as it is sometimes called, varies in width from three to twelve or fifteen miles, and is about twenty-five miles long. It is remarkably beautiful to the eye, and a large portion of the valley is as rich and fertile as it is beautiful. The stage road from Sacramento to Portland runs the whole length of this valley, crossing the Rogue River at Rock Point, and continuing along down the banks of that stream twelve miles before it leaves the valley. The points of interest along this great thoroughfare from California to Oregon, from where the road comes down the Siskiu Mountains into Bear Creek Valley to where it leaves the Rogue River Valley to strike off into

Josephine County, are the Mountain House, Ashland, a thriving town, Eagle Mills, Phœnix, Jacksonville, Willow Springs, a rich mining locality, Dardanelles, Rock Point, Evans's Creek, Dry Diggings, and Croxton's Station, or Grant's Pass. Southwest from Jacksonville, on the upper waters of Applegate Creek, are the mining towns of Sterling and Williamsburgh; while in the northeastern portion of the county are the valleys of Antelope, Little Butte, and Big Butte Creeks, and on the north side of Rogue River is a settled locality rejoicing· in the name of Sam's Valley. There are other valleys of less extent, beautiful and fertile, which a want of space will not allow to be particularly mentioned. These, running into those already described, and becoming one in connection with the main river, constitute what is known as the Rogue River Valley, one of the most delightful upon which the sun ever shone.

This county has been of immense value to the Pacific coast, and especially to the state of Oregon, from the immense amount of gold which has been taken annually from its gulches and hill-sides. The yield of gold has varied somewhat from year to year; but the experience of sixteen years of mining in this locality abundantly proves the durability of the Jackson County mines. Besides this the county is rich in agricultural, pastoral, and manufacturing resources, so that if the mines were to fail, of which there is no ground for fear, the county would still constitute an important part of the state of Oregon. Already an extensive woolen factory is in process of erection, and nearly completed, at Ashland, on Bear Creek, and the extended valleys, hills, and even mountains, covered with grass, afford ample fields for the production of wool; and when the iron horse shall come neighing through the valley, which will doubtless be the case before many years, then this delightful valley will be placed, in point of value, upon an equality with the most favored portions of the state.

•MARION COUNTY.

This county is bounded on the north by Clackamas County, east by Clackamas and the Cascade Mountains, by which it is separated from Wasco County, on the south by Linn County, and on the west by Polk and Yamhill counties, from which it is separated by the Willamette River. The central position of Marion County, its abundant agricultural resources, the superiority of its soil, in connection with its excellent commercial advantages, render it one of the most, if not the most prosperous county of the state. It covers an area of from two thousand five hundred to three thousand square miles. Of this there is forty-six thousand acres under cultivation. The population of the county is now estimated at ten thousand, and at the last election there were cast some two thousand two hundred votes. Salem is the county seat, as also the capital of the state. It is situated on the east bank of the Willamette River, and very near the center of the valley; and no city in this or any other country has a more delightful location. It is fifty miles southwest from Portland, the commercial emporium of the state, and sixty-two miles from the Columbia River. It contains a population of four thousand five hundred, ranking next to Portland in size and commercial importance. The scenery around the city has been considered in the general description of the country, and nothing need here be added but to say, that it would be utterly impossible to conceive of a picture more variegated, beautiful, and magnificent than is here presented to the eye. The blue limpid waters of the Willamette, which wash the western side of the city, the prairie plains and hills in the immediate vicinity, and the dark lines of forest through which the river flows, added to the bolder outlines of the distant mountain ranges, present a picture to the eye at once charming and instructive.

The site of the city is a gradually inclined plane, bordered around with forest outlines. Here the oak, the fir, the maple, and the balm blend together in harmonious beauty; and, indeed, nature has been so lavish of the adornments with which she has decked the locality, that the efforts of art seem but to mar and deface, rather than beautify. Salem is laid out on a grand scale. Her streets are from ninety to a hundred feet wide, and cross each other at right angles. Extensive avenues are also provided, and these are beautified by rows of fine cottages and splendid mansions, which appear on every hand. The public buildings for the state have not yet been erected, but will doubtless be commenced in 1868.

The penitentiary, located here, and now a temporary building, will be erected first, and the State House, Insane Asylum, and others contemplated, as soon as the bricks can be manufactured by the convicts of the prison. At present the state rents apartments in a brick block owned by Joseph Holman, Esq., for the use of the legislature, which answers for the time being a very good purpose.

Salem has laid the foundations to become in the future, and that at no distant day, a great manufacturing city. By the excavation of a ditch or canal of less than a mile in length, water is brought from the Santiam River the distance of about fourteen miles, and intersects the Willamette River at this place. By this arrangement a fall of forty feet or more has been secured, all within the limits of the city. It constitutes the best, and, perhaps, the easiest applied water-power in the state. This hydraulic privilege is owned, by a charter from the state legislature, by the Willamette Woolen Manufacturing and Milling Company. The water is exhaustless, easily controlled both summer and winter, and it is estimated that this water possesses a driving capacity sufficient to drive the machinery for a chain of factories miles in extent. Already an extensive woolen factory, with four sets of carding machinery, one thousand six hundred and eighty spindles, and thirty-three looms, is driven constantly by this power. It employs one hundred and fifty operatives, uses four hundred thousand pounds of wool annually, and produces one thousand yards of cloth per day. In addition to this the company own an extensive flouring mill, which they have erected at a cost of about seventy-five thousand dollars. This company has been remarkably successful, and has added immensely to the wealth of Salem. It is composed of some of the most energetic business gentlemen on the coast. No business operation that has ever been commenced in Oregon has done more to awaken the dormant energies of the people, and give a spur to the enterprise of the country, than this. And, as it has conferred a great financial benefit upon the people generally by a large increase of operatives, and opening a market for wool and other produce, so, on the other hand, it has laid the foundation for the accumulation of a fortune upon the part of all the stockholders of the company.

In addition to this, Salem is blessed with extensive lumbering manufactories, sash factories, founderies, machine shops, and every other branch of mechanism and industry which the necessities of the country demand. Stores of all kinds—hotels, livery stables, photograph galleries, saloons, meat markets, druggists, booksellers—and all other business establishments which are requisite to give life, energy, and activity to a growing town, abound in all parts of the city of Salem. Merchandising especially, as Salem is the center for a large extent of country, rich in every agricultural resource, is carried on very extensively, and becomes the medium through which men beginning with a small capital in a few years raise themselves to independence.

The legal profession has a very strong representation in the little capital of Oregon, especially as to the number of lawyers in comparison with the population. Twenty disciples of Blackstone ought to be sufficient to set the whole population of Salem, of less than five thousand, by the ears; and yet it would be difficult to find a more well-disposed, peaceful, and quiet community in any country than constitute the society of this growing town. Perhaps this is to be attributed to a kind of counteracting influence exerted by an equal number of ministers of the gospel of peace whose residences are within the precincts of the city. At any rate, the people of this community, under the discipline and instruction of these two professions, filled by so able and influential a body of men, ought to be, as they really are, a gospel-loving and a law-abiding people.

The medical profession constitute another "institution" in Salem which should receive a passing notice. Comprising an equal number with the two professions of which we have spoken, according to the theory of some, it is quite remarkable that Salem and vicinity should remain in so healthy a condition. There are certainly doctors enough, and poisonous drugs enough, not only to keep the people all sick, but rapidly to remove them to another clime. And yet few communities are blessed with more uniform and unbroken health; and the people when taken sick, and under the care of the doctors, live, as the man said about his wife, "beyond all account." Perhaps, after all, this state of things is, at least in part, to be attributed to the care exercised by the very able and excellent corps of physicians and surgeons who preside over the sanitary interests of this rising community. If so, we cheerfully accord to them all the credit for the healthfulness of our town and country to which they are entitled.

With three such bodies of men, the lawyers to take care of our temporal interests, the physicians to take care of our bodies, and the ministers to take care of our souls, it might reasonably be expected that we would be exempt from many of the ills to which flesh is heir. "But this too," as the preacher saith, "is all vanity and vexation of spirit."

The publishing interests of Salem deserve also a separate notice. Here are three papers published, one daily and two weekly. Of course they cater to the different political tastes and appetites of the people among whom they are published. The Salem *Daily Record* is issued at twenty-five cents per week, and is devoted to politics and local and general news. D. W. Craig, Esq., is the publisher and proprietor.

The *Capital Chronicle* is published every Saturday, Upton & Noltner, proprietors, the former filling also the editor's chair.

The *American Unionist*, William Morgan, proprietor, is published every Monday, and is the present official paper of the state. These papers are well sustained, and contribute much to the development of the resources and the advancement of the interests of the entire country.

The schools of Salem constitute an important interest worthy of special mention.   There are four public schools already established in the four quarters of the city, some of which are graded institutions, and all promising much for the numerous children everywhere thronging the streets.   There are also a number of private schools well patronized; indeed it would be very difficult to find a community in any state where more general attention is paid to educational interests than in this, or where the youth are more generally taught or further advanced in science and the fine arts than they are in the city of Salem. Much of this, I am aware, is to be attributed to the presence in their midst of the Willamette University, the particulars of whose history are traced in the subsequent chapters of this work.

Another institution in Salem just rising into notice, and already beginning to be of service to an unfortunate class of the children and youth of the country, is the Orphan Asylum.   This institution originated in the action of several benevolent ladies of the city of Salem, who were moved in this direction by contemplating the situation of a number of orphan children, whose parents had died upon the plains or elsewhere without leaving them any adequate means of support.   Mrs. Elizabeth Parrish, wife of Rev. J. L. Parrish, of the Oregon Conference, who is the president of the association, has donated, near the city, a valuable piece of ground of sufficient dimensions to accommodate the institution, and energetic measures are being taken to erect upon it a suitable edifice.   In the hands of the ladies of the city of

Salem it will doubtless be carried forward to completion, and become the means of great good to the bereaved, afflicted, and suffering orphan.

Of Christian Churches there are eight in Salem, which, in the consideration of the institutions of the country, require a passing notice.

The Methodist Episcopal Church justly stands at the head of the list, not only because of superiority of numbers, but also of priority of organization. It was established at Salem mainly by removals from the old mission station, ten miles below, in 1841, and was at that time under the pastoral care of Rev. David Leslie. Its original members were Rev. Jason Lee and wife, Rev. L. H. Judson and wife, Rev. H. Campbell and wife, Rev. James Olley and wife, Joseph Holman and wife, Rev. G. Hines and wife, and Webley Hauxhurst, who was the first white man converted to Christianity through the labors of the first missionaries. In the spring of 1842 G. Hines received the appointment of superintendent of the mission school, and pastor of the Church at Salem, which he retained until the fall of 1843, when Salem again fell under the pastorate of Mr. Leslie, who also had the care of all the societies in the Willamette Valley.

The present church edifice, which, when erected in 1850, was considered large and commodious for the population, is now too small to accommodate the multitude that attend the service. Since its first organization in 1841 the Church has shared in a good degree of prosperity, and for several years past its membership has varied from one hundred and fifty to two hundred and fifty persons. At the present time, under the pastorate of Rev. J. H. Wythe, M. D., it has enrolled a membership of over two hundred, and a Sabbath-school varying from three hundred to four hundred members. This Church owns a property consisting of the house of worship and lot, valued at ten thousand dollars, and a parsonage property, the result of a donation from the Missionary Society of the Methodist Episcopal Church in 1845 through their agent, Rev. George Gary, worth five thousand dollars. It is in contemplation soon to erect a neat and commodious church edifice, which will seat from eight hundred to a thousand persons, at a cost of about twenty thousand dollars.

THE CONGREGATIONAL CHURCH.

This Church was permanently organized in 1853 by Rev. O. Dickinson, who, under the auspices of a missionary society, then took charge of the infant Church, having only four members, and no church building. Until the present year he has remained the pastor, and has labored with great diligence, perseverance, and success in building up the interests of his denomination. The Church was greatly prospered under his administration, and now comprises a membership of about one hundred persons, and a flourishing Sunday-school connected with the congregation. Mr. Dickinson also saw erected a very neat and suitable church edifice in a central part of the city for the accommodation of his rapidly-growing Church. Rejoicing in these abundant fruits of his labors, he applied for and received a dismission from his charge in 1866. Soon after this the Rev. P. S. Knight, one of the alumni of the Willamette University, received and accepted a call to the pastorate of said Church, where he is laboring with great acceptability and usefulness.

THE BAPTIST CHURCH.

This Church was organized in 1859 by laymen in the absence of ministers, and commenced with nine members. Its first regular minister was Rev. J. L. Fisher, and under his administration the Church rapidly "grew and prevailed." A beautiful church edifice was commenced in 1862, and finished in 1864. The Church property is estimated as being worth six thousand dollars. The Rev. J. P. Hungate is the present incumbent, and has now in charge a large congregation, a good Church membership, and a flourishing Sabbath-school.

ST. PAUL'S CHURCH.

This is an Episcopal Church, and was established here by Bishop Scott, under the auspices of the Missionary Board of the Protestant Episcopal Church of America. This climate seems not to have been favorable to the kind of Christianity inculcated in this Church. It has never prospered much. It is said that the communicants now number thirty-nine, and the congregation is correspondingly small. The Sabbath-school numbers about sixty-eight.

THE ROMAN CATHOLIC CHURCH.

This Church was established in 1862, and finds enough of the Catholic element in the town to sustain it in all its peculiar interests. Rev. Father Goens is the present priest of this Church, and labors diligently to build up all of its interests. Connected with it is a kind of nunnery, under the name of the Academy of the Sacred Heart, which is under the direction of the Sisters of the Holy Names of Mary and Jesus. This latter, however, is for educational purposes, and its advantages are enjoyed only by young ladies. This Church contemplates the enlargement of their institutions, and they possess the power beyond any other organization to carry out their designs.

THE CHRISTIAN CHURCH. (CAMPBELLITE.)

This Church has recently been organized, and have erected a fine substantial brick building for the accommodation of the large number of people of that faith in the vicinity of Salem. In relation to the present condition of the Church as to numbers, Sabbath-school interests, etc., the writer is not informed.

ZION'S CHURCH.

This is a Church which was started by the Rev. James Croasman, a missionary of the "Evangelical

Association of North America."   Mr. Croasman commenced his efforts in the midst of a city of churches, and in a few months had completed one of the handsomest in the town, had dedicated it, and organized a society of about fifty members, and secured the attendance of a good congregation; a measure of success that might well be coveted even in the midst of circumstances vastly more favorable than surrounded him.

THE METHODIST CHURCH, SOUTH.

This denomination has a church building in Salem, but it is not much occupied, and the association does not seem to prosper. This gives the city eight churches; a number, perhaps, as great in proportion to the population as commonly falls to the lot of such towns to possess, even in the Atlantic states.

Embraced in the institutions of Salem, and requiring a passing notice, are those associations which, though not strictly religious, are designed to promote the moral and financial interests of all connected with them, and commonly known as secret societies. These are the following:

Of the Masonic Fraternity there are two departments: Salem Lodge, No. 4, and Multnomah Royal Arch Chapter, No. 1.

Of the Independent Order of Odd Fellows there are three departments: Chemeketo Lodge, No. 1, Anniversary Lodge, No. 13, and the Willamette Encampment, No. 2.

Of the Good Templars there are two lodges: Capital Lodge, No. 11, and Salem Lodge, No. 30.

These institutions are all in good repute, and are well sustained, comprehending many of the most influential and best men in the country. The I. O. O. F. have established, for the benefit of the fraternity, a library association, and have already placed upon the shelves, in Holman's block, five hundred volumes. They have also purchased ground one mile from town, which they have neatly improved, for the purposes of a cemetery.

The institution of Good Templars was introduced into the state mainly through the labors of Rev. George B. Taylor, of California; and lodges have been established in almost every neighborhood, and the result has been beneficial to the country.

The State Library also deserves special notice. This is kept also in Holman's block, and, according to the report of P. H. Hatch, Esq., the state librarian, numbers three thousand one hundred and thirty-seven volumes. These consist mostly of law books and public documents and state papers, published by authority of Congress or of the respective states.

The county of Marion, of which Salem is the seat of justice, as well as the capital of the state, has been surveyed, somewhat, in the general descriptions we have given of the Willamette Valley; but to a proper understanding of the country embraced within its limits, it will be necessary to call attention to a few additional particulars. To accomplish this we will start from Salem on a tour of observation, and take the stage road leading north toward Portland, and passing through a skirt of timber of some four miles, we cross a low marshy place called Lake La Bish, and strike the upper end of the French Prairie, so called, because it was first settled by Canadian Frenchmen from the Hudson's Bay Company. This we find is an extensive, fertile, and beautiful prairie, from four to six miles in width, and about twenty miles long. We traverse the whole extent of it, noting the rich and well-cultivated farms on each side of the way, the fine farm buildings, with every other sign of prosperity. We have passed a few snug school-houses, and now we stop a moment at a little town called Waconda, twelve miles from Salem. To the left of us, our faces to the north, the flourishing town of Fairfield, five miles distant, stands upon the river's brink. To the right of us, two miles distant, Fowlerville, with her mills, driven by the water of Pudding River, enlivens the eastern border of the prairie; while between the two places the country is as beautiful as any the sun ever warmed. Proceeding a few miles, we pass Belpassi, a lovely point, where stands a Christian church and academy, sustained by the Cumberland Presbyterians; ten miles further, bring us to the flourishing town of Aurora. The country through which we have passed we pronounce to be little, if any, inferior to the best portions of the state. The French Prairie is now mostly occupied by Americans, the first occupants having sold out and left for other quarters.

Aurora was settled, and is now owned, by a

German Association, who are bound together by a community of interests. They are a very wealthy company, and have done much to enliven, develop, and enrich that portion of the country where they live.

Butteville, on the bank of the Willamette River, some five miles west of Aurora, is a point of some importance, situated near the northwest corner of Marion County. Eastward from Aurora, along the northern line of the county, the country is diversified by timbered land and prairie, plains and rising grounds, for more than thirty miles to the foot hills of the Cascade Mountains. The whole distance the country is good, and being brought into a state of cultivation. We will not attempt to trace the eastern line of the county, as that runs along on the summit of the Cascade Range, but will turn southward, and pass along over what we have called the foot hills of these mountains. These we find to be occupied some distance back from their base, and to constitute a fine country both for farming and grazing purposes. As we proceed southward we pass over a number of dashing streams, clear as the crystal and cold as the bubbling spring, which come leaping down from the mountains, in their course forming many beautiful cascades, and hurrying on to unite their waters with the Willamette. Among them is Butte Creek, Abaquaw, and Silver Creek. These all fertilize delightful portions of the country, and on the latter, where the stream leaves the Waldo Hills, is situated the beautiful and flourishing town of Silverton.

Not stopping to survey particularly this delightful locality, we pass for several miles over the round, smooth, elevated summits of the Waldo Hills, which we find to be under a very fair state of cultivation; and on the southern border of these hills, and over-looking a most delightful country, we reach a little town which, from its locality, but more especially from the grandeur of the mountain scenery in its rear, is called Sublimity. From this point we descend into the Mill Creek Bottom, and pursuing a well-traveled road for some fourteen miles, along which farms are scattered at convenient distances, we reach Jefferson City, nestling among the evergreens of the Santiam Valley, and on the southern border of the county of Marion. Contemplating for a moment the business-like aspect of this little town, and especially surveying the fine flouring mill built and run by the indefatigable Jacob Conson, Esq., and the fine lumbering establishment and carding machine conducted by Absalom Smith, Esq., and the several stores and shops of various kinds, not forgetting the Methodist church, built entirely by the benevolence of Rev. Father Parrish, as he is familiarly called, we then step down a mile below, and find another little town which goes by the name of Santiam. We are now fifteen miles directly south of Salem, and, as there is not sufficient importance in Santiam to detain us at that point, we will pass over the Salem Hills, which we have already described, along the great thorough-fare tracked by a daily stage in each direction, noting the many substantial improvements which dot the country in all directions, and descending an inclined plane, we again enter, from its southern side, Salem, the pride of Oregon; soon to be numbered among the most beauteous of the cities of America.

LINN COUNTY.

This county is bounded north by Marion County, east by the Cascade Mountains, south by Lane, and west by Benton, from which it is separated by the Willamette River. Embracing the portion of the Cascades that would come within its limits, it contains an area of not less than one thousand five hundred square miles, equal to nine hundred and sixty thousand acres of land. The whole number of acres under cultivation is forty-nine thousand four hundred and five. The population of Linn is second only to Marion, and amounts to about eight thousand souls, there being an excess of males over females of about six hundred. The number of voters at the last election was two thousand two hundred and fifty. The value of assessable property was two million five hundred thousand dollars. Albany is the county seat, and is situated on the east bank of the Willamette River at the mouth of Callapooia Creek, twenty-five miles south of Salem, and seventy-five miles south of Portland. It occupies a beautiful locality, and is one of the most prosperous towns of the state. It is adorned by a magnificent court-house, which the people of the county have erected at a cost of thirty-one thousand dollars. It is aided by extensive flouring mills and other manufactories. The spires of four churches point heavenward, as if to indicate the religious character of the inhabitants. The public schools are of an elevated character, and a college, established under the auspices of the Old School Presbyterian Church, promises great usefulness to town and county and state. The private dwellings of Albany are more tastefully ornamented than those of any other town in the state. The exportations of produce from Albany are greater than from any other inland town. In fine, Albany possesses all the elements of a continued and an enlarged prosperity. It is now the third city in the state.

The county of which it is the seat of justice is one of the best on the Pacific. The Santiam River divides this county from Marion. This river comes down from the Cascades in two branches, the north and south, and there is quite an extent of country between these branches. This is called the " Forks " of Santiam. This is in Linn. The scenery is fine, and the country is not undesirable. The land is rich, and well adapted to farming and grazing purposes. At a central point in the Forks, on a beautiful tributary of the Santiam, is the little flourishing town of Scio. Rapidly growing, and blessed with manufactories, schools, and Churches, it will advance to a place of considerable importance.

Leaving the Forks, and crossing the south branch, we come to the growing little town of Lebanon, standing on the borders of the largest and most beautiful prairie in the state of Oregon. This town contains several stores, workshops, etc., and is the locality of an academy which is under the patronage and control of the Oregon Conference of the Methodist Episcopal Church. This is an institution that would be creditable to a place of much higher pretensions, and is now under the able management of the Rev. J. B. Calloway. Its influence for good in the vicinity where it is located is great, and, in preparing students to enter the advanced classes in the Willamette University, it is becoming a useful adjunct to that institution. The building is of wood, of fine appearance, and sufficiently large to accommodate the school for years to come.

Three miles from Lebanon, in a southerly direction, is a bald prairie eminence known as Washington Butte. Beyond this, and further out in the prairie, are Ward's Butte and Saddle Butte. These are elevations of great beauty, somewhat isolated from the foot hills of the Cascades, and from their summit command a view of the largest, the most beautiful, and the best prairie in the state of Oregon. This prairie is, on an average, about ten miles broad and forty-five miles long, being cut, in two or three places, by streams that meander through it. This prairie is all divided up into beautiful farms, the most of which are under a good state of cultivation, and, with their beautiful and cozy farm dwellings, their capacious and well-filled barns, their broad and fruitful fields, their apples, peaches, plums, and grapes, and their numerous flocks and herds, constitute most delightful homes for their occupants, conferring upon them not only a competency of the good things of earth, but even a superabundance.

Brownsville is another important town in this county, and is situated on the Callapooia Creek, twenty-two miles southeast from Albany, and fourteen miles south from Lebanon. This flourishing town has excellent water privileges, which are beginning to be extensively used. Here is a large woolen factory in successful operation, a fine grist mill, and other manufacturing establishments, with a number of stores and business shops of various kinds, all of which give satisfactory evidence that this town, up among the foot hills of the Cascades, possesses the elements of a certain prosperity. It is surrounded by an excellent farming and grazing country, and for many miles up the Callapooia, east of Brownsville, the valley is broad, and composed of the best of farming land, and the foot hills are very fertile, and are settled up for miles back, and constitute one of the best grazing districts in the state. There are several small valleys on the tributaries of the Willamette, among the foot hills of the mountains, which are worthy of mention : Brush Creek, which is a better valley than its name would imply; Mohawk Valley, which for some reason took its name from the Mohawk of New York state; and "Sweet Home" Valley, hidden among the mountains, yet as delightful as its name would indicate.

Leaving this eastern portion of the county, and

traveling westward over a most delightful plain, and taking a survey as we pass along of the nice farms, the splendid orchards, and other objects of interest, keeping within the limits of Linn County, we at length, after proceeding some fifteen miles, reach a point of interest on the east bank of the Willamette River. This is Harrisburg, another prosperous little town, commanding very considerable trade from the rich and extended prairie over which we have just passed. Here also is a large flouring mill, and all the appurtenances of a fine growing town. Steamboats reach this point quite regularly for six months in the year. Now we will turn to the northward, and travel down along the east bank of the Willamette River; and we will look at the pretty farms, the snug cottages, the noble barns, now and then looking down upon the silvery river flowing at our left as we pass along, and twelve miles below Harrisburg we come to another point of interest called Peoria. It is a little town close upon the river's brink, on a beautiful spot, and commanding considerable trade from the fertile prairie on the margin of which it is located, and will doubtless grow in proportion to the advancement of the country around. Again we will proceed northward, and passing through a country of surpassing loveliness for fifteen miles more, we reach Albany again, and here, climbing to the elevated dome of the court-house, we will take a parting view of the county of Linn from that altitude. Looking south, we have a distinct view of Spencer's Butte, and the range of hills forming the southern boundary of the Willamette Valley, fifty miles distant. We see the mighty Cascade Range, with Hood and Jefferson and the Three Sisters, stretching along to the right and left, and casting their shadows against the eastern sky the distance of at least one hundred and fifty miles. And we also see every foot almost of the beautiful county of Linn, checkered with farms, traversed with roads, dotted with cottages, and teeming with industry, and with the whole panoramic scene before us we are ready to exclaim, " Surely this is a scene of natural beauty and grandeur worthy of the pencil of the most skillful master properly to portray.

Scattered over the fine and extended prairie which we have been surveying are quite a number of houses of worship which have been erected by different denominations, and on the Sabbath day nearly all the people are in the house of God.

Numerous white school-houses dot the prairie in every direction, neat, tasteful, and commodious, where the children rally to receive the rudiments of an education. In fine, here, as in every portion of Oregon, are seen on every hand the evidences of an advancing Christian civilization. A few years only have elapsed since an unbroken solitude reigned over these extended plains; but now the solitary places are rejoicing with gladness, and the wilderness is budding and blossoming like the rose. Leaving our high post of observation we come down to the common level of the country, and finish our description of Linn.

There are two weekly papers published in Linn, both in the city of Albany: the *Albany Journal*, by Wm. Pickett & Co., and the *States Rights Democrat*, by Abbott & Brown. Both are popular with the respective parties in whose interest they were established, and both are useful in developing the resources of the county and state.

MULTNOMAH COUNTY.

This county is principally embraced in the city of Portland, so far as its population is concerned. It lies on the banks of the Willamette River in the north part of the state, with Clackamas on the south, Washington on the west, and Columbia on the north. This county contains a population of near eight thousand souls, with a large preponderance of males over females, as in all other counties on the Pacific. As the land outside of Portland is mainly heavily timbered, there are only four thousand one hundred and fifty-one acres under cultivation. The total value of assessable property, by a recent valuation, is four million dollars. This makes the county of Multnomah the wealthiest one in the state. Portland is the county seat, as well as the commercial emporium of the state. It stands upon the western bank of the Willamette River, on ground that but a few years ago was covered with a dense and heavy body of fir timber. It extends for two miles up and down the river, and the ground is mainly covered with buildings one half mile back. It has many very beautiful and substantial blocks of stores and private dwellings, and it is affirmed that, in proportion to its population, it is the wealthiest city on the Pacific coast, if not in America. There is a road extending from Portland by the way of Salem and Jacksonville, to the city of Sacramento in California, the distance of over six hundred miles, and a line of daily stages ply between the two points. This is a very important fact in the description of Oregon. This line of stages was first owned by a California company, but by purchase became the property of H. W. Corbett, who was subsequently elected a United States senator from Oregon, and was himself a resident of Portland. This place is greatly benefited by this line, as is also the entire country. Portland also constitutes a center for Washington Territory and Idaho, and there are daily departures to and arrivals from these portions of the country.

Besides this, Portland is at the head of ship navigation on the Willamette River, and here sailing vessels and steamboats from San Francisco land all their freight and passengers. If Portland can retain these advantages she must continue to be the commercial center of this part of the Pacific coast. Portland, like Salem, has her "institutions," and we call attention to a few of them.

HER SCHOOLS AND SEMINARIES OF LEARNING.

Portland, like all other towns in Oregon, pays great attention to the subject of education. Her public schools, of which there are several, under the management of competent teachers, rank with the best in the country, and are, indeed, decidedly popular.

There are also private schools, concerning which we have little information.

Besides these, there are denominational institutions which are exerting an extensive influence.

The Catholics here also, under the direction of a society of sisters, have established a school, as usual, for the exclusive benefit of girls. They are influenced, doubtless, by the consideration that if they can get the girls they will soon have the mothers, and if the mothers, the children that may follow, and consequently the country.

The Portland Academy and Female Seminary deserves particular notice. This institution is the property of the Methodist Episcopal Church, and is under the control and patronage of the Oregon Conference. It is almost coeval in existence with Portland itself, having been built as early as 1849 or 1850.

The Rev. James H. Wilbur was the agent, in the hands of Providence, in originating and carrying forward to completion this important educational enterprise. He bared his arm to the physical labor, as well as the superintendency of the business, and as a result, before leaving Portland for a southern field he saw the building prepared for occupancy, and a school in successful operation, under the tuition of one abundantly competent to sustain its interests. Rev. C. S. Kingsley was the successful principal and conductor of this institution for several years, and it attained to a high position as a seminary of learning under his skillful management. It has, however, with all such institutions in Oregon, on account of the smallness of the population, and a want of adequate means of support, experienced some reverses; but at the present time, under the able management of T. M. Gatch, A. M., formerly president of the Willamette University, it is sharing an unusual degree of prosperity.

The Churches of Portland are a distinguishing feature of its institutions.

The following are the principal, though there may be other associations claiming to be Churches not here named: the Methodist Episcopal Church, the Old School Presbyterian, the Congregational, the Baptist, the Methodist, South, the Protestant Episcopal, the Roman Catholic, and a Synagogue of the Jews. Most of these are flourishing Churches, and are doing much for the cause of Christianity in Portland and the surrounding country. As in most other places on the Pacific coast, the Methodist Episcopal Church is the oldest in the place, being in existence coeval with the town itself. As it claims priority of occupancy, so it has been regarded as the leading Church in Portland in its influence upon the masses of the community. In its early history, and under the skillful management of Rev. J. H. Wilbur, the society erected for that period a good and comfortable house of worship. Subsequently, under the administration of Rev. David Rutledge, now of Tennessee, this house was reconstructed and improved.

It is now being displaced, under the pastorate of Rev. C. C. Stratton, by the erection of a splendid brick gothic church edifice, which would not be disparaging to one of the fine avenues in the city of New York.

The periodicals of Portland constitute another of its important institutions. These are the daily and weekly Herald, by the Oregon Herald Company; the daily and weekly Oregonian, by Henry L. Pittock; the weekly Pioneer, a German paper, by Walther & Landenburger; the Pacific Christian Advocate, edited by Dr. H. C. Benson; and M'Cormick's Almanac, which has become of itself a permanent institution of the country, having been published annually for fourteen years.

The above periodicals are all important as auxiliaries in the great work of developing and advancing the interests of our young and growing state, and some of them have become so identified with all our operations, and linked with all our interests, that it would be impossible to discontinue them without seriously impairing all those interests. This is emphatically true in reference to the Pacific *Christian Advocate*. This important aid to the propagation of Christianity in general, and the advancement of the denominational interests of the Methodist Episcopal Church in particular, has become to the country a fundamental necessity. Scarcely more so are either our institutions of learning, or our active, living ministry. An extent of country six hundred miles in length and five hundred in breadth depends mainly upon the *Pacific Christian Advocate* for its religious reading and news. In all that vast region nothing could possibly supply its place. Nothing from the eastern states, nothing from any other portion of the Pacific coast. The *Pacific Advocate*, like leaves from the tree of life, falls at the doors of hundreds of families, blessing them with its healing virtue, and bearing to their hearts the messages of peace and love. It is vital to every interest connected with the Methodist Episcopal Church within the limits of the Oregon Conference. It has now entered the thirteenth year of its publication.

In this enumeration of the institutions of Portland the National College of Business and Commerce should not be omitted, as it has become one of the permanent establishments of the city. Its object is to confer upon all who desire to avail themselves of it the advantage of a thorough business education. The institution is under the presidency of M. K. Lauden, Esq., whose reputation for ability and extensive business acquirements are a sufficient guaranty for the thoroughness of the instructions given. An ordinary English education is all that is required to enter the school, and the average time to complete the whole course is from twelve to sixteen weeks, according to the advancement and application of the student. This young institution is in a flourishing condition, having its pupils from all parts of the state. It must be of incalculable benefit to the future business of our young commonwealth. This, with those we have already mentioned, together with mutual insurance companies, publishing houses, banking establishments, Masonic, Odd Fellows, and Good Templar Lodges, not forgetting the Oregon Fire Works Company, with its laboratory near Port land, constitute the principal institutions of the flourishing county of Multnomah, and its beautiful and thriving city Portland of the Pacific.

CLACKAMAS COUNTY.

The country included within the limits of this county is diversified by hills, valleys, prairies, and woodlands, the latter, however, predominating. It is an interesting portion of the state, and is bounded north by Multnomah, east by the Cascade Mountains, south by Marion, and west by Washington and Multnomah counties. It has a population of four thousand two hundred, there being a large preponderance of males over females.

By the last assessment the property was valued at one million six hundred and five thousand five hundred and ninety-four dollars. The land cultivated in 1867 was only six thousand and sixty-two acres.

Oregon City is the county seat, and boasts of being the oldest incorporated city of the state.

This city has many advantages, arising from the fact that it is located in the very channel of trade through the country, and commands one of the most extensive water privileges in the state. Here the whole Willamette River plunges down a precipice of thirty feet perpendicular, forming a most valuable power, as well as an object of great beauty.

This city, commencing at the falls, stretches along down the east bank to the river for a mile and a half, and back some distance on to the hill, and, containing many beautiful private dwellings, several churches, a large and commodious public school-house, a court-house, and other interesting objects, it presents a delightful appearance as you approach it from the direction of Portland. It is twelve miles from the latter place, and steamers ply between the two every few hours. A daily line of stages also passes through the town.

Its manufacturing character has been mentioned elsewhere, and need not be repeated here.

The first frame Christian church that was ever erected on the northwest Pacific coast was located here. It was commenced in 1842 by Rev. A. F. Waller, who was then a missionary at this point, and so far completed in 1844 as to be opened for public worship by the writer of this sketch. The church is indeed an historical one, and to be considered among the permanent institutions of the country. Connected with the church is a parsonage property of considerable value, and, taken altogether, this constitutes one of the pleasantest stations in the Oregon Conference. This county derives its name from the Clackamas River, which divides it into two nearly equal parts. The other points of interest in the county are Milwaukee, six miles below Oregon City on the Willamette River, Clackamas, Clear Creek, Beaver Creek, and Baker's Prairie. The county is every way capable of sustaining a vast increase of its present popu-

FIRST CHURCH IN OREGON.

lation. Oswego, which is also in Clackamas County, with its extensive iron works, has been considered in the general account of the valley.

This county, from the position which it occupies, commanding as it does the main channel of trade through the state, possessing almost boundless water power, and combining extensive agricultural and mineral interests, should be classed among the most important and valuable portions of the state.

COLUMBIA COUNTY.

This county is bounded on the north by the Columbia River, on the east by the Columbia and Multnomah, on the south by Washington County, and on the west by the county of Clatsop. Its population is small, amounting to about five hundred. The number of voters at the last election was one hundred and seventy-three. This county is very long, extending for many miles along the south bank of the Columbia, embracing a broad range of timbered hills that reach back for several miles from the river. These hills are many of them rich in soil, and afford great lumbering facilities on account of the excellence of timber that adorns their summits, and the ease with which this timber can be cast into the river. There is less than one thousand acres of land under cultivation in the county, and according to the last assessment the assessable property amounted to one hundred and fifty-nine thousand nine hundred and seventy dollars. St. Helens, named after a snow-crowned mountain of the same name—a beautiful view of which may be had from this locality—is situated on the south bank of the Columbia River, north of Portland the distance of thirty miles. It is the seat of justice, and, besides occupying a very beautiful locality, is a place of growing importance. Religious and educational institutions keep pace with the improvements of the town, and the time is not far distant when the extensive and beautiful plateau in the rear of the town will be adorned by delightful cottages and country seats. Rainier, named after another snow-covered mountain, and some twenty miles below St. Helens, is also a point of some interest, though commanding no very cheering prospect of future growth.

BAKER COUNTY.

The name of the patriot, orator, and statesman, the gallant Colonel E. D. Baker, who fell at Ball's Bluff, in the late civil war, and whom Oregon delighted to honor, is perpetuated in the name of this county, which is situated in the eastern portion of the state. The topography of this county is exceedingly variegated and beautiful. It embraces within its limits extensive tracts of excellent agricultural and grazing lands, which are now occupied by an intelligent and energetic people. This county has come into existence in its political organic character very suddenly, and mainly through the discovery of valuable gold and silver mines, which already have yielded large amounts of money, and are being rapidly developed. Auburn is the county seat, and is located three hundred miles from Salem, the capital of the state, by the usual route, and two hundred and fifty miles from Portland. Baker City, another important point, is delightfully situated in the Powder River Valley, ten miles southeast of Auburn. This valley comprehends a vast amount of excellent and beautiful country, as also inexhaustible stores of mineral wealth. Religiously and morally, it is purely a missionary field. Its religious and literary institutions—its churches and school-houses—are yet to be established.

GRANT COUNTY.

This county is situated directly west of Baker County, and between it and the Cascade Mountains. It embraces an excellent pastoral and grazing country, with considerable tracts of good land for agricultural purposes. It is also rich in mineral wealth, and large quantities of gold are taken annually from its gulches and cañons. The character of its surface is similar to many other portions already described, so far as relates to its scenery. Its population by the last census was two thousand two hundred and fifty; two thousand males and two hundred and fifty females. Number of voters thirteen hundred. Its assessed property was two hundred and ninety-five thousand dollars. The seat of justice of this county is Cañon City, which is built on the middle fork of John Day's

River, and is about three hundred and sixty miles from Salem, by the usual route, and three hundred and ten from Portland. This is a new county, and, with Baker, is in a state of formation in respect to all of its interests. It has but five thousand acres of its land under cultivation, while tens of thousands await the implements of husbandry to develop their ample though hidden stores, and confer upon their occupants homes and plenty.

POLK COUNTY.

This county is bounded south by Yamhill County, east by Marion, from which it is separated by the Willamette River, south by Benton County, and west by the Pacific Ocean. It has an area of about twelve hundred and fifty square miles, equal to about eight hundred thousand acres of land. It embraces a section of the Coast Range of mountains, in which there are many depressions, and narrow valleys of excellent land, which, however, is covered with a dense growth of timber. The eastern half of the county is well adapted to grazing and agricultural purposes, and is already being brought into a state of handsome cultivation and improvement. Indeed, some of the finest farms in the state are to be found in some of the valleys of this county. There are two streams that have their source in the Coast Range of mountains, which, running east, and empty into the Willamette River, and, with their tributaries, water the eastern half of the county; these are the La Creole and Luckimute : and there are other streams that run westward from the same source and empty into the Pacific Ocean. Situated on the La Creole is the beautiful town of Dallas, which is the county seat. This town is within fifteen miles of Salem, the capital, and is sixty miles southwest from Portland.

The eastern half of the county is as densely populated as any of the farming portions of the state, and contains a population of about five thousand souls. The votes cast at the last election numbered eleven hundred and twenty-five. Acres of land under cultivation, ninety thousand one hundred and twenty-seven, being nearly twice as much as any other county in the state. The assessable property was valued at one million thirty-three thousand one hundred and seventy-nine dollars. This county, besides possessing abundant agricultural resources, is finely situated for commerce, the steamboats plying on the Willamette River all along her eastern border affording her ample means for both importation and exportation. Besides Dallas, there are a number of places of considerable importance within the limits of this county. Eola, on the opposite side of the river, and five miles above Salem ; Independence, seven miles further up; Monmouth, two miles back from Independence; and Buenavista, seven miles up from Independence, are all beautiful and flourishing little towns, and are sustained by a fine farming country around them.

This county has made of late, as indeed it may be

said of nearly all the counties in the state, very great advancement in regard to schools and academies. Common schools are numerous and well sustained, and there are several schools that have attained to the dignity of academies. Dallas and Bethel are the seats of institutions of the latter kind. Monmouth, which is really the most delightful location in Polk County, is the seat of an institution which is laboring with some success to sustain the character of a college. This institution is under the patronage of the Christian Church, better known outside of that particular denomination as Campbellites. The school, with all other institutions of the kind in Oregon, has had its reverses; but, on the whole, promises to become a successful auxiliary in the promotion of the educational interests of the state.

UNION COUNTY.

This county is also situated in the eastern part of Oregon, and comprehends a section of the Blue Mountain Range. It is most remarkably diversified in its scenery, and embraces one of the handsomest and most fertile valleys in the state. This valley is called the Grand Round. It is circular in its form, and about twenty miles in diameter. It is now occupied by a farming and pastoral population.

The town of Le Grande is situated in this valley, and is the seat of justice for the county. It is about three hundred and fifty miles east from Salem in a direct line, and about the same distance from Portland. The county contains a population of about two thousand, and cast at the last election seven hundred and five votes. The county, with respect to all its interests, is in an embryo state, but it has a basis in its agricultural and mineral resources which will enable it to grow into one of the most flourishing and wealthy counties east of the Cascade Mountains.

UMATILLA COUNTY.

This county lies mainly in the great valley between the Blue Mountains and the Cascade Range. It is a fine county of land, wonderfully diversified and interesting in its scenery, and is destined ultimately to contain a heavy population. The present population is about two thousand, and the number of votes cast was seven hundred and ninety-seven. The number of acres under cultivation is five thousand seven hundred and seventy, while the assessable property is valued at eight hundred and eighty-seven thousand one hundred and forty-eight dollars. Umatilla City is the county seat, and is situated directly on the Columbia River, and is two hundred and twenty-five miles east from Portland, and two hundred and seventy-five miles from Salem by the usual route. It is a place of very considerable importance, as it constitutes a landing-place for all the supplies of goods and people destined for the mining camps in Eastern Oregon and the southern part of Idaho.

Within the limits of this county is the Umatilla

Indian reservation, which includes one of the most valuable parts of the county.

This county also is in a forming state, and requires a few years for its resources to become developed, and then it will doubtless take rank among the best counties of Oregon.

WASCO COUNTY.

This interesting portion of Oregon derived its name from the tribe of Indians who occupied the country when the whites began to settle within their territory. These Indians were called the Wasco tribe, and the principal point or portion of their country, embracing the Dalles of the Columbia, was called Wascopam. Hence the name of the county. It lies immediately east, and embraces the foot hills, and even much of the higher portions of the Cascade Mountains. In its topography it is remarkably diversified, and in point of interesting and impressive scenery is equal to any county within the limits of the state, and probably to any canton in far-famed Switzerland. It is not necessary for an American to go to Switzerland nor Italy, to the Alps nor to the Apennines, nor to any other foreign country, to enjoy the divine sensations resulting from the contemplation of scenery infinitely more grand than it is possible for the imagination to paint; he only needs to perform a passage from Vancouver up the Columbia River through the tremendous cañon of more than eighty miles in length, and gaze upon rocks piled upon rocks, abutments on the top of abutments, basaltic columns rising above columns, and mountains heaped on mountains, and old Hood lifting his hoary head far up into the blue vault of heaven, and looking down upon the clouds that hang around him thousands of feet below his shimmering summit, and he cannot fail to be convinced of the utter insignificance of the works of art, and of the impossibility of the most skillful artist ever being able to copy to the life the picture here painted by the hand of the great Artist of the universe. Such is the scenery presented to the eye of the traveler in passing up the Columbia to Dalles City, the county seat of Wasco County. Indeed, the whole county, as to its surface, presents a picture in which is blended beauty, romance, sublimity, and grandeur in equal proportions, and like the kaleidoscope, offers to the traveler an ever-varying scene.

This county is bounded north by the Columbia River, east by Umatilla County, south its limits are indefinite, and west by the Cascade Mountains. Its population is about two thousand souls. Number of voters six hundred and four. Value of assessable property one million seven hundred and seventy-one thousand four hundred and twenty dollars.

Dalles City, the county seat, is situated on the south bank of the Columbia, and is distant from Salem, by the way of the Willamette and Columbia Rivers, one hundred and sixty-five miles, and from Portland one hundred and fifteen miles. The town pays considerable attention to schools and churches, and other means of improvement. The Mountaineer, a lively weekly paper, is published by Mr. William Hand, and receives its share of public patronage.

WASHINGTON COUNTY.

This county embraces the country drained by the Tuality River, known as the Tuality Plains. These plains have been considered in the general description of the country, and here it may only be said that they are second to none in beauty and fertility in any part of the state. They now constitute, perhaps, the most thickly settled of any of the farming communities. The population of the county by the last census was three thousand four hundred and ninety-one. Number of voters eight hundred and twenty-four, and the amount of land under cultivation is twenty-six thousand three hundred and forty-three acres. The county seat of Washington County is Hillsborough, which is built on a most delightful plain near a branch of Tuality River.

Hillsborough is sixty miles north of Salem, and eighteen miles west from Portland. Besides Hillsborough, there are many other points of interest in this county which might be considered if space would permit. Among these Forest Grove should not be omitted. This place, situated twenty miles west of Portland and fifty-six north from Salem, is the location of an institution of learning under the patronage of the Congregational Church, called the Pacific

University. It was established at an early day in the history of Oregon, being only second in age to the Willamette University. The Rev. Harvey Clark, of whom mention has been made in this work, was the principal instrument of bringing this university into existence, but he did not long live to see its advancement.

It has often felt the pressure arising from a sparse population and limited means. The Rev. Dr. Marsh, who for some years has been the president of this university, has succeeded in placing it upon a more permanent basis by raising an endowment fund of some forty thousand dollars. This was done in the Atlantic States. Dr. Marsh made two visits to the East, spending in all some three years of time, during which he visited many portions of the country, the eastern cities, New York, Boston, and other cities, presenting before the people, privately and publicly as he had opportunity, the claims of that institution upon the benevolence of the Church, and as a result bore with him to the Pacific coast the funds which he had raised, thereby placing the institution upon a firm footing, and establishing a power for the conferment of blessing upon untold generations.

There are also many flourishing public schools within the limits of this county, and the children are generally brought within the means of acquiring an education.

Religious institutions abound and flourish in this county. There are several prosperous Christian Churches established here, and some of the earliest efforts which were made on the coast to build up religious societies were made on these beautiful plains. On a pleasant Sabbath, early in April, 1841, the Rev. A. F. Waller and the writer preached the first sermons that were ever heard in this portion of the land, and from that time until the present religion has had a place within what is now Washington County.

The Methodists, Congregationalists, and Baptists all have comfortable houses of worship, and the people are generally liberal in supporting the institutions of the Church.

These delightful plains have easy access to the waters of the Willamette River at Oregon City and Portland, and to the Columbia River at St. Helens, by good roads leading to these places. Washington County, in fine, embraces a very valuable portion of the state, and is second to none in everything relating to improvements in all the departments of husbandry, as well as in respect to all those institutions which are designed more especially for the promotion of the moral and intellectual wellbeing of its population.

YAMHILL COUNTY.

A tribe or class of Indians who were the original proprietors of the land embraced in this county, and a beautiful river which runs through its entire extent, were known by the name of Yamhill by the aborigines long before the country was occupied by the pale faces. This accounts fully for the origin of the name of the county. This county is bounded on the north by Washington and Clackamas, on the east by the Willamette River, on the south by Polk County, and on the west by the Coast Range of mountains, which separate it from Tilamook and Clatsop counties. It comprises not only a very magnificent, but also a very rich, fertile, and lovely portion of the state of Oregon. It is, as with many other counties, wonderfully diversified by lovely valleys, extended plains, gentle undulations, rising grounds, and lofty eminences, and these are all characterized by a naturally rich and productive soil.

The county contains a population of upward of four thousand souls, with a preponderance of four hundred males over the females. At the last election the votes cast numbered one thousand and eighty-two.

The number of acres of land under cultivation was twenty-six thousand three hundred and forty-three. Assessable property was valued at one million dollars.

Lafayette, situated on the left bank of the Yamhill River, and five miles from where that river empties into the Willamette, is the county seat. It is located twenty-four miles northwest of Salem, and thirty miles southwest of Portland. It is most delightfully located in the midst of a fine agricultural country, and is yearly advancing in commerce and population. It has a court-house, a church, and an academy, which imply that its financial, spiritual, and intellectual necessities are provided for and secured. Below Lafayette two miles, on the same river, is the town of Dayton, which is also a growing place. A steamer runs regularly to this place from Oregon City. Here is a commodious Methodist church and parsonage, and from this point, in a circuit of some fifteen miles, there are three other Methodist churches, besides those that belong to other denominations. South of Lafayette some four miles is situated the beautiful village of M'Minnville. This is one of the most delightful spots in the Yamhill country, and the agents of the Baptist Church in Oregon, to whom the responsibility was committed, displayed not only good judgment, but fine taste in selecting this place for the location of their principal literary institution in Oregon. This is called the M'Minnville College, and will doubtless work its way into a permanent university. This institution has for some years been under the general direction of the Rev. Dr. Chandler, aided by a corps of professors and teachers fully qualified not only to elevate the character of the school, but to insure its future permanence and prosperity. Common schools, those fruitful adjuncts of academies and colleges, abound also in this county in every neighborhood able to support them. The other places of note in this county are Amity, Mountain House, North Yamhill, Sheridan, and West Chehalem; but they must be passed with the general remark that they help to make up one of the most beautiful, fertile, and desirable counties included within the limits of the Willamette Valley.

OREGON INSTITUTE.

CHAPTER VI.

HISTORY OF THE OREGON INSTITUTE AND WILLA-METTE UNIVERSITY.

THE history of all nations proves that science and literature flourish most where the foundations of society are laid in the principles of a pure Christianity.

For untold ages the great Pacific slope of the North American Continent had been enveloped in almost impenetrable darkness, and the wandering tribes of savage barbarians which roamed over its extended plains were as untamed and ignorant as the wild beasts by which they were surrounded; but at length was heard over this region of the valley and shadow of death the voice of Providence, saying, " Let there be light," and there was light.

Heathen hands were outstretched from these Cimmerian realms, and heathen voices were heard imploring for the Christian's book and the white man's God. Connected with the introduction of Christian civilization into the Pacific world, and leading to that important event, was one of the most interesting circumstances that ever transpired in the history of any heathen nation. It was this: A deputation of Indians from one of the principal tribes inhabiting this vast region of night, who had heard of the existence of the white man, and of his superior knowledge, traversed the whole distance from the waters of Oregon to the frontiers of Missouri, exposed to the fury of hostile clans and beasts of prey, for the purpose of learning from General Clark, who was then the superintendent of Indian affairs for the whole western world, the truth of what they had heard concerning the white man's worship and civilization. This wonderful event was hailed by the Methodist Episcopal Church in the United States as the clear expression of the will of heaven that a gospel mission should be at once established in the benighted regions bordering the Pacific Ocean. Measures were taken to carry a resolution formed to this effect into immediate execution, and in the month of June, 1833, the Rev. Jason Lee, of Stanstead, Canada East, was ordained in New England by Bishop Hedding, and was appointed to the superintendency of a mission which he was authorized to establish in the territory of Oregon. In the following August Rev. Daniel Lee, a nephew of Jason, was appointed to accompany his uncle, and early in March, 1834, they left New England for the Pacific shores, accompanied by Cyrus Shepherd, a lay member of the Church. On reaching what was then considered the far West, they were to accompany the expedition of Captain Nathaniel Wyeth, of Massachusetts, who was intending to proceed to Oregon for purposes of traffic among the Indian tribes. On their progress westward from New England they held missionary meetings in all the principal towns through which they passed, and great interest was excited in the public mind in relation to the enterprise. On the twenty-fifth of April they had reached the frontiers, and on that day, having been joined by P. L. Edwards, of Missouri, also a lay member, they left civilized society behind them, and started on their perilous journey across the trackless wilds. They penetrated the deepest recesses of savage life, and experienced all manner of hardships and deprivations and exposures incident to journeyings over thousands of miles of almost unexplored regions, beset on every hand by hostile savages and beasts of prey; but, preserved in the midst of the imminent and multiplied dangers by which they were surrounded by a merciful Providence through the many months of their wearisome toil across the arid deserts, on the twenty-first day of September, 1834, they found themselves in the territory of Oregon, on the banks of the beautiful Willamette River, ten miles below the spot where the city of Salem now stands, and there they commenced laying the foundations of Christian civilization in this western world.

Up to that period unbroken heathenism had reigned from Arkansas to the waters of the great Pacific, and from the hyperborean regions of Alaska to the country of the Montezumas. But in the order of the divine economy another state of things was now to be introduced. The dominions of darkness were to be invaded, "the wilderness and the solitary places were to be glad for them, and the desert to bud and blossom as the rose." Simple were the means employed, but grand have been the results secured.

At the time these missionaries of the cross located themselves on the Willamette there were no white children on all the Pacific slope of the continent of North America, and but very few white men. There were, however, a few Englishmen, Scotchmen, and Canadian French, who were connected with the Hudson's Bay Company, and had married Indian wives, and rejoiced as the fathers of half-caste children; and at Vancouver there were a few children that were three fourths white, their fathers being white men and their mothers half-caste. These were also connected with the Hudson's Bay Company. So soon as these devoted missionaries had established themselves at their post on the Willamette, and had thrown up a log-cabin to shelter those that might remain from the storms of winter, one of their number proceeded to Vancouver and commenced a school for the benefit of the half-breed and other children at that post, and the others commenced teaching the children of the natives of the country the rudiments of science and religion, and preaching the Gospel to the members of the Hudson's Bay Company, and to such other straggling white men as had preferred to remain in the country rather than return to civilization with the companies with which they had been connected, and also to the Indians as far as it was possible to get their attention. They gathered together some dozens of Indian children in the little log school-house which they had erected for the purpose, and immediately established what was denominated the "Oregon Mission Manual Labor School."

This school, and the one at Vancouver already men
tioned, were the first that were opened on the Pacific
coast for instruction in the English language.

The school on the Willamette in a few years became a flourishing institution, and gave great promise
of future usefulness to the Indian race. Mr. Slocum,
who, under the auspices of the government of the
United States, visited Oregon in 1837, remarks in
relation to this school as follows: "It is indeed a
source of regret that I could continue no longer at
your mission on the banks of the Willamette, for
the visit was to me one of exceeding interest. On
my return to the civilized portions of our country I
shall not hesitate to express my humble opinion that
you have already effected a great public good, by
practically showing that the Indians west of the
Rocky Mountains are capable of the union of mental
and physical discipline as taught at your establishment. For I have seen with my own eyes children
who two years ago were roaming their own native
wilds in a state of savage barbarism, now being
brought within the knowledge of moral and religious
instruction, becoming useful members of society by
being taught the most useful of all arts, agriculture,
and all this without the slightest compulsion." The
prosperity of the school and the general state of the
country seemed to demand an increase in the number
of Christian laborers; accordingly Mr. Lee addressed
letters to the Missionary Board in New York, earnestly soliciting them to send out a reinforcement.
In compliance with this request, the Board appointed

Dr. Elijah White and wife, Mr. Alanson Beers and wife, Miss Ann Maria Pitman, Miss Susan Downing, Miss Elvira Johnson, and Mr. W. H. Wilson, assistant missionaries. This company sailed from Boston in July, 1836, and performing the voyage round Cape Horn, arrived safely in the Willamette Valley on the 27th day of May, 1837. On the 20th of September following the mission settlement was again increased by the arrival of Rev. David Leslie and family, Rev. H. K. W. Perkins, and Miss Margaret Smith.

Sixteen adult persons were now connected with the mission, and at the close of 1837 they were all at or near the Willamette station, and were laboring in their respective departments, not without effect; some in sustaining the interests of the mission school, some in preaching the Gospel to the Callapooias and other Indians and to the few white men who had begun to gather around the mission, some in the mechanical branches, and some in taking care of the mission farm and the rapidly increasing stock of cattle and horses. Though some of the members of the mission school had died during the year, yet, in view of all the circumstances surrounding them, the missionaries were greatly encouraged, and began to take measures for the enlargement of their work. A new mission station was established at the Dalles of the Columbia, and it was the unanimous opinion of all the missionaries, expressed in a meeting held for general consultation, that provision should be made for the supply of other portions of the extended field. They considered that "the harvest was plenteous, while the laborers were few;" and they passed a unanimous resolution advising the superintendent, Rev. Jason Lee, to make a visit to the United States for the purpose of representing before the Board of Managers of the Missionary Society of the Methodist Episcopal Church, and the public generally, the true condition of the country and of the Indians, and soliciting the men and means which, in their judgment, were necessary for the successful prosecution of the missionary work.

Mr. Lee concurred in the opinions thus expressed by the members of the mission, and accordingly took leave of his wife and brethren on the Willamette on the 26th of March, 1838, and commenced the long and hazardous journey back across the Rocky Mountains. He was accompanied by P. L. Edwards, of the mission, Mr. Ewing, of Missouri, and two Indian boys. Mr. Lee and his company made the tedious and dangerous transit in safety, and on the 1st of September he arrived at the Methodist mission among the Shawnees, then under the superintendency of the Rev. Mr. Johnson, and having at night retired to his room, he was offering up a tribute of thanksgiving to Him who had been his preserver while on his toilsome journey through the hostile tribes of the mountains, when he heard a rap at his door. Rising, he admitted the stranger, who placed a package of letters in his hands and immediately left the room. He broke the black seal of one, and the first line conveyed to him the heart-rending intelligence that his Ann Maria and her little son were numbered with the dead.

Sorely afflicted by the loss which he had sustained, a knowledge of which had been communicated by an express sent by his friends in Oregon, after resting a few days he proceeded on to New York, where he arrived about the 1st of November, and at once zealously engaged in accomplishing the objects of his visit to the United States. On the 14th he was present at a meeting of the Missionary Board, and stated at length the object of his visit. He urged with much earnestness the importance of extending the missionary work in Oregon; and, in view of this, he pleaded with great zeal the necessity of sending to that country a large reinforcement. In his opinion it was essential, for the prosperity of the mission, to supply it with the requisite means to furnish itself with all the means of support, and all the necessary implements for husbandry and mechanical purposes should be sent out by the Board. To meet all these demands would require a very heavy outlay, and for this and some other reasons Mr. Lee met with strong opposition from some of the members of the Board, who sincerely doubted the expediency of the measure; but the superintendent, who had just come from the field of operations, perseveringly and powerfully urged the claims of the mission until he succeeded in obtaining all, and more than all he requested.

As a result of his interviews with the Board, the latter, at a meeting held on the 6th of December, 1838, passed a resolution to send to Oregon five additional missionaries, one physician, six mechanics, four farmers, one steward or accountant, and four female teachers, making thirty-six adult persons. Connected with the different familes were seventeen children, making the aggregate fifty-three. These were all selected and appointed within a few months, the laymen by Dr. Bangs and Mr. Lee, and the missionaries by Bishop Hedding, who at the time had the charge of the foreign missions. This company was collected from almost every part of the United States, and was the largest mission family that had ever sailed at one time from any American port. They left the port of New York, accompanied by Mr. Lee himself, on the 9th of October, 1839, in the ship Lausanne, and going by the way of Cape Horn and the Sandwich Islands, arrived in Oregon in May, 1840. The following are the names of the persons belonging to this expedition who subsequently were connected with the great educational enterprise of the country, whose history it is the object of the following pages to trace: Rev. A. F. Waller, Rev. Gustavus Hines, Rev. J. L. Parrish, Rev. L. H. Judson, Rev. James Olley, Doctor J. L. Babcock, Mr. George Abernethy, Mr. Hamilton Campbell, M. H. B. Brewer, Mr. W. W. Raymond, and their families; and Miss C. A. Clark, (now Mrs. Wilson,) Miss Elmira Phillips, Miss Almira Phelps, (now Mrs. Holman,) and Miss Orpha Lancton, (now Mrs. M'Kinney.) There were other persons connected with this large reinforcement who came out as missionaries, but as they remained in the country but a short time, and had nothing to do in the matter of providing for the educational wants of the population, it is not necessary to mention them particularly in this history. Some of the members of the last reinforcement were sent into other portions of the work, but most of them received their appointments within the Willamette Valley.

At this time the missionaries themselves and their families constituted quite a large colony, their number being about seventy-five, embracing upward of twenty children. Situated as they were, the parents could not educate their own children, and they began already to feel the necessity of having a public school established, where they could place their children for education, and have them separated from those influences arising from the heathenism by which they were surrounded. Besides those already named, all of whom were directly connected with our missionary establishment, there were beginning to be, as early as 1841, some immigrants from the Eastern States, and other portions of the world, who had settled in various parts of the country, constituting already quite a growing community. Children and youth were becoming somewhat numerous, and were growing up in comparative ignorance, and the general voice seemed to call loudly upon the friends of science to make one united effort in some way to furnish means to supply the pressing educational demands of the infant though rising colony.

The community generally looked to those who were connected with the Oregon Mission to take the lead in the grand enterprise, and, accordingly, a meeting of the members of the mission, and all others interested in the subject, was called on the 17th day of January, 1842, by the Rev. Jason Lee, superintendent of the mission, at his own house at what was then known as Chemekete, now North Salem, for the purpose of consultation upon the subject of English education in Oregon, and to prepare the way for the speedy establishment of a literary institution which should meet the wants of the growing community.

Little more was done at this first meeting than to discuss the general question of education as the great want of the country, and to appoint a committee to call a public meeting, and to prepare business for the consideration of such meeting in reference to the contemplated institution.

Dr. J. L. Babcock, David Leslie, and Gustavus Hines were appointed that committee. According to instruction, general notice was given, and the meeting was called to be held at what was then beginning to be known as "the Old Mission," on the 1st day of February, 1842. The house where this primary public meeting for the promotion of education in Oregon was held was the original mission house which was erected by Mr. Lee in 1834 on the eastern bank of the Willamette River, near the place known in past years as Garrison's Landing, and one half mile above the present little town of Wheatland.

The tide of influence which was then and there set in motion by the action of that meeting will roll on

OLD MISSION HOUSE IN OREGON.

in its elevating and purifying course, increasing in volume and power to the end of time; but the house itself, made memorable by many other hallowed associations, and the ground upon which it was located, by the ceaseless action of the waters of the river have long since been swept away. In addition to the members of the mission, the meeting was well attended by the friends of education in the country generally, among whom was the Rev. Harvey Clark, of precious memory, a minister of the Congregational Church, who, by his judicious counsel contributed much to the promotion of the objects of the meeting. After a careful survey of the whole ground, and a thorough investigation of all the difficulties in the way of accomplishing the object, it was unanimously resolved not simply to make the attempt, but positively to proceed to establish a collegiate institution for the benefit of the rising generation of Oregon. Retreat and failure were terms that were entirely rejected from the vocabulary of the men who were the originators of the important measures that were to result in the establishment of the first collegiate institution on the waters of the great Pacific.

The name by which the institution should be known became a subject of considerable discussion, and it was finally moved by G. Hines, and seconded by J. L. Babcock, that it should be called The Oregon Institute. This motion prevailed, and the meeting then proceeded to organize the institution by the election by ballot of a board of nine trustees. After balloting twice the following persons were declared duly elected the first board of trustees for the Oregon Institute :

Rev. Jason Lee, Rev. David Leslie, Rev. G. Hines, Rev. J. L. Parrish, Rev. L. H. Judson, Mr. George Abernethy, Mr. Alanson Beers, Mr. H. Campbell, and Dr. J. L. Babcock.

A committee was also elected by this meeting called the committee of location, consisting of Rev. Jason Lee, Rev. G. Hines, Rev. D. Leslie, Rev. H. Clark, and Dr. J. L. Babcock.

This committee proceeded at once to survey various localities in the valley to find a suitable place at which to locate the buildings of the institute, and reported in favor of the upper end of the high prairie known as the French Prairie, a very beautiful locality, but defective in the accommodation of living water. For this reason it was subsequently abandoned ; and it was finally resolved that the Oregon Institute be located on what was then called the " Wallace Prairie." The land selected for the claim of the institute was the same that is now owned by Asahel Bush and the gentlemen Keizer, two miles and a half below the city of Salem.

To set the whole thing in motion, the next step taken was to adopt measures to draw up a prospectus to present to the public, and a constitution and code of by-laws for the government of the school. Accordingly, at a meeting of the Board held on March 9th, 1842, it was resolved to appoint a committee of three to accomplish the above object, and report at the next meeting of the Board. The persons appointed on this committee were L. H. Judson, J. L. Parrish, and G. Hines.

Without anything to guide them in the accomplishment of their work except their own judgment, this committee produced the following prospectus, constitution, and code of by-laws, and reported them at a meeting of the Board held on the 15th of March, at the house of L. H. Judson, in North Salem. This report, with slight alterations by the Board, was unanimously adopted:

PROSPECTUS.

To all whom it may concern. Whereas it is believed to be highly important, and indispensably necessary to the future welfare of this rising community, that a permanent literary institution be established in this valley, of such a character as fully to meet the present and prospective wants of the children and youth of Oregon, in which they may receive that intellectual and moral training which alone can prepare them for respectability and usefulness; therefore a respectable number of the inhabitants of the Willamette settlement have entered into arrangements for the purpose of raising funds and carrying into operation a respectable boarding-school.

It is also contemplated, so soon as the community and the resources of the institution shall justify it, that it will become a university. The contemplated institution is to be called the "Oregon Institute," and to be located on the Wallace Prairie, on an eminence about one half mile south of the place occupied by Baptist Delcour, near a fountain of living water. A constitution has been adopted which, in order to secure the best education of the pupils in science, morality, and piety, places the institution in the hands of that society of evangelical Protestant Christians which shall first pledge itself to sustain it, and also making it the right of any person who shall subscribe at any one time fifty dollars or more, and pay the same according to the terms of subscription, to be associated with said society in the transaction of all business pertaining to the institution.

A board of nine trustees has been appointed, whose terms of office are to expire as follows: three at each annual meeting of the society pledged to sustain the school, at which time there shall be three others elected to fill their place.

CONSTITUTION OF THE OREGON INSTITUTE, ADOPTED
MARCH 15, 1842.

ARTICLE I.

Whereas the Oregon Institute is designed not
only to promote science, but morality and piety,
therefore this institution shall always be under
the supervision of some evangelical branch of the
Protestant Church.

ARTICLE II.

The institution shall be an academical boarding
school as soon as practicable; and whenever it shall
be deemed expedient by the proper authorities to
make it a university it shall be so constituted.

ARTICLE III.

The primary object of this institution is to educate
the children of *white men;* but no person shall be
excluded on account of color, provided their character
and qualifications be such as are required in the
by-laws of the institution.

ARTICLE IV.

There shall be nine trustees for this institution,
who shall be elected tri-annually by the society which
shall first pledge itself to sustain the institution, two-
thirds of whom shall be members of said society,
whose duty it shall be to hold in trust for said society
all the property of said institution, consisting of real
estate, notes, bonds, securities, goods and chattels,

etc., belonging to it; and any person who shall subscribe at any one time fifty dollars or upward shall
be entitled to a voice in all the business meetings of
the society which relate to the institution.

Article V.

There shall be a visiting committee appointed by
the society contemplated in the fourth article, or by
such organized body of the same Church as shall be
selected by said society, whose duty it shall be to
examine all the departments of the institution, and
report the result to the public at large.

Article VI.

There shall be a steward connected with the institution, who shall have the charge of the boarding
department, and also of all the children who board
in the institution while they are not under the
care of their instructors.

Article VII.

In the literary departments there shall be a male
and female branch, subject to the control of male
and female teachers, and so conducted as best to
promote science, morality, and piety.

Article VIII.

This Constitution may be altered at any annual
meeting of the society above named by a vote of
two thirds of the members present, excepting article
first, which shall not be altered or amended.

ARTICLE IX.

There shall be an annual meeting of the society pledged to sustain the institution, to be held the last Monday in May in each year. Said annual meeting shall fill all vacancies in the Board of Trustees, and either appoint the visiting committee or make choice of some organized body for that purpose, and transact such other business as may be deemed proper which does not contravene this Constitution.

ARTICLE X.

Should no society pledge itself to sustain the institution previous to the last Monday in May, A. D. one thousand eight hundred and forty-two, then the business of the institution shall be transacted by those who subscribe fifty dollars or upward at any one time for the support of the institution, till some society shall give a pledge to sustain it.

BY-LAWS ADOPTED MARCH 15, 1842.

SECTION I.

As soon as four thousand dollars shall be subscribed the trustees shall proceed and erect buildings, and prepare for the contemplated school.

SECTION II.

Any person of color who may desire to be admitted as a pupil shall procure testimonials of a good moral character, and that the candidate can read and write so as to be understood, and speak the English language intelligibly.

Section III.

The present trustees shall divide themselves into three equal classes by casting lots. The offices of those composing the first class shall terminate in May, A. D. 1843, the second class one year, and the third class two years thereafter, at each of which times there shall be three trustees chosen to fill such vacancies; and there shall be annually thereafter as many trustees chosen as shall fill all vacancies which may be occasioned by death or otherwise.

Section IV.

Any person who shall subscribe to the funds of the institution fifty dollars or more at any one time, and shall pay the same according to the terms thereof, shall receive a certificate of patronage, signed and sealed by the president and secretary of the Board, which certificate shall entitle the receiver to a voice in all the business of the society relating to the institution during his natural life.

Section V.

Any person who shall subscribe to the funds of the institution at any one time five hundred dollars, and pay the same according to the terms thereof, shall receive a certificate of scholarship, signed and sealed as in the above, which certificate shall entitle him or his heirs to the tuition of one scholar perpetually in the institution.

Section VI.

All subscriptions less than fifty dollars shall be paid within six months from the time of subscribing.

Section VII.

All subscriptions of fifty dollars, and not exceeding three hundred dollars, shall be paid in four equal installments, due semi-annually from the time of subscribing.

Section VIII.

All subscriptions of three hundred dollars or more shall be paid as follows: One fourth at the annual meeting next succeeding the time of subscribing, the remainder in semi-annual payments of fifty dollars each till the whole shall be paid.

Section IX.

Any person who has subscribed to the funds of the institution at any one time one hundred dollars or more shall be allowed at any one time thereafter to increase his subscription to five hundred dollars, in which case his former subscription shall be reckoned as a part of the sum necessary to entitle him to a certificate of scholarship as provided for above.

Section X.

No person shall be eligible to the office of trustee, or steward, or visiting committee, or receive employment as a teacher, who denies the authenticity of the sacred Scriptures.

Section XI.

The steward and teachers shall draw up a code of regulations for the internal management of the institution, which shall be laid before the Board of Trustees for amendment or approval.

Section XII.

The above sixth, seventh, and eighth sections of by-laws shall not take effect until the pledge of support contemplated in the constitution shall be given.

Section XIII.

The chairman of the Board of Trustees is hereby authorized to call a meeting of said Board whenever he shall be requested to do so by three of the members of the Board.

Section XIV.

The chairman and secretary of the Board shall be elected annually, at which time there shall be three trustees elected.

Section XV.

It shall be the duty of the trustees to report the state of the finances to each annual meeting.

For the purpose of carrying into effect the objects set forth in the foregoing prospectus, constitution, and by-laws, a subscription paper was drawn up and circulated through the community to raise the necessary funds.

The history would not be complete if this paper in its original form were not to be printed.

The following is a true copy of this first subscription raised in Oregon for the establishment of a literary institution, and the names of all the subscribers, with the amounts donated.

SUBSCRIPTION.

We whose names are hereunto appended promise to pay to the collector of the Board of Trustees the sums set to our names, according to the following conditions: All subscriptions less than fifty dollars within six months after subscribing; subscriptions of fifty dollars, and less than three hundred, in four equal semi-annual installments from the time of subscribing; subscriptions of three hundred dollars, and upward, one fourth at the first annual meeting succeeding the time of subscribing; the remainder in semi-annual installments of fifty dollars each.

The above conditions of payment are not to take effect until some evangelical branch of the Protestant Church shall pledge itself to sustain the institution.

All donations to the institution shall be paid as follows: At least one third in cash orders on the mission or Vancouver, and the remainder in tame neat cattle, lumber, labor, wheat, or cash, according to the choice of the donors, said property to be delivered at the institution at the market prices.

SUBSCRIBERS' NAMES.	AMOUNT.
L. H. Judson	$500
Joseph Gale	100
Jason Lee	500
Gustavus Hines	300
Hamilton Campbell	100
Elmira Phillips	50
James Olley	100
Joseph Holman	100
David Leslie	500
J. L. Parrish	200
W. W. Raymond	200
Joseph L. Whitcomb	100
J. L. Babcock	160
A. Beers	300
Daniel Lee	100
H. B. Brewer	200
Robert Shortess	100
James Bates	50
James S. O'Neil	50
Orpha Carter	10
W. H. Gray	50
A. F. Waller	200

At the time this subscription was raised the entire business of the community was done by the way of barter trade, as, properly speaking, there was no cash or money in the country, and the cash mentioned in connection with the subscriptions simply means accepted orders either upon the mission store at Oregon City, or upon the Hudson's Bay Company at Vancouver.

To show the earnestness and liberality with which this enterprise was carried forward it will be proper to observe that, in proportion to the means possessed, perhaps there never was a better subscription raised for any similar purpose, many of the persons cheerfully giving from one quarter to one third of all they possessed in the world. The subscription, amounting to about four thousand dollars, was thought to be sufficient to warrant the erection of buildings; but there were difficulties in the way; the whole matter was yet afloat.

The constitution which the Board had adopted provided that the school should always be under the supervision of some branch of the Christian Church; and further, that it should be that branch that should first come forward and enter into a pledge to patronize and sustain the institution. And the by-laws also provided that no subscription was binding until this pledge of patronage and support was duly given. It was therefore very clear that until some Church should assume this responsibility, and adopt this institution as its own, all the efforts of the Board to build up the school would be greatly trammeled, and perhaps prove entirely abortive. The Congregational Church had already been organized, with its center at the Tuality Plains, but it was yet too feeble to sustain such a charge; and as there was no other branch of the evangelical Church in Oregon that seemed either disposed or prepared to occupy such a position, and as the public generally seemed to be looking to the Methodist Episcopal Church to take the initiation in this grand enterprise, a meeting was held at the house of Rev. Gustavus Hines, known as the "Old Parsonage," in which it was resolved that the Rev. Jason Lee, the superintendent of the Oregon Mission, be respectfully requested to call a meeting of the Methodist Episcopal Church in Oregon, both ministers and laymen, to take into consideration the importance of receiving the Oregon Institute under its care, and pledging itself to patronize and support it. Accordingly the Church and friends of the enterprise were called to meet at the place of the above meeting on October 26, 1842, and there, after a most thorough investigation of the whole subject, on a motion made by Dr. Elijah White, and seconded by Rev. A. F. Waller, it was unanimously resolved that, as a branch of the Methodist Episcopal Church in the United States, we take under our care, and pledge ourselves to make every reasonable effort to sustain, the Oregon Institute. Previously to this act of the Methodist Episcopal Church as a body, of receiving the institute under a pledge of support, the property was in the hands of an irresponsible Board; but the conditions of ownership expressed in the constitution and by-laws having been complied with by this action of the Church, the school, and all that appertained to it, was transferred to the proprietorship of that body. Lest there might be some doubt as to the propriety and validity of this course of procedure another general meeting of the Church and community was called on May 20, 1843, at the institute premises on Wallace Prairie, and a resolution was presented by Rev. David Leslie, and seconded by L. H. Judson, that this meeting, in behalf of the Methodist Episcopal Church and the subscribers to the Oregon Institute, do hereby recognize the present Board of Trustees, and approve of their doings. Nearly every subscriber was present on the occasion, and voted in favor of the resolution; and henceforth the Oregon Institute was regarded as the property, and under the exclusive control of the Methodist Episcopal Church. Immediately after this action the Church, then assembled, proceeded to fill the vacancies which had occurred in the Board by resignation, and the expiration of the term of service of the first class. W. H. Wilson was elected to take the place of J. L. Babcock, who had resigned, and W. Hauxhurst, Alanson Beers, and W. H. Gray to fill the first class. Mr. Gray was a member of the Presbyterian or Congregational Church, and had been for some years connected with the mission in the interior among the Cayuses, under the direction of the American Board; but he had applied for and obtained a release from any further service to them, that he might become the general superintendent and secular agent of the Oregon Institute. He was accordingly engaged by the Board at a salary of four hundred dollars per annum. A building committee had also been constituted to take measures to erect a suitable house for the purposes contemplated, and Mr. Gray was authorized to draw upon the Board for the requisite funds, and up to November 16, 1843, there had been expended upon the house about three thousand dollars.

At this date ceased the action, in connection with the Board, of one of its most prominent and efficient members, and one whose name is to occupy in the history of Oregon the first place among the pioneers of Christian civilization upon the Pacific slope, namely, Rev. Jason Lee. This indefatigable laborer in the cause of humanity received his birth in the township of Stanstead, Canada East, but was mainly educated in the Wilbraham Academy, in the state of Massachusetts, under the tuition of the lamented Dr. Wilbur Fisk. When it was determined by the Church to send missionaries to Oregon over the Rocky Mountains, he was selected by the authorities of the Church as a suitable person to be placed at the head of the grand enterprise. Yielding to the solicitations of Dr. Fisk, from a conviction of duty he left the domains of civilization, and, accompanied by a few self-denying and kindred spirits, in the year 1834 he penetrated the deepest recesses of savage barbarism, and finally emerging from the defiles of the Cascade Mountains into the lovely valleys of Oregon, he commenced the work of laying the foundations for the erection of a Christian civilization upon these western shores. Oregon became at once the country of his adoption and the country of his love; and from the beginning he showed clearly that he had all the moral, religious, and educational interests of the country deeply at heart.

At the first annual meeting Mr. Lee had been elected president of the board of trustees, and, as he was about to visit the Atlantic States for the purpose of promoting both the civil and religious interests of Oregon, he proposed to accept an agency from the Board if it should be their pleasure to confer it upon him. Accordingly it was resolved that the Rev. Jason Lee be requested and authorized to act as agent in the United States to solicit funds and donations for a library, philosophical apparatus, etc., for the Oregon Institute. Mr. Lee had buried two wives and an infant son beneath the evergreens of Oregon, and his affections now, in all their strength, twined around a little daughter of two years old, whom he had committed to the care of a friend, and who constituted the only family tie that bound him to earth; yet he considered the objects to be accomplished in Oregon's advancement and elevation to be of such paramount importance that he could, under the conviction that duty called him, tear himself away from all he held dear on earth to secure this one desire of his heart. On taking leave of this western world he indulged the pleasing hope, that after accomplishing his mission in the East he would be permitted to return to the land he loved better than life, and employ his waning energies in the cause of humanity on the Pacific shores, and finally to lay his bones by the side of those of his two companions who had fallen as martyrs in the work to which they had consecrated their all. But an inscrutable Providence ordered it otherwise. In April, 1845, he fell in the midst of his friends, and they dug his grave near the shores of Lake Memphremagog, in the province of Lower Canada. A marble slab, bearing a suitable record of his life and labors, marks the spot where his dust reposes; but while vitality remained his heart dwelt in the regions of the setting sun. Possessing but little of this world's goods, he donated to the Oregon Institute six hundred dollars, one hundred of it just before he breathed his last.

In the month of May, 1844, energetic measures

were taken to advance the interests of the Board by the survey, appraisal, and sale of lots; and by forwarding the institute building, so that early in the season a school might be put into successful operation. But an event was about to transpire which was destined to change the whole aspect of things in relation to the locality of our school, and show conclusively that the interests we sought to promote were under the immediate supervision of the wise providence of God. This event was the revolution that was effected in our missionary policy in Oregon. This revolution originated in the action of the Missionary Board in New York, which, for reasons which appeared justifiable, at a regular meeting held July 19, 1843, recommended to the bishop having charge of foreign missions either the appointment of a special agent to proceed to Oregon, and investigate the financial concerns of the mission, or supersede Mr. Lee by a new superintendent. The latter course was decided upon by the bishop, and in September following it was announced that the Rev. George Gary, of the Black River Conference, was appointed to the superintendency of the Oregon mission. The instructions of the authorities of the Church to the new superintendent were few, but he was clothed with discretionary power, and had the destiny of missionaries, laymen, property, and all, put into his hands. With this almost unlimited authority Mr. Gary arrived in Oregon on the first day of May, 1844, and entered at once upon the delicate and responsible duties devolved upon him. It was a somewhat singular coincidence that Mr. Lee, not knowing that he had been superseded, was on his way to New York at the same time that Mr. Gary was approaching the Pacific shores. They never saw each other. Mr. Lee, as above stated, fell in Canada, and Mr. Gary assumed the responsibilities of superintendent of the mission in Oregon, which had devolved upon Mr. Lee for the period of ten years.

After Mr. Gary had given himself sufficient time to survey the ground, and form some just conception of the magnitude of the work committed to his hands, on the 7th of June following his arrival he called a meeting of all the missionaries, ministers and laymen, at the old parsonage, in what is now Salem, then occupied by Rev. David Leslie, for the purpose of consultation concerning the various departments of our missionary work. The meeting commenced at an early hour of the day, and such was the importance of the interests involved that the investigation continued until daylight the next morning.

The principal points arrived at, however, in this instance, was a decision to sell the mission property at Clatsop, near the mouth of the Columbia River, consisting of a farm, buildings, and stock. Mr. Gary also informed the laymen connected with the mission that he intended to dismiss them, and proposed to defray their expenses home if they wished to return, or pay them an equivalent in such property as the mission possessed in Oregon. With the exception of one, Dr. J. L. Babcock, they preferred to remain in the country, and accordingly mission property was distributed among the different families to the amount to each family of from eight hundred to a thousand dollars. And here it should be observed that the course adopted by Mr. Gary in disposing of the laymen belonging to the mission was as satisfactory to the latter as it was just and honorable in the superintendent.

It will have been already discovered that one of the objects of the missionary enterprise of the Methodist Episcopal Church in Oregon was the establishment and maintenance of a Mission Manual Labor School for the benefit of Indian children. This school had been established by Mr. Lee, in the fall of 1834, on the old mission premises, ten miles below Salem, and, under the care of Cyrus Shepherd and others it assumed an interesting and promising aspect. In 1841 this Indian school had increased to about forty children, and these were crowded into a small log-house, and it became evident that more commodious quarters must be provided for it. It was also ascertained, by an experience of a few years, that the original locality of the mission was comparatively an unhealthy one, and it was determined in council to remove the headquarters of the mission to Chemeketo, now the city of Salem. In connection with this removal it was determined by Mr. Lee, by the consent and advice of the Missionary Board in New York, to build a suitable house for the accommodation of the Indian Mission School. Accordingly, in 1842 this determination was carried into effect by the erection of the old wood house still standing upon the institute grounds, and costing the Missionary Society of the Methodist Episcopal Church when erected ten thousand dollars. The Indian Mission School moved into this building in the fall of 1842, and for a few months it seemed to be flourishing; but a strange fatality finally fell upon it. A fatal disease carried away many of the children, others ran away, and some were stolen by their parents, until but few were left, and these withering under the influence of the fatal scrofula; so that, on the arrival of Mr. Gary in 1844, a dark cloud rested upon the prospects of our Mission School. On the 26th of June the superintendent called a general meeting of the missionaries and members of the Methodist Episcopal Church at the Mission School-house, to take into consideration the subject of the school, and determine whether it should be continued or disbanded. The matter was thoroughly investigated pro and con, and it was finally determined to bring the Indian Mission Manual Labor School to a close. This was immediately done, and now the house and premises, which had cost the Missionary Society more than ten thousand dollars, were in the hands of Mr. Gary, to be disposed of and put to some other use. The question, How can this property be best employed to promote in Oregon the true objects contemplated by the Church in this expenditure? became a matter of grave investigation, and as a result, Mr. Gary proposed to sell the Oregon Mission School-house and lands connected with it to the trustees of the Oregon Institute for the sum of four thousand dollars. It was exceedingly desirable on the part of the trustees of the Oregon Institute to secure this property, as the location was far more eligible, and the lands, embracing a mile square, were far more valuable than the place on Wallace's Prairie. Besides this, the house itself, which was new, had cost the Missionary Board more than twice the amount for which Mr. Gary proposed to sell to the trustees of the institute the entire property.

Fortunately for the interests of the Oregon Institute, the Board was presented with an opportunity to sell the property on Wallace's Prairie, which, through a committee appointed for that purpose, was done for the sum of three thousand dollars ; and by the same committee, duly authorized by the Board, the Oregon Mission School-house and lands connected with it were purchased for the sum of four thousand dollars, and became the property of the Oregon Institute.

It should be distinctly understood that up to the time of this purchase the name Oregon Institute was known only in connection with the property on Wallace Prairie, but now the name was transferred from the old locality to the present locality within the city of Salem, and the Oregon Mission Manual Labor School became, by virtue of said transfer, the Oregon Institute. It may here be properly observed, that Mr. Gary had an opportunity to sell the Mission School property to the Catholics for double the amount of that he was to receive for it from the trustees of the Institute, but in that case it would have been converted into a nunnery; and every evangelical Christian will say, "Rather destroy it entirely than desecrate it to so impious a purpose."   For the promotion of the interests of the Church of Christ, and for the general welfare of this rising country, a more judicious appropriation of the property could not have been made than to place it in the hands of the trustees of the Oregon Institute.   This, by a most singular train of providences, was finally done, the Oregon Institute receiving the property for less than one half of its real value, the other half being in effect a free donation to the Board from the Missionary Society through its agent, the Rev. George Gary.

About the time this transfer was made, or a few months after, twenty-three years ago, the author of this sketch wrote the following in relation to this school; and the reader cannot fail, in contrasting the present with that period, to see clearly the correctness of the views then and there expressed:

" The institution stands upon an elevated portion of a beautiful plain, surrounded with the most delightful scenery, and at a point which, at some future day, is destined to be one of great importance.   The building is beautifully proportioned, being seventy-five feet long and forty-eight feet wide, including the wings, and three stories high.   When finished it will not only present a fine appearance without, but will be commodious, and well adapted to the purposes intended to be accomplished within.   It is already so far advanced that a school is now in successful operation, under the tuition of one well qualified to sustain its interests. Already it numbers more students than did either the Cazenovia Seminary or the Wilbraham Academy at their commencement, and who can tell but that it may equal, if not exceed, both those institutions in importance as well as usefulness. Though I cannot say that it is the only hope of Oregon, for whether it lives or dies Oregon will yet be redeemed from the remains of Paganism and the gloom of papal darkness by which she is enshrouded; but the sentiment forces itself upon the mind, that the subject of the Oregon Institute is vital to the interests of the Methodist Episcopal Church on the Pacific coast. If it lives, it will be a luminary in the moral heavens of Oregon, shedding abroad the light of knowledge long after its founders shall have ceased to live. But if it dies, *our* sun is set, and it is impossible to tell what will succeed. Perhaps a long and cheerless night of papal darkness; but, more probably, others, more worthy of the honor than ourselves, will come forth to mold the moral mass according to their own liking, and give direction to the literature and religion of Oregon."

As the house which had thus fallen into the hands of the trustees of the Oregon Institute had but recently been occupied by the Indian school, it was in such a state of forwardness as to render it practicable to open a school for white children without delay, and consequently a committee was appointed by the Board to employ a teacher, and put the school into immediate operation. Mrs. C. A. Wilson was the person upon whom devolved the honor, by the employment of this committee, to open, as a teacher, the Oregon Institute. Mrs. Wilson commenced her school early in the fall of 1844, under very favorable auspices, having more students than some of the academies in the Eastern States had at their commencement, which subsequently became very flourishing institutions. The committee to whom was delegated the power to commence and conduct the school during the winter, were David Leslie, Alanson Beers, L. H. Judson, and John Force; and, at a meeting of the Board held the 7th of April, 1845, a resolution was passed approving the action of the committee, and assuming the responsibilities of the school, with all its contracts and liabilities. The school at this time was conducted on the principle of a boarding school, most of the pupils coming from a distance and living in the institution, and under the supervision of W. W. Raymond, whom the Board had employed as steward of the concern. At this time also there were enacted thirteen rules for the general management of the establishment.

At the annual meeting of the Board, May 25, 1845, D. Leslie was re-elected president, W. H. Wilson was elected secretary, and A. Beers treasurer. As the house was still unfinished measures were taken to advance it toward completion, and provide for a school during the following winter, and also for the survey and sale of lots. Previously to this, the Board had conceived the plan of laying out a city embracing most of the land claim which it held by virtue of its purchase from the Missionary

Society through its agent, and this survey was in accordance with the plan and under the direction and at the expense of the Board of Trustees.

In the fall of 1845 there came into the valley a large emigration from the Eastern States, and though the country was generally open for settlement, yet the Oregon Institute being now in successful progress, and the business operations in the vicinity affording facilities for livelihood, the lands in the immediate vicinity of the institute soon were all occupied, and jumping claims became, to some extent, the order of the day. The recent purchase was considered by many as very desirable, and was looked upon with longing eyes; and the validity of the claim of the institute began to be questioned both by the old residents and the new-comers, and a strong disposition was manifested to jump the claim. The country at this time was very deficient in regard to law, as the provisional government had not provided for the incorporation of such bodies as the Board of the Oregon Institute. Indeed, this body, at this time, had no existence in law, and advantage was taken of this fact in attempts to wrest the land from the possession of the Board, which if successful would have ruined the institution. With this state of things it required all the wisdom and vigilance of the friends of the school to retain possession of this land, so that it would not be lost to the institution. Fortunately for the interests of education in Oregon, the provisional government had enacted a law providing for the holding of land by a partnership of two or more persons, and the friends of the institution took advantage of this law to secure the land. It so happened that the claims of W. H. Wilson on the north, H. B. Brewer on the east, Rev. D. Leslie on the south, and Rev. L. H. Judson on the west, all staunch friends of the institution, encompassed the institute claim on all sides, and arrangements were made with these gentlemen by the Board to extend their personal claims, so as to cover the entire claim of the institute, and have the same recorded as a claim held by them in partnership, according to the requirements of the provisional law. These gentlemen entered into heavy bonds with the Board of Trustees to hold the premises as a partnership claim, until such times as the Board should become an incorporate body, and be competent to receive back and hold the property according to law.

In March, 1846, it was arranged by the Board, in connection with the partnership, that W. H. Wilson, one of the partners, should, as agent of the concern, take personal charge of the premises for safe keeping. On the twenty-sixth of May, Mr. Wilson, by a unanimous vote of the Board, was confirmed in the agency, and empowered to transact the business of the Oregon Institute, and he was authorized to sell lots and receive pay for the same, and as a compensation for such service he was to receive seven per centum on all the sales effected. It should be distinctly understood that at this time the institute land which was held by the partnership arrangement embraced the whole of the present site of the city of Salem. The city is indebted entirely to the Board for the magnificent plan upon which the plat was surveyed, a plan that will ultimately make Salem of Oregon one of the most beautiful cities upon the continent of America. The liberality of the Board appeared not only in respect to the town survey, but also in the encouragement given to mechanics and others to settle and improve within the city limits. Instruction was given to the agent, W. II. Wilson, to make a donation to worthy individuals of one lot to each, to the number of twenty lots, according to his discretion. This was designed both to encourage individuals, and to give a start to the embryo town.

For some time after the middle of 1846 various matters of business more or less affecting the interests of the institute engaged the attention of the Board, the particulars of which it will not be necessary to incorporate into this history. It will be sufficient simply to allude to them, such as providing for the finishing of the outside of the institute building, the erection of out-houses, the inclosing of yards, the donation of lands for church and yard purposes, the selection of a cemetery, and the adjustment of certain matters relating to the sale of lands to D. Leslie, J. L. Parrish, and C. Craft. The business pertaining to these last mentioned sales does not appear to have been completed until June, 1847. The price for which the lands mentioned were sold was fixed at twelve dollars per acre. At the same time a resolution was passed by the Board empowering D. Leslie, L. H. Judson, and W. H. Wilson to dispose of the water-power or mill-seat belonging to the institute premises, and as much land with it as they might think proper. It was also resolved that the agent, W. H. Wilson, be instructed to commence the sale of lots by public auction, after giving at least ten days' notice through the columns of the "Oregon Spectator." The committee authorized to sell the water privilege was also instructed to sell to applicants any portion of the land embraced in the town survey, previous to the public sale by the agent, at such prices, not less than the minimum price fixed by the Board, as in their judgment they might think proper. These measures were, as far as practicable, carried out by the Board through the committees appointed, and in the mean time the school was kept for the most part in successful operation.

The civil changes that occurred in respect to Oregon, as regarded the land interests of the country, produced a marked effect in their final results upon the institution whose history we are endeavoring to trace. When the Board of the Oregon Institute was first organized in 1842, it was not only self-constituted, but entirely an irresponsible body, based upon no law, as, indeed, the country then was wholly without law, every man being left to do that which was pleasing in his own sight. The original members of the Board, however, were men who considered that a "higher law" than any mere civil enactment had its claims upon them, and to that law, in all their operations affecting the interests of the Oregon Institute, they held themselves strictly accountable. To hold the property and secure it to the interests of the school through all the changes that took place from a state of no law up to the establishment of legitimate government among us, required, as has been seen, integrity of purpose, added to perseverance, foresight, and great watchfulness. These qualities having been brought into constant requisition for its advancement and security, the Oregon Institute is found at the close of the fifth year of its existence to occupy a very promising position, and bidding fair to become the leading literary institution on the Pacific coast.

In 1848 the Oregon Donation Land Law, through the agency of the Hon. Samuel Thurston, delegate to Congress from the territory of Oregon, passed both houses of Congress, and opened the way for the rapid settlement of the Willamette Valley. This act, important as it was to the general interests of the country, not only became the occasion of serious and protracted trouble and difficulty to the Board of Trustees, but in its final results became the cause of inflicting a very serious injury upon the financial interests of the institution.

At the time of the passage of the Donation Law W. H. Wilson, with his family, lived upon the claim, and in the institute building, and, as has been stated, were in the employment of the Board of Trustees, he as agent, while Mrs. Wilson was conducting the school as teacher. Mr. Wilson was also a member of the Board of Trustees, and had acted doubtlessly in all good faith with the other members of the Board in all the struggles of the past to sustain the institution, and, as they were in the occupancy of the land when the Donation Law was passed, it was natural for the Board to look to them as the proper persons through whom to secure the premises by a fulfillment of the provisions of that law; but as the primary object of this history is not so much to make an exposition of all the particulars which have entered into it, and the errors and mistakes of those who have been connected with the enterprise, as to promote its present and future interests, we deem it not important to trace in all its minutiæ the tedious and unpleasant controversy in regard to this land claim between the Board of Trustees of the institution on the one hand, and Dr. Wilson and his wife on the other.

There were indeed two sides to the question; but the interests involved, so far as the institution was concerned, were of such a nature as for many months to constitute subjects of grave, earnest, and extended investigation in the meetings of the Board. But the character of these investigations, and the opinions entertained and expressed by the different parties, are not so important matters of history as the manner in which, finally, the whole controversy was settled. We shall therefore dismiss the whole subject after stating a few facts in relation to this point.

At a meeting of the Board, held November 1, 1854, a committee was appointed consisting of A. F.

Waller, G. Hines, and J. L. Parrish, to take into consideration the subject of difference between William H. Wilson and the trustees of the Oregon Institute, and all the interests of the university growing out of the land claim, and report at a subsequent meeting of the Board a plan for the full adjustment of all the interests involved in the premises. This committee at once attended to the work assigned them, and had an interview with Mr. Wilson, and as a result, the latter, at the next meeting of the Board, made the following proposition:

"Feeling as I do a very deep and anxious solicitude for the welfare of the institution of learning in our midst, and feeling most seriously the embarrassments under which it labors in consequence of questions in which I am involved, I propose to submit the following as the basis of a final settlement: You perceived by the exhibit of yesterday, admitting its correctness, that I had received from the sales upon my part of the claim but three thousand three hundred and five dollars, and had paid out over five thousand. I propose first to relinquish to you that excess. I propose to secure to you, or the trustees of the Willamette University, the sixty acres called for in the bond you hold, or if it has been encroached upon, to make it good, to be held in trust as per bond. I propose in the next place to divide the unsold remains of that portion of the claim lying on the south side of the street, which runs east from the river in front of the Methodist meeting-house, so as to secure to you, or the trustees of the Willamette

University, two thirds in value of such unsold remains, to be held or disposed of by the said trustees at their discretion, for the endowment of said university. If the above propositions are acceded to, then, and in that case, mutual releases shall be passed, showing a final settlement of all the interests growing out of the land claim.

"Signed, WILLIAM H. WILSON."

As matters stood the Board had no alternative; and, acting upon the principle that a half loaf is better than no bread, acceded to this proposition as the best that probably could be done under the circumstances, and a committee consisting of W. H. Wilson, A. F. Waller, and G. Hines, was appointed, whose duty it was to proceed and view the premises, and divide the land, and designate by metes and bounds that which was awarded to the institution, and that which was awarded to said W. H. Wilson. This committee immediately performed the task imposed upon them, and the apportionment thus made was accepted by the parties as a final settlement of the interests involved in the land claim of the Oregon Institute and Willamette University. The Board then ordered the president and secretary to receive from Mr. Wilson all conveyances and instruments necessary and proper for the carrying out of the propositions of Mr. Wilson, and to execute to him all receipts and acquittances necessary to the adjustment and cancellation of all claims of said Board against him. This instruction was subsequently carried into effect by the constituted authorities, and the legal questions involved in the matter were in this manner forever put to rest.

We are not in these representations disposed to be rigid, nor at all uncharitable. We would accord to all parties good intentions in all that they have done touching this matter. In the statements that have been made we have not designed to call in question the motives of any. We have simply dealt in facts as far as we have gone, and upon this subject, as upon all others, we would say, let the public first understand, and then judge. And here it will be proper to observe that during the whole history of the institution up to this period no persons in the country showed a more lively interest in the welfare of the school, and none were more liberal in the use of time and money in its support, than were Mr. and Mrs. Wilson. Dr. Wilson himself was one of the early secretaries of the Board, and officiated in that capacity for some years. He was also for years the efficient agent of the Board, and contributed much by his counsel as well as means to carry forward the enterprise toward ultimate success. He came to Oregon as a layman in connection with the first reinforcement to the mission in 1837. An active member of the Church, an efficient leader and steward, he was also licensed to preach as a local preacher in Oregon, and officiated in that capacity for a number of years. In 1840 he was married to Chloe A. Clark, who was a member of the large reinforcement of that year. Dr. Wilson was one of the earliest permanent settlers on the Pacific coast, and from the beginning took a deep interest in every enterprise for the promotion of the moral, intellectual, and physical development of the country. True to the interests of the Church, and faithful in the observance of all religious duties, from his geniality and kindness, and the vein of good feeling that always seemed to be running through his entire nature, he was remarkably popular in all the associations of life. He died very suddenly in the city of Salem by an apoplectic stroke, leaving a widow and three children to mourn his unexpected and premature departure.

CHAPTER VII.

ORGANIZATION OF THE WILLAMETTE UNIVERSITY.

It has been already observed that the original design of the founders of the Oregon Institute was to place it under the control of some organized religious body that would enter into a pledge to patronize and sustain it.   This pledge was given, so far as it was possible, in 1842.   True, there was not an organized conference at that time in the country, yet there was a Methodist society which had been organized by Rev. Jason Lee and his associates according to the constitution of the Methodist Episcopal Church. This society or branch of the Methodist Episcopal Church in Oregon, thus organized, formally received the institution under the pledge required, and in this form, as a simple society, had the entire management and control of the school up to September, 1849. In the mean time the provisional government had given place to the territorial form of government, and the Methodist society established in the country had grown into the Oregon and California Mission Conference, which had been organized under the direction and by the authority of the General Conference of the Methodist Episcopal Church.   During the first session of the Mission Conference thus organized, which was held in the chapel of the Institute building, measures were taken to adopt the institution as a conference, and provide for the security of the property belonging to it. It was also resolved to make application to the legislature of Oregon Territory for a suitable charter for the government of the institution.

Rev. Wm. Roberts, who was the superintendent of the mission at that time, and the preacher in charge of Oregon City, were appointed a committee to carry out these measures. Whatever this committee may have done in the premises does not appear upon the records, but it is evident that they did not succeed in obtaining a charter, for we find that during the third session of the Oregon and California Mission Conference, held in the Institute building, September 3, 1851, that a committee of five was appointed, consisting of J. II. Wilber, C. S. Kingsley, N. Doane, F. S. Hoyt, and Wm. Roberts, to procure from the next legislature of the Oregon Territory the incorporation of the Oregon Institute and University; and to take measures, in connection with the executive committee, to secure their speedy endowment.

At the same conference the following persons were elected members of the Board of Trustees for the Oregon Institute and University: David Leslie, Wm. Roberts, A. F. Waller, W. II. Wilson, J. L. Parrish, J. H. Wilber, J. Q. Thornton, Thomas Nelson, George Abernethy, C. S. Kingsley, J. Flinn, J. Stewart, F. S. Hoyt, and Amory Holbrook.

There was also a Board of Visitors elected, which

shows that the institution had fully passed into the hands of the conference.

The committee of five, appointed by the Board to procure a charter of incorporation from the Legislative Assembly of 1853, made application to that body for that purpose, and as a result reported to the Board of the Oregon Institute

AN ACT TO ESTABLISH THE WILLAMETTE UNIVERSITY.

Whereas the happiness and prosperity of every community, under the direction and government of Divine Providence, depend in an eminent degree on the right education of the youth who must succeed the aged in the important offices of society, and the principles of virtue and elements of liberal knowledge fostered and imparted in the higher institutions of learning tend to develop a people in those qualifications most essential to their present welfare and future advancement; and whereas it appears that the establishment of a university in the town of Salem, in the county of Marion, with a suitable preparatory department for the instruction of youth in the arts and sciences, is likely to subserve the intellectual development and enlightening of the youth of this territory; therefore,

SECTION I.

Be it enacted by the Legislative Assembly of the Territory of Oregon, That there shall be established in the town of Salem, in the county of Marion, a university, to be called the Willamette University, and that David Leslie, Wm. Roberts, George Abernethy, W. H. Wilson, Alanson Beers, Thomas H. Pearne, Francis S. Hoyt, James H. Wilber, Calvin S. Kingsley, John Flinn, E. M. Barnum, L. F. Grover, B. F. Harding, Samuel Burch, Francis Fletcher, Jeremiah Ralston, J. D. Boon, Joseph Holman, James R. Robb, Cyrus Olney, Asahel Bush, and Samuel Parker, and their associates and successors, are hereby declared to be a body corporate and politic in law, by the name and style of the "Trustees of the Willamette University."

SECTION II.

And be it further enacted, That said corporation shall have perpetual succession, and shall have power to acquire, receive, and possess, by donation, gift, or purchase, and to retain and enjoy property, real, personal, and mixed, and the same to sell, grant, convey, rent, or otherwise dispose of at pleasure; *Provided*, that no part of the resources thereof shall ever be used for any other than educational purposes, as herein contemplated: *and provided further*, That the yearly income of which, accruing to said institution, shall not exceed twenty-five thousand dollars. They shall have power to contract and be contracted with, to sue and be sued, to plead and be impleaded in all courts of justice, both at law, and in equity. They shall cause to be made for their use a common seal, impressed with such devices and inscriptions as they shall deem proper, by which said seal all deeds, diplomas, and acts of said corporation shall pass and be authenticated, and they shall have power to alter or amend the same at their pleasure. They shall have power to form and adopt a constitution and by-laws for their government, to make and to carry into effect all necessary regulations for the management of their fiscal concerns, to appoint subordinate officers and agents, to make, ordain, and establish such ordinances, rules, and regulations as they may deem necessary or expedient for the good government of said institution, its officers, teachers, and pupils; *Provided*, that such ordinances, rules, and regulations shall in no manner contravene the constitution and laws of the United States nor the laws of this Territory.

Section III.

And be it further enacted, That said trustees shall meet at least once every year, and shall manage the concerns of said institution as they shall judge most advantageous to the cause of education; that seven of their number shall form a quorum, at any regular meeting, for the transaction of business. The said trustees shall elect one of their number to be president of their Board; and when it may be deemed advisable to add to the number of said trustees, or become necessary to fill vacancies, which may occur by death, resignation, or otherwise, the Annual Conference of the Methodist Episcopal Church in Oregon, within whose bounds said institution is located, shall elect such additional trustees, and fill such occurring vacancies. The first meeting of said Board of Trustees after the passage of this act, shall be called by David Leslie, and held at the Oregon Institute. They shall divide themselves into three classes; the term of office of the first class shall expire in one year, the second in two years, and the third in three years; and thereafter, each class shall hold its term of office for three years.

Section IV.

And be it further enacted, That all deeds and other instruments of conveyance shall be made by the order of the Board of Trustees, sealed with the seal of the corporation, signed by the president, and by him acknowledged in his official capacity, in order to insure their validity.

Section V.

And be it further enacted, That the Annual Conferences of the Methodist Episcopal Church in Oregon may appoint seven visitors, to visit and examine into the affairs of said institution, and each year to meet and confer with the Board of Trustees at some convenient time during its annual meeting; and the governor of this territory, judges of the Supreme Court, and president of the Council, and speaker of the House of Representatives of the Legislative Assembly, next preceding each annual meeting of said Board, shall be *ex-officio* visitors, having equal rights and privileges with the herein beforementioned visitors.

Section VI.

And be it further enacted, That, in order to con-
titute the university, established by this act, a general and efficient seminary of learning, there shall be
included within it a preparatory department, known
by the name of the "Oregon Institute," which shall
be open to persons of both sexes, and over which
said Board of Trustees shall have entire supervision
and control; *Provided,* that they shall respect all
contracts heretofore made and now existing in regard to said Institute; *And provided further,* that
said Board of Trustees shall have power to add such
other departments in the arts and sciences, law,
and medicine, and theology, as in their judgment
may be suitable to the wants and condition of the
country.

Section VII.

And be it further enacted, That the principal or
president, and professors of said institution, shall be
styled the "Faculty of Willamette University,"
who shall have power, with the advice of and in
accordance with the rule adopted by the Board of
Trustees and Visitors, to grant and confer degrees
in the liberal arts and sciences to such pupils of the
institution and others as by their proficiency in
learning, or by other meritorious consideration, shall
have entitled themselves to academic honors; and
the said faculty and board shall have and exercise
generally all such powers and privileges of conferring
honorary degrees, and other marks of literary and

scientific distinction, as are exercised by other similar institutions in the United States.

Section VIII.

The president of the Board of Trustees shall annually, in the month of December, make a report to the secretary of the Territory of the names and officers of the faculty, the names of the teachers, and the branches taught by them, the number of pupils taught in the university during the year, the number in the several classes respectively, and the names and degree of the graduates. And it shall be the duty of the secretary to place and keep on file in his office such report, which shall at all times be open for the inspection of any person or persons wishing to examine the same.

Section IX.

And be it further enacted, That the legislature shall have power at any subsequent session, when the necessities of the institution or considerations of public good require it, to alter or amend this act at pleasure.

Section X.

This act to take effect and be in force from and after its passage.

Passed by the House of Representatives, January 11, 1853. Passed by the Council, January 12, 1853. P. F. HARDING, Speaker of the House of Representatives; M. P. DEADY, President of the Council.

By this act of incorporation the Oregon Institute is absorbed in the Willamette University. True, the name is retained in connection with the academical department; but the distinguishing designation of the institution by this act, which originated with the Board of Trustees, became the Willamette University, endowed with all the rights and privileges belonging to universities of the first grade in the United States. But eleven years had passed since the idea of such an institution originated in the minds of a few voluntary exiles in a then heathen land, and found expression in measures taken with great diffidence and trembling as to their ultimate success; but now the institution had become a chartered university, according to the original design of its founders, and was evidently marching on to the accomplishment of a high and noble destiny.

To adapt the action of the Board to the new order of things, a meeting of that body was called by David Leslie, according to the provisions of the charter, in the chapel of the Institute, March 16, 1853.

At this meeting, as the third section of the act of incorporation required a division of the Board into three classes, the Board proceeded to make such classification.

First class, to continue one year: B. F. Harding, A. F. Waller, Cyrus Olney, J. Holman, F. S. Hoyt, John Flinn, S. Burch, Asahel Bush, W. Hauxhurst.

Second class, two years: L. F. Grover, J. Corson, J. Ralston, William Roberts, George Abernethy, W. H. Wilson, C. S. Kingsley, D. Leslie.

Third class, three years: E. M. Barnum, J. R.

Robb, Samuel Parker, A. Beers, J. Stewart, F. Fletcher, J. D. Boon, T. H. Pearne, J. H. Wilber.

As a new name and university powers had been conferred upon the institution, it was found, as a matter of course, that the old constitution and by-laws under which the school had been conducted would no longer answer the purpose; consequently, at this first meeting of the Board under the charter a committee was appointed, consisting of A. F. Waller, W. H. Wilber, T. H. Pearne, C. S. Kingsley, and F. S. Hoyt, to draft a constitution and code of by-laws.

The Board also by a resolution requested Bishop Ames, who was then in attendance, to appoint at the coming session of the Oregon Annual Conference a member of said conference to the presidency of the Oregon Institute, the old name being still used in the action of the Board, doubtless more by habit than otherwise.   The design of this request was carried out at the ensuing Annual Conference by the appointment of Rev. Francis S. Hoyt as president of the Willamette University.

The first officers of the Board under the charter were elected March 19, 1853: David Leslie, President, T. H. Pearne, Secretary, and J. L. Parrish, Treasurer.   T. H. Pearne resigned, and E. M. Barnum was elected in his place.

The committee that was appointed to draft a constitution and by-laws made their report at a subsequent meeting, but the constitution reported seemed to require further investigation, and was deferred

until some future time; but the by-laws which were
presented were thoroughly discussed, and adopted
as follows:

BY-LAWS OF WILLAMETTE UNIVERSITY.

1. The University shall consist of two departments,
namely, a Collegiate Department, and a Preparatory
or Academic Department

COLLEGIATE DEPARTMENT.

2. Until the wants of the institution require
further provision for a board of instruction, the following shall be the faculty of the Collegiate Department:

(1.) A president, whose title shall be the president
of the Willamette University, who shall act as professor of Mental and Moral Philosophy.

(2.) A professor of Ancient and Modern Languages.

(3.) A professor of Natural and Exact Sciences.

3. The president shall, in addition to his duties as a
professor, have the entire supervision and direction of
the disciplinary conduct of the Collegiate Department,
subject at all times to the counsel of the faculty and
to the ordinances of the trustees, and he shall receive
for his services the annual salary of one thousand
dollars, ($1,000.)

4. The professor of Ancient and Modern Languages,
and the professor of Natural and Exact Sciences, shall
give diligent instruction in their proper departments,

shall have the entire disciplinary control of students while under their immediate instruction, shall counsel the president in relation to the government of the institution, and shall severally receive as compensation for their services the annual salary of nine hundred dollars, ($900.)

PRELIMINARY, OR ACADEMICAL DEPARTMENT.

5. The president of the University shall act as principal of the Academical Department, and shall have the same supervisory control of it as of the Collegiate Department, and until further provision be made, he shall give such instruction, not inconsistent with his duties as a professor in the Collegiate Department, as the wants of the institution require.

6. The Preliminary, or Academic Department, shall be divided into two divisions: first, the male; second, the female.

7. The male division, except in the care and instruction of boys under the age of ten years, shall be under the tuition of a preceptor.

8. The female division, except in case of advanced scholars desirous of pursuing collegiate or ornamental branches, which may be by the regulation of the institution be taught by a preceptor, shall be under the tuition of a preceptress, whose salary shall not be more than seven hundred and fifty dollars, ($750.)

A rule was also passed requiring each teacher to keep a faithful record of the daily attendance, recitations, and conduct of each pupil, grading them so that their standing should range from one hundred to five hundred, according to their propriety of conduct, or merit of recitations. Other rules were also adopted in relation to giving marks of demerit for absence and other causes, and to regulate the conduct of students in their rooms, and in relation to the price of tuition, and public examinations and exhibitions.

The school was conducted the first year of its history under the charter with some good degree of success, though every thing pertaining to it was in a crude and imperfect state, or rather in a state of formation.

There were no other means for the support of the school than was furnished by the tuition paid by the pupils, and the receipts from this quarter were so limited that it was necessary to place the salaries of the teachers at a very low figure. But improvement marked the progress of the institution, and a better day seemed to be dawning.

The first annual meeting of the trustees of the Willamette University under the charter was held in the chapel of the Oregon Institute March 1, 1850. Up to this period no special efforts had been made to raise an endowment fund aside from endeavoring to secure the interests involved in the land claim, already described. This, if it could have been secured according to the original purpose of the trustees, would have made a splendid endowment, at least for some years; but as the amount arising from the land which could be made available as an endowment fund from the loss of more than one half of the claim was necessarily small, amounting to but a few thousand dollars, it became absolutely necessary to enter with energy into other measures to accomplish the same object. Accordingly at this first annual meeting under the charter, as the duty of developing the Willamette University as an institution of learning was devolved upon the trustees of the same, and as, in the judgment of the Board, the time had come when the wants of the community and the interests of the institution demanded an immediate effort to provide an endowment thereof, it was therefore resolved to raise a fund as soon as practicable, additional to the interest arising from the land, to consist of two parts.

1. A fund for the support of the Board of Instruction of said university, which shall be irreducible, and the income of which shall amount to at least five thousand dollars, ($5,000.)

2. A building fund, which shall amount in total to twenty-five thousand dollars, ($25,000,) and which shall be at the direct disposal of the trustees, to be devoted to the purpose of erecting suitable buildings for the convenience of the university.

These funds were to be raised by the sale of scholarships, entitling the holders thereof to the privilege of sending a pupil to be instructed free of tuition in the institution for the term of time mentioned in the certificate of each of such scholarships, and to the department mentioned in the same. Three orders of scholarships were to be sold, as follows: The first should entitle the holder thereof to the tuition of one pupil in the Preparatory Department for the period of ten years, and should be sold for one hundred and fifty dollars, ($150;) the second should entitle the holder to the privilege of sending one pupil, free of tuition, to either the Preparatory or Collegiate Department, or both of them, for ten years, and should be sold for two hundred dollars, ($200,) provided always that no such holder should be entitled to the tuition of more than one pupil at a time in said institution on account of said scholarship, and provided that such scholarship shall not entitle any person to instruction in the ornamental branches.

The third order was that of perpetual scholarships, entitling the holders to tuition of pupils in any of the departments of said institution during the existence thereof, should be sold for five hundred dollars, ($500,) and subject to the same restrictions as the former. These scholarships were made assignable, and when assigned entitled the assignee to the same privileges and interests in said institution as were vested in the original or in any subsequent holder thereof at the time of the assignment.

The energy with which the Board entered into this endowment enterprise may be further seen in the fact that the bishop presiding at the next annual conference was to be requested to appoint the presiding elders of this conference agents to procure funds for the institution. It was further arranged by the Board that the funds accruing to the institution from the sale of scholarships should be divided, so that one third should be appropriated to the building fund until the same should amount to twenty-five thousand dollars, ($25,000,) after which all moneys accruing from the sale of scholarships shall accrue to the irreducible fund, and the other two thirds of all moneys accruing as before stated should continue to accrue to the said irreducible fund for the support of the Board of Instruction.

The agent of the university was instructed and authorized to secure lands, or any other gifts to the institution, either by donation, or as security for the payment for the same, under the direction of the executive committee. Another act of importance by the Board at this time was the passage of a resolution requesting the bishop at the next session of the conference to appoint F. S. Hoyt president of the Willamette University.

With the experience of the past, the Board found it necessary to improve upon the police of the school, and consequently under the same date the following rules to regulate the general conduct of the students as far as possible were enacted:

Drinking wine or intoxicating liquors, smoking, card-playing, swearing, immorality of any kind, quarreling, rude and unkind treatment of fellow-pupils, the throwing of stones, disobedience, indolence, and any other acts or behavior calculated to injure the reputation and peace of the university, or the moral habits of the students, were entirely prohibited. The disciplinary arrangements of the institution further provided that in cases of the violation of the rules, after due admonition, the president shall, where circumstances permit, notify the parents of such pupils, after which, if the faculty judge it necessary, said pupil may be suspended from the privileges of the institution for any period of time not exceeding fourteen days, within which time the executive committee shall be called together and decide upon the relation of such pupil to the institution, provided that in extreme cases of violation of rule, or of improper behavior, the president, by and with the consent of the faculty, shall have the power summarily to expel.

The institution had possessed a twofold character, being partly a boarding-school and partly not, some of the young men occupying rooms in the third story of the institute building, and boarding themselves, and some young men and young ladies boarding in private families, and some of the pupils boarding with their parents or guardians at home, and it was difficult to adapt any given set of rules to such a variety of circumstances; but to meet some of the exigences of the case, and to produce uniformity as far as possible, it was ordained that study hours both for the evening and the day should be announced by the president at the beginning of each quarter, and during such hours students were required to attend closely to their studies. And those who studied in their rooms were required to maintain the same quietness and diligence as though under the eye of the teacher. And all business, work, paying or receiving visits, were prohibited during study hours. And no visiting about town, or at stores, shops, or hotels, were to be allowed during the evening. And to render this arrangement effective, parents and guardians of pupils residing in the vicinity were requested to have their children and wards who attended school conform to this rule as far as possible, both for their own improvement and for good example.

Up to this period the school had been of a mixed character, the different departments not having been well defined, the smaller pupils being connected with the larger in the same rooms; but now a primary division was established, including boys and girls under and about ten years of age, which were to be under the tuition of a male or female teacher, as might be judged proper by the executive committee.

CHAPTER VIII.

SCHOLARSHIPS AND INTERNAL HISTORY.

ON the 31st of May, 1854, pursuant to a call of the president, the Board of Trustees met at the chapel of the institute for the purpose of perfecting, if possible, the scholarship system, already to some extent described, and of introducing some other arrangements which might serve as a basis of action in our efforts to advance the financial interests of the university. As the scholarship system which has been introduced into the financial plans of the Willamette University constitutes one of the main pillars of its support, it would not be proper in this history to omit a particular description of this policy. The general principles have been referred to on a previous page, and to provide for the application of these principles was the object of the present action of the Board. It had been resolved to issue three kinds or degrees of scholarships, one of one hundred and fifty dollars, ($150,) one of two hundred dollars, ($200,) and one of five hundred dollars, ($500,) the first two ten years' scholarships, and the last perpetual. It was necessary to execute a form of certificate adapted to each one of these grades, according to the design of the scholarship. This was done by the Board, and the following are the forms adopted for the three kinds:

FIRST FORM FOR A TEN YEARS' SCHOLARSHIP.

Having paid to the undersigned, an authorized agent of the Willamette University, the sum of one hundred and fifty dollars, —— has entitled himself or his order, upon the presentation of this certificate, to one scholarship, for the term of ten years from the date hereof, in the Preparatory Department of said university.

SECOND FORM FOR A TEN YEARS' SCHOLARSHIP.

Having paid to the undersigned, an authorized agent of the Willamette University, the sum of two hundred dollars, —— has entitled himself or his order, upon presentation of this certificate, to one scholarship, for the term of ten years from the date hereof, in the Preparatory or Collegiate Department of said university, or in both.

THIRD FORM—PERPETUAL SCHOLARSHIP.

Having paid the undersigned, agent of the Willamette University, the sum of five hundred dollars, —— has entitled himself or his order, upon the presentation of this certificate, to one perpetual scholarship in the Preparatory or Collegiate Department of said university, or in both.

To carry out these and other financial arrangements contemplated, the Board appointed, perhaps, the most formidable phalanx of agents that ever was employed by any single university at the same time. It consisted of Rev. A. F. Waller, Rev. T. H.

Pearne, Rev. James H. Wilber, Rev. William Roberts, and the Hon. George H. Williams. These were all regularly appointed agents of the university, and authorized to receive donations of money or property for said university, to sell scholarships and receive pay or security therefor pursuant to the resolutions of the Board instructing them relative thereto, and to execute all necessary receipts, certificates, and instruments of writing for the transaction of such business. As it was contemplated to receive lands as well as money in payment for scholarships, it was necessary to have a form of deed or bond suited to the case; accordingly Judge Williams, being a legal gentleman, was requested by the Board to draft a form suited to the circumstances. The following is the form adopted by the Board :

Know all men by these presents, that I, ——, am held and firmly bound unto the Willamette University in the penal sum of —— dollars, to the payment of which sum I bind myself, my heirs, executors, and administrators. Sealed with my seal, and dated this —— day of ——, 18—.

The condition of the above obligation is such, that if the above named —— shall convey, by good and sufficient deed, within ——, from the date hereof, the following described lands, to wit, ——, as a donation to said university, then this obligation to be null, otherwise of force.

The agents were further instructed to make the securities for ten years' scholarships in the Preparatory Department payable, the interest annually, and principal in two years; and those for ten years' scholarships in the Preparatory or Collegiate Department, or both, payable, interest annually and principal in three years; and the securities for perpetual scholarships, interest payable annually and principal in five years; the rate of interest to be not less than the legal rates, and both interest and principal payable to any authorized agent of the Board, or to the treasurer of the same.

The securities which the agents were authorized to receive were to consist of promissory notes, with one or more sureties, or mortgages upon real estate; and the seal which was adopted by the university was the eagle side of a United States ten dollar gold coin. With this financial system of operations thus far introduced, and with such an array of talent in the corps of agents to carry out the plan to practical effect in the sale of scholarships and in the use of other measures to establish an endowment fund, we will leave them for the time being to the accomplishment of the important work committed to them, and for a while attend to some other matters of historical interest connected with the Oregon Institute and Willamette University.

In the regular course of our history we now approach an important matter of financial interest to the university, with which stands connected a name, the mention of which will excite emotions of deep interest in the minds of all that were favored with his acquaintance, and especially of all the early Oregonians. The name is that of Alanson Beers, and the interest referred to is that which was connected with what was called the Beers House. The name of Alanson Beers ceased to appear in connection with the acts of the Board in the spring of 1853, simply because he was no longer an inhabitant of earth. After a very severe illness of a few days only, he passed at that time from the scenes of earth to the rewards of eternity. Alanson Beers came to Oregon as a lay member of the Oregon Mission of the Methodist Episcopal Church. He sailed with his family, in connection with a number of other persons, from Boston in July, 1836, and entered the mouth of the Columbia River in May, 1837. Though he was connected with the mission as a blacksmith, yet the superintendent placed him in charge of the mission farm near Matheny's Ferry. He entered at once into all the moral and religious reforms of the day which promised good to the people, and he was especially active and efficient in the formation of the provisional government. He was a member of the first legislative committee of the territory, and also of the executive committee of three who acted as a kind of triune governor of Oregon. He was efficient, reliable, and honest in all these relations, winning the favor and the confidence of all with whom he had intercourse. In February, 1842, he was present at a public meeting where the Oregon Institute received its birth, and was elected one of the members of the original Board of Trustees. At an annual meeting he was elected treasurer of the Board, and served a few years in that capacity, always showing that he had the interests of the institution deeply at heart.

He conceived the idea that a boarding house connected with the institution, properly conducted, would do much to promote its interests, and he applied to the Board for the privilege of erecting a suitable house for that purpose on the northwest corner of what is known as the sixty acre reserve. The Board consented to the erection of such a house, but did not either sell or lease Mr. Beers the land upon which the house was located. The house was therefore the property of Mr. Beers before his death, and was recognized by the Board as belonging to his estate. Consequently, on November 1, 1854, the question was brought before the Board, " What disposition can be made of the property belonging to the estate of Alanson Beers situated on the lands of the university?" Rev. J. L. Parrish was the administrator of the estate, and having made various statements in relation to the circumstances under which the building was erected, the Board proceeded to adopt the following preamble and resolution :

Whereas Mr. Alanson Beers, in pursuance of an arrangement made with the Oregon Institute, did erect on the premises of said institute a house to be permanently occupied as a boarding house for the accommodation of the institute; and whereas said Alanson Beers has subsequently deceased, and, therefore, cannot carry out the contract made with the institute; and whereas the power of controlling the interests of the Oregon Institute is now vested in the trustees of the Willamette University, therefore, *Resolved*, that we proceed to elect a committee to take into consideration the subject of the interests of the Institute in the premises above-mentioned, and report at an adjourned meeting of the Board a plan for the settlement of the questions involved.

This committee, after a full investigation of the subject, recommended that, in adjusting the interests of the institution in the Beers House, the original intention of the parties in the erection of the house should be strictly observed; and if it were necessary in carrying out this design to lease the land for a term of years, it should be so leased, and the Board at first adopted this recommendation. Subsequently, however, the Board reconsidered this action, and provided an agent to be present at the administrator's sale of said house, with discretionary authority to purchase it, which he did by bidding it off at three thousand dollars. But it is not necessary to trace all the action of the Board from time to time in relation to the Beers House. It will be sufficient to say that after a number of trials to use it for the purposes for which it was constructed, it was finally decided that the time had probably not yet come when a boarding house could be sustained in connection with the Willamette University. Accordingly, the whole property was sold to Mr. John Ford, and by him conveyed to its present occupant, General John F. Miller. Thus the object contemplated by the builder of this house, Mr. Alanson Beers, was, in part at least, defeated; and yet it is quite probable that if the originator had survived it would have been a great blessing to the institution. But he fell; just as he was preparing to move into the building, all finished, and its capacious rooms waiting occupancy, he fell; and when he fell society lost a most valuable member, the young and rising territory one of its most useful and cherished citizens, and the Willamette University one of its warmest and most faithful friends. As has been stated, he was one of the original nine who constituted the first Board of Trustees for the Oregon Institute, and he remained a member of the Board by re-election from time to time until his death.

At a meeting of the Board, held November 1, 1854, Rev. William Roberts, who had at a previous annual meeting been elected secretary, resigned his position in consequence of his having been appointed presiding elder in Washington Territory, and at an adjourned meeting the Board elected Gustavus Hines to fill his place until the close of the year.

The second annual meeting under the charter was held in the chapel of the institute March 7, 1855, and the following persons were elected officers of the Board for the ensuing year:

Rev. DAVID LESLIE, President; Rev. J. D. BOON, Vice-President; Rev. GUSTAVUS HINES, Secretary; Mr. ELISHA STRONG, Treasurer.

Rev. A. F. Waller, Rev. J. D. Boon, Hon. G. H. Williams, Hon. E. N. Cook, and William H. Wilson, were elected members of the executive committee.

At this meeting President Hoyt presented his resignation to the Board, desiring it to take effect at the close of the summer term. The resignation was referred to a select committee. At an adjourned meeting the constitution was so amended as to require seven to be on the executive committee, and Gustavus Hines and F. S. Hoyt were elected to fill up that committee, and the following persons were nominated and recommended to the Oregon Annual Conference for election to fill the class in the Board whose term of service had expired: L. F. Grover, W. H. Wilson, A. M. Belt, C. Bennet, William Roberts, A. C. Gibbs, J. G. Wilson, D. Smith, John C. Peebles, George H. Jones, C. A. Reed.

The executive committee during the year had made some repairs in the foundation and chimneys of the institute building, and recommended that measures be taken for further improvement in both the building and grounds the ensuing year.

The Board also resolved to appoint seven agents to solicit scholarships and donations for the institution during the coming year, and the following persons were elected said agents: T. H. Pearne, F. S. Hoyt, A. F. Waller, L. F. Grover, Samuel Parker, T. F. Royal, and E. M. Barnum; and the executive committee was instructed to procure printed certificates of scholarships, to be given to those who purchase the same, and action was taken to change the certificates so as to agree with the present arrangements of the Board.

At this time the select committee to whom was

referred the matter of the resignation of President Hoyt reported adversely to the acceptance of the resignation, and recommended to the Board the election of a professor of mathematics, and appointed a committee of correspondence on the subject. The report was adopted; but at a subsequent meeting of the Board so much of it as related to the election of a professor of mathematics was reconsidered, and finally amended so as to provide for the election of a professor to take his place in the institution at the commencement of the fall term.

It is in connection with the operations of the school during the present year that the name of Mrs. Thurston appears upon the records. She had been associated with the school as one of the faculty for some time previously, and the Board, placing a high estimate upon her services, and receiving an intimation that she would probably retire from the school, passed a resolution respectfully inviting her to remain in connection with the institute as preceptress.

The Board received a communication at this time from Rev. T. H. Pearne, Financial Agent of the Missionary Society of the Methodist Episcopal Church, requesting payment of whatever sum might be due on the four thousand four hundred and thirty-seven dollars and eighty-three cents, ($4,437 83,) secured by bond executed by W. H. Wilson and others to said Missionary Society. This communication was referred to a committee, which was instructed to correspond with the Board of Managers of said society, and secure the formal relinquishment to this

Board of Trustees of the claim and bond above referred to.

Questions from time to time had arisen since the incorporation of the institution and the adoption of the name of Willamette University, and the scholarship system under the charter, in regard to the rights of the original subscribers to the funds of the Oregon Institute in relation to scholarships; whether they were entitled to scholarships by virtue of their former subscriptions, or whether those subscriptions were to be ignored in the sale of scholarships, and the old subscribers be required to pay the same as others who had never subscribed in aid of the institution. To ascertain the facts in relation to the matter, so that the Board could come to a just conclusion in the premises, a committee was appointed to procure and take into consideration certain papers relating to the origin and early history of the institution. This committee consisted of Rev. Gustavus Hines, Rev. J. L. Parrish, Rev. A. F. Waller, and Hon. L. F. Grover. This committee obtained the original papers of the Oregon Institute, and upon them made their report. In their report they gave the history of the institution from its incipiency up to that time, and on the facts presented the committee found, 1. That in the establishment of the Oregon Institute in 1842 on Wallace's Prairie the institution was intended as a progressive one, with an express intent of advancing the same to our present organization; that at no time since has the object of the institution been abandoned, however embarrassed its condition or informal its proceedings; and, 2. That the early patrons of the Oregon Institute, who entitled themselves to scholarships in the same, were equitably as well as legally entitled to scholarships in the Willamette University in value equal to the amounts paid by them into the treasury of said institution. This proved to be acceptable to the Board, and was consequently adopted; and a meeting, held August 15, 1855, in carrying out the principles of the report of the Board, took action, granting Rev. David Leslie, Rev. L. H. Judson, and Rev. Jason Lee (deceased) perpetual scholarships for having paid five hundred dollars each to build up the Oregon Institute. And it was furthermore decreed that all who had heretofore entitled themselves to scholarships in full, or in part, be entitled to avail themselves of the benefit of such scholarships from the date of the certificates of said scholarship issued or to be issued by virtue of the late action of the Board in the premises. In the case of Rev. Jason Lee, deceased, the action of the Board at this time was eminently just and proper It was as follows:

Whereas the Rev. Jason Lee by his last will donated to this institution the sum of one hundred dollars over and above the amount of five hundred dollars ($500) personally donated by him in his lifetime; therefore,

Resolved, That a perpetual scholarship be issued to the estate of said Jason Lee, and that all tuition heretofore accrued due from said estate be remitted in consideration of said bequest of one hundred dollars. And further, in acting upon this principle, it was determined that, in view of the deep interest which Alanson Beers took in the establishment and maintenance of the institution, each of his children be presented with a ten years' scholarship, not to be transferred.

The Board of Instruction for the past two years had varied somewhat from time to time, as it was found quite impossible as yet to obtain permanent teachers. It had consisted of Mr. Hoyt, who was both president and principal of the academical department; Mrs. Thurston, preceptress; and Miss Julia Bryant, teacher in the primary department. But changes had taken place, so that at the close of the year ending February, 1856, we find Rev. F. S. Hoyt president and professor, Rev. Charles Hall Professor of Exact Sciences, and Mrs. Hoyt preceptress, and teacher in the primary department.

CHAPTER IX.

POPULATION, NEW CONSTITUTION, AND ENDOWMENT

WE have now reached the fifteenth year of the his
tory of the Oregon Institute, and the fourth of the
Willamette University.   During that period we have
been passing through great changes, civil, political, and
religious; but especially in regard to the population
of our country.   In 1842, when the Oregon Institute
sprang into being, there were not two hundred white
persons of American origin, all told, on the Pacific
slope of our continent.   Indeed at that time, taken
as a whole, the country was in a state of comparative
barbarism.   A more heterogeneous class of humanity,
small as it was, could not have been found in any
land than had sought an asylum in the wilds of the
Pacific coast.   Here were the Indian, the legitimate
proprietor of the soil, Englishmen, Scotchmen, Irish-
men, Americans, Germans, Prussians, Italians, Spanish, Frenchmen, Danes, Canadians, Hawaiians, Ota-
heitans, Africans, and Chinese.   From intermarrying
with one another, and particularly with the natives
of the country ever since white men first visited
these shores, an amalgamated population had been
introduced, presenting every variety of color, disposition, and character of which the human species is
capable.   The English, Scotch, French, and some

others, had been introduced into the country mainly through the Hudson's Bay Company.

Many persons had found their way to Oregon from the numerous vessels which, from the earliest discoveries, had touched at various points along this extended coast. Scarcely a ship had visited the Columbia River for years from which two or more had not made their escape, and, secreting themselves until the vessel had left, they would come forth to mingle with the motley inhabitants as citizens of Oregon. Some had deserted their ships on the coast of California, and had fought their way to the valley of the famed "Multnomah" through the hostile tribes that roamed among the Klamath and Umpqua Mountains, and some had found their way to the fertile valleys of Oregon from the Rocky Mountains themselves; men who, in connection with the American companies established for purposes of traffic with the Blackfeet, Nez Perces, and other Indian tribes, had for many years been ranging the mountainous regions of the vast interior, experiencing the most surprising adventures among the Indians, and enduring every variety of hardships which human nature is capable of suffering, and at last had found a peaceful and quiet retreat on the banks of some beautiful river or streamlet meandering through the vales, where they were secure from savage violence and treachery, and where most of them proposed to close their earthly career. Some of these mountaineers had Indian wives, and formed an attachment for the mothers of their sons and daughters, and consequently, on leaving the scenes of their savage life, they took with them their wives and children, anxious that both might be benefited by mingling with civilized society; and they had heard that civilization was springing up in the midst of the mixed population of the valleys of Oregon. The most fruitful channel, however, for the supply of population for Oregon was the immigration channel from the United States east of the mountains to the Pacific coast. It had long been a problem whether the unknown regions west of the Rocky Mountains would or could ever be populated by immigrations across the continent, direct from the Atlantic States. The problem, however, was about to be solved. Lewis and Clark found their way across. Wilson Price Hunt and company scaled the barriers. Bonneville and Wyeth passed the stupendous gates, and traced the waters as they flowed westward to the ocean. The intrepid Lee, the pioneer missionary, and his companions, explored the South Pass through the mountains on their passage toward the setting sun. Whitman and Spaulding, with their wives and associates, followed in the train, and found no insuperable barriers. In 1839–41 parties comparatively small made the transit in safety. In 1842 the immigration numbered one hundred and thirty-two persons in all. Up to this period the transit had been made either on foot, or on the backs of mules or Indian ponies; but now another question was to be settled. Can wheeled carriages perform the trip over the mountains, from the Mississippi River to the Pacific Ocean? The emphatic answer is, They can;

for in 1843 the immigration, consisting of over eight hundred persons, performed the trip in wagons drawn by oxen. The gates were now open, the bars were all let down, the problem was fully solved. Oregon and the whole Pacific coast were to be peopled by immigration from the Eastern States. In 1844 another eight hundred was added to the population in the same manner. In 1845 three thousand souls sought the "better country," "not an heavenly," fanned by the breezes of the western ocean. In 1846 and 1847 the immigrations were respectable as to numbers; and in 1848 the donation land law was passed, and, but for the wonderful discovery of gold on the Sacramento, in California, doubtless an overwhelming tide of immigration would have set in to Oregon; but as it was, for the time being the stream was turned aside; some thousands, however, annually were added to the population of Oregon. In 1852 twenty thousand men, women, and children found homes and rest in these lovely valleys. In 1853 ten thousand were added to the former. In 1854 and 1855 the number, though respectable, was very much smaller. The aggregate of all these immigrations, diminished by just so many as from dissatisfaction had left the country or had died, had occupied the whole country, sparsely in many places, from Puget's Sound to Siskiu Mountains, and from the Cascade Mountains to the Pacific coast.

We have taken this cursory glance at the population of Oregon at this time for the purpose of showing the basis upon which we were operating, the causes which impelled us forward, and the increasing importance of the institution which we were laboring to establish. The Oregon Institute had been located in the most delightful and fertile portion of the entire country, at a very central point in the unrivaled valley of the Willamette. The population throughout the whole country, and especially in the vicinity of the institution, was continually increasing, and the demands upon the school seemed correspondingly to increase. And hence the energy that was thrown into the action of the Board, and hence the conception and vigorous application of the plans for properly endowing the University, so that it would, according to the original design, so far as literature and science were concerned, meet the growing demands of the country.

At the annual meeting of the Board, held March 5, 1856, the following persons were elected officers for the ensuing year:

Rev. DAVID LESLIE, President; Hon. G. H. WILLIAMS, Vice-President; Hon. L. F. GROVER, Secretary; ELISHA STRONG, Treasurer.

An executive committee and an auditing committee were also elected; a committee was also appointed to revise the constitution, and, at a meeting held Sept. 10, 1856, the Board adopted the constitution, as follows:

CONSTITUTION.

To secure a regular and efficient discharge of their duties, the Trustees of the Willamette University adopt, and agree to be governed by, the following constitution :

ARTICLE I.

SECTION 1.—This association shall be called the Board of Trustees of the Willamette University, pursuant to the provision of the Act of Incorporation granted by the Legislative Assembly of the territory of Oregon, bearing date January 12, 1853.

SECTION 2.—The recognized duties of this Board of Trustees shall be to secure to the Willamette University the possession and perpetuity of an adequate endowment, to manage its fiscal affairs, and to organize and exercise such supervision over its departments of instruction as shall best secure its usefulness as an institution of learning.

ARTICLE II.—OFFICERS.

SECTION 1.—The officers of the Board of Trustees shall be a president, a vice-president, a secretary, and a treasurer.

SECTION 2.—It shall be the duty of the president to preside at all meetings of the Board, to call such special meetings as are hereinafter provided for, to subscribe his name to all acts and proceedings of the Board when necessary and proper to give validity to the same, to visit during each term the several departments of instruction connected with the university, and to make a written report of their efficiency at the next ensuing meeting of the Board

Section 3.—It shall be the duty of the vice-president to perform the duties of the president in his absence.

Section 4.—It shall be the duty of the secretary to give due notice of the meetings of the Board, to keep a full record of its proceedings, to attest and affix the seal of the university to all instruments of writing, whenever necessary to give them validity, to receive and file all papers and documents, collect all moneys due the university, and pay the same to the treasurer, taking his receipt therefor, and make report to the Board at each annual meeting.

Section 5.—It shall be the duty of the treasurer to keep a full, accurate, and complete account of the fiscal affairs of the university, to receive all moneys due the institution for tuition or otherwise, and account for the same; to make such exhibit thereof at each meeting as shall furnish the Board a proper and satisfactory knowledge of the same; to make a written report in detail at each annual meeting, the same having been submitted to and received the approval of the auditing committee, and he shall in no case pay out money except on the order of the Board, signed by the president, and countersigned by the secretary.

Section 6.—The officers of the Board shall be elected by ballot at a regular meeting, and shall hold their several offices until the next ensuing annual meeting, or until their successors are elected and qualified.

ARTICLE III.—MEETINGS.

SECTION 1.—The Board shall hold its annual meetings on the Tuesday preceding the collegiate anniversary, and quarterly meetings on the third Wednesday in November, February, and May, and such other meetings as may be called by the president upon the application of two or more members of the executive committee. This article was amended so that the third quarterly meeting could be held at the close of the winter term.

ARTICLE IV.—COMMITTEES.

SECTION 1.—There shall be two standing committees, an auditing committee that shall consist of three, and an Executive Committee to consist of seven, to be elected annually from among the members of the Board. The president of the university shall be *ex-officio* member of the executive committee.

SECTION 2.—It shall be the duty of the Auditing Committee to audit the accounts of the treasurer.

SECTION 3.—It shall be the duty of the Executive Committee to have the general supervision of the University and the business of the Board in the interim of its meetings, and to make report thereof at each regular meeting of the Board.

ARTICLE V.

This constitution may be altered or amended by a two thirds vote of all the members of the Board present at any regular meeting.

In connection with the adoption of the above constitution, a course of study, which had been thoroughly digested by a qualified committee, of whom Rev. F. S. Hoyt, the president of the institution, was the chairman, was also adopted, and the collegiate year was divided into three terms; and it was further provided that the course of instruction should extend through four years in the College proper, and three years in the Preparatory Department; the college years to be designated according to well-established usage in such institutions, by the names of Senior, Junior, Sophomore, and Freshman.

As the course of study which was adopted was subsequently revised, it is not necessary to give it in detail in this place. It may be proper to observe, however, that it compared well in its comprehensiveness with that of older and more mature institutions in the Atlantic States; and, in connection with the amended constitution, and the arrangements in reference to the proper designation of the collegiate years, shows the advancement of our cherished school from the character of a mere primary and academical institution, to the position and characteristics of a real college. It was now passing from its chrysalis condition into a new-fledged university, and was preparing to plume its wings for an upward flight.

In the progress of this history it has been necessary frequently to revert to the efforts which the Board of Trustees was putting forth to create an endowment fund by the sale of scholarships, and otherwise; and here we shall resume the subject, and present in one view the struggles of the Board in relation to the endowment up to the present time.

The Missionary Society of the Methodist Episcopal Church was still in possession of considerable property in Oregon in lands, having a claim on the land upon which the city of Dalles is located, and also having secured a title to land to the extent of a quarter section in the vicinity of the city of Salem.

The Missionary Society had expended an immense amount of money since the beginning of missionary operations in Oregon, and the country had been vastly benefited, both religiously and financially, by such expenditure, and it was proper and right that the lands which the missionaries had occupied should be confirmed to the Board.

This was done so far as the land at Salem was concerned, and, as this land lay adjoining the university campus, it was valuable in itself, and might be used greatly to the advantage of the university; and as the Board of Trustees had been greatly disappointed in respect to their original claim, it was very desirable on their part to secure this land, and use it to the best advantage for the enlargement of the endowment fund of the university.

The property was in Oregon, and had been secured to the Missionary Board through the instrumentality of those men "who counted not their lives dear unto them so that they might finish the ministry committed to their hands; and it was thought by all that the avails of that property should be appropriated to the promotion of religion and science in Oregon ; and if so, that it could not be employed better than to put it into the hands of the Trustees of the Willamette University.

The subject of the endowment of the university was one of the deepest possible interest to the state of Oregon and the Pacific coast generally, and consequently it was proper for the Board to use all lawful and Christian means to compass so desirable an end. Little, however, had been effected previously to 1856, but at that time the Rev. T. II. Pearne, who had been elected as a delegate to the General Conference from Oregon, was authorized by the Board of Trustees to make application in the Atlantic States for aid toward the endowment of the Willamette University. Mr. Pearne presented the subject before the Missionary Society in New York, and that body received it with their usual liberality, and proceeded to pass the following resolution :

" *Resolved*, That our agent in Oregon who, for the time being, may hold legal power from the Board to act for it, be authorized to pay over to the Trustees of the Willamette University the sum of five thousand dollars toward the endowment of said university out of any moneys in his hands arising out of the mission property in Oregon belonging to the Missionary Society of the Methodist Episcopal Church ; "*Provided*, that before said agent shall pay over as aforesaid, the Board shall be informed and satisfied that the sum of fifteen thousand dollars has been invested in good and sufficient and productive securities, other than simply individual liabilities, said securities to be free from all claims against them, and to have arisen out of sources not heretofore granted by this Board, but from other and different sources."

This resolution was reported to the Board of Trustees in Oregon in September of 1856, and was hailed by them as an act worthy of the Missionary Board of the Methodist Episcopal Church, and it afforded them very great encouragement in their efforts to raise funds for the endowment of the university. Prompted by the necessities of our institution, and this generous offer of the Missionary Board to aid us in its endowment, we proceeded through our agent, the Rev. A. F. Waller, to canvass the country for the purpose of raising the funds requisite to entitle the Board to the five thousand dollars.

The principal method adopted to raise the fifteen thousand dollars was the sale of perpetual scholarships at five hundred dollars each, though other measures, with some degree of success, were also employed. It was found to be a very difficult matter in the sparsely settled and undeveloped state of Oregon to raise so large a sum; but by energetic and unceasing efforts for nearly three years, it was found on the fifth of August, 1859, that the whole amount of fifteen thousand dollars had been raised and invested in good securities. So soon as this was ascertained by the report of the agent, the Board of Trustees passed, in substance, the following preamble and resolution :

" Whereas it has been understood that the Missionary Society of the Methodist Episcopal Church proposed to secure to the Willamette University the sum of five thousand dollars on condition that said university would raise the sum of fifteen thousand dollars; and whereas the sum of fifteen thousand dollars was raised on or before the first day of August, 1859, therefore,

" *Resolved*, That a committee be appointed to correspond with said Missionary Board, and secure as soon as possible the said five thousand dollars, so that it may be funded, and the interest thereof used for the support of said university."

- Rev. William Roberts was appointed that committee, and he addressed a letter to the Missionary Board informing them that we had substantially fulfilled the condition upon our part, and consequently were ready to receive the five thousand dollars according to the offer of the Missionary Board.

After this correspondence several years passed by, and the matter remained unadjusted; but at the session of the Oregon Conference held in Salem, 1864, Rev. T. H. Pearne, who was the authorized agent of the Missionary Board in Oregon, informed the conference that the Board proposed to convey to the Trustees of the Willamette University a certain piece or parcel of land lying in the vicinity of Salem, containing some eighty acres, more or less, in lieu of the five thousand dollars in cash, and requested the conference to take action upon the subject. The action of the conference was favorable to this arrangement, and immediately after the adjournment of the conference a special meeting of the Board of Trustees was called to take into consideration the proposition of the Missionary Board. At this meeting, which was held August 20, 1864, the Board of Trustees passed a resolution accepting of the land as a full satisfaction for the five thousand dollars in cash.

The land proposed to be given possessed a value which would justify the Missionary Board in conveying it and the Trustees of the University in receiving it as an equivalent for the five thousand dollars. The impression had gone abroad that this land possessed an immense value in consequence of a certain water privilege which it contained. This, however, was an entire mistake. The water which ran through the premises in a ditch which had been excavated for that purpose, did not belong to the premises, but was the property of the Oregon Milling Company, subject to their control, and liable to be removed into another channel at their option. The premises, therefore, were not made more valuable, but rather injured in value by the ditch which was dug through them. Consequently, in conveying that land to the Board of Trustees, the Missionary Board would not be giving more than was first proposed, and the Board of Trustees would receive what they could ultimately use to about the same advantage as would have resulted from the investment of the five thousand dollars.

There arose between the Missionary Society and the Board of Trustees, doubtless more from a misapprehension of each other's views and intentions than from any other cause, a somewhat protracted controversy in relation to this business operation, and, consequently, there was a delay of the final arrangement until the present year, (1867.) Early in this year the Missionary Board through their secretary, W. L. Harris, D.D., and much to the satisfaction of the Board of Trustees, took effectual measures to transfer to that body, by a good and sufficient deed, the said tract of land, comprising eighty acres, more or less, in lieu of the five thousand dollars. This transfer was eminently wise and just upon the part of the Missionary Society, first, because the property thus appropriated becomes a permanent fund for the accomplishment of good to the end of time; and second, by a reflex influence it doubtless will tend directly to the promotion of the future interests of the missionary cause by returning fourfold into the treasury of the Missionary Society; third, because this arrangement becomes the occasion of greatly increasing the confidence of the public in our institution, and will contribute greatly toward relieving the Board from all embarrassment arising from a want of income, and open the way for the Willamette University finally to enter upon a career of great usefulness and prosperity. In this connection it may be proper to observe, that while the negotiation between the two Boards was going on, the Board of Trustees was laboring faithfully and constantly for the maintenance and advancement of their beloved institution, and they had succeeded, entirely outside of all sources granted to them by the Missionary Board, in raising the endowment fund up to the amount of twenty-four thousand dollars, nearly all of which was amply secured. Besides this, the Board of Trustees had but recently invested in real estate, in the form of a splendid brick edifice located on their college campus, which in size and beauty when finished would do honor to any state in the Union, the sum of twenty-five thousand dollars. This was nearly all provided for by subscription, and the entire property, amounting to about fifty thousand dollars, was, indeed, free from all incumbrance. This amount does not include the college campus of sixty acres, nor the lands which the Board received in their settlement with Dr. W. H. Wilson, the value of which it would be difficult at this time to determine; but the fact, in itself of considerable importance to the Board of Trustees, which here should be clearly exhibited, is, that at the time the Missionary Board made the transfer of the land spoken of, the Board of Trustees had raised and invested in real estate, and funded as the beginning of an endowment, from the resources of the country, independent of any and every thing that had ever been received from any other source, the sum of fifty thousand dollars. To accomplish this, and to keep the building which we were erecting free from debt, or rather, unembarrassed with debt, it was necessary to pull upon every string and to move with great precaution. Also, by this constant and unusual draft upon the people it was extremely difficult to sustain the other financial departments of the university. The population of Oregon was small, the people were poor, and money was scarce, and the Willamette University felt the pressure; and the bestowment by the Missionary Board of the eighty acres of land spoken of, from its present, but especially from its prospective value, was indeed a godsend to our cherished institution, for which the Board of Trustees and the friends of religious education generally in Oregon cannot be too thankful.

The Missionary Society of the Methodist Episcopal Church and the Book Concern have, under God, been the greatest benefactors of the Pacific Coast. Aside from that part of the coast embraced in the state of California, they have paid in cash for the religious and civil benefit of the country within the limits of the Oregon Conference, since the first missionaries went there in 1834, not less than five hundred thousand dollars. Oregon should not forget her benefactors; and the friends of the Willamette University should remember that but for the benevolence of the Missionary Society, and the interest it has ever taken in the advancement of the Church and its institutions, the success which has crowned the effort to establish the institution is to be, in part, attributed to the timely and efficient aid which that society has afforded.

It seemed proper to indulge in these reflections while considering the manner in which the unpleasant controversy between the two Boards in relation to the five-thousand-dollar donation was closed up. Surely, the final issue was of such a nature as that the Board of Trustees of the university has been laid under lasting obligation to the Missionary Society; while at the same time they claim, in all the protracted controversy, to have been actuated by honesty of purpose, and a sincere desire to promote the best interests of humanity in Oregon. And here the old adage. may be properly inserted, " To err is human ; to forgive, divine."

Having traced the history of the five-thousand-dollar donation to the endowment fund, it will be necessary to revert back to the period when the Board of Trustees considered that they had fulfilled the condition in relation to the fifteen thousand dollars. This was in July 28, 1859. At a meeting of the Board held at this time it was ascertained from the report of Rev. A. F. Waller, who had been acting as agent without remuneration for two years, that the endowment of twenty thousand dollars, embracing the five thousand, was completed, and it was resolved forthwith to raise an additional endowment, if possible, of twenty thousand, and a request was voted to the next annual conference of the Methodist Episcopal Church to appoint Rev. A. F. Waller as agent of the university for the ensuing year, to carry out the wishes of the Board in reference to the endowment. According to this request the bishop presiding at the ensuing conference appointed Rev. A. F. Waller agent, and he continued his efforts, as circumstances would permit, to enlarge the endowment fund by the sale of scholarships. As he had already thoroughly canvassed the ground in raising the fifteen thousand dollars, and as the community was quite limited, and the people of wealth few and far between, it was found, after years of effort, to be quite impossible to raise an additional twenty thousand dollars. A few thousand, however, was added to the former collections, and the following is a list of the names of all the persons who, by the payment of five hundred dollars, have entitled themselves to perpetual scholarships:

Francis Fletcher	$500	Rev. William Roberts	$500
Rev. C. S. Kingsley	500	Rev. J. H. Wilber	500
Rev. T. H. Pearne	500	Fletcher Crabtree	500
Hon. ——Lansdale	500	W. W. M'Kinney	500
Hon. J. S. Smith	500	William Odell	500
Rev. J. L. Parrish	500	Martin Vaughn	500
Rev. David Leslie	500	W. O. Gibson	500
Mrs. C. A. Wilson	1,000	George Belknap	500
Rev. Jason Lee	600	Orrin Belknap	500
Hon. L. F. Grover	500	Ransom Belknap	500
E. Strong	500	M. Swank	500
Rev. A. F. Waller	500	Hon. Jeremiah Lampson	500
M. Swegle	500	Elias Buel	500
J. N. Gilbert	500	James M'Kain	500
Joseph Waldo	500	Mrs. Jane Armstrong	500
Joseph Holman	500	Hon. John H. Moors	500
Rev. J. D. Boon	500	Abijah Carey	500
Thomas Cross	500	Hon. Joseph Lane	500
Rev. Gustavus Hines	500	Hon. S. Stout	500
Webley Hauxhurst	500	Hon. E. D. Baker	500
Hon. J. M. Harrison	500	Rev. L. H. Judson	500
W. S. Ladd	500		

CHAPTER X.

THE INTERNAL HISTORY OF THE UNIVERSITY.

FROM the imperfection of the records kept during a number of the early years of the school's history, and the fact that some of the records have been lost, it will be quite difficult, if not utterly impossible, to refer to the names of all who have taken a part in the internal management and conduct of the institution. I now refer to those persons who have been employed in the very responsible positions of presidents, professors, and teachers in the institution from the beginning in 1844 up to the present time. Some of the teachers who have been connected with the school have remained but a very short time, and considerable teaching has been done during some of the years of the school's history in the lower departments by persons who have at the same time been pursuing their studies in the higher departments of science. If the names of any who have been regularly employed as teachers in any department shall be omitted in this chapter, such omission will be the result of the absence of the proper data. Some of the names of the early teachers have already been mentioned in this work; but I shall run the hazard of being charged with repetition for the purpose of presenting the internal history of the school in one connection. The patrons of the Oregon Institute were very fortunate in the teacher that was employed to open the school. Mrs. Chloe E. Wilson has the enviable reputation of having been the first teacher in the Oregon Institute. The school was opened August 16, 1844, with some twenty pupils. These were mostly primaries, as up to this period but slight opportunities for the acquirement of even the fundamental principles of education had existed. Mrs. Wilson continued in the school as the only teacher for two years, during which there was a large increase of population, and a corresponding growth of the school. In the spring of 1846 the number of pupils had increased to sixty, and at that time it was found necessary to employ an additional teacher. Accordingly Mr. Hinman, now the Hon. Mr. Hinman, of Washington County, was employed to assist Mrs. Wilson, and continued in the institution for one year. In August, 1847, Mr. J. S. Smith, now the Hon. J. S. Smith, of Salem, and a most active and efficient member of the present Board of Trustees of the University, became connected with the school as teacher, and remained until February, 1848, when he left in consequence of ill health. Mrs. Wilson remained the principal conductor of the school until 1848, when the names of Rev. James II. Wilber and his daughter are found connected with the institution. How long the two latter taught in the institution does not appear.

Mr. St. J. M. Fackler, an Episcopal clergyman, who subsequently married the daughter of Mr. Wilber, but now deceased, though very much of an exclusive churchman, favored the institution for a short period with his experience as a teacher. In the estimation of many it was thought that it was a little doubtful which of the twain commanded most of the attention of the reverend gentleman, the school itself, or the accomplished daughter of Mr. Wilber. Judging, however, from the fact that so soon as the young lady was secured Mr. Fackler ceased his connection with the institution, it is natural to conclude that to win this inestimable prize was the principal motive that influenced him to condescend to become a teacher in the Oregon Institute. I do not intend by any means to cast reflections upon Mr. Fackler. He had an undoubted right to use all lawful and religious means to procure the blessing of a good wife, and having accomplished this somewhat difficult task in the manner above indicated, he settled in Oregon, and became the most active and efficient Episcopal clergyman in the country. Providence, however, did not long permit him to cherish the prize which he had won. An only daughter, and a fond and doting wife, her friends wept over her grave in the church-yard in the city of Portland ere she had attained her twentieth year. Mr. Fackler subsequently married a second time; but on a passage from Oregon to New York, after leaving the Isthmus of Panama, he died, and was buried at sea.

After those already mentioned, the names of the Rev. M. Eells and his wife, formerly connected with the mission in the Walla Walla country, established by Dr. Marcus Whitman under the direction of the American Board, appear among the teachers of the institute. This mission was broken up by the Indian war which followed the Whitman massacre, which occurred in the fall of 1847, and the surviving members were scattered to other portions of the country. Mr. Eells and his wife found employment for a while as teachers in the Oregon Institute, where they exerted an excellent influence, and contributed much while they remained to give character and stability to the school. The precise time when they commenced their services and when they ceased their connection with the school do not appear upon the records; but it is presumable from what does appear that they were officiating in the winter of 1849 and 1850.

At the second session of the Oregon and California Mission Conference, held at Oregon City September 4, 1850, the Rev. F. S. Hoyt and the Rev. Nehemiah Doane were appointed as teachers in the Oregon Institute. Mr. Hoyt had received his appointment from the Eastern States to Oregon with a view of taking charge of the Oregon Institute as the principal whenever he should arrive in the country. He had not yet arrived, and Mr. Doane was placed in charge until Mr. Hoyt should reach the coast. Mr. Doane continued in the school for one year, Mrs. Doane assisting him as teacher during the same time. They were efficient and active, and gave excellent satisfaction to the patrons of the school; but it was not necessary to continue both Mr. Hoyt and Mr.

Doane in connection with the school at the same time, consequently the latter left the institution for other service, and Mr. Hoyt, after his arrival, which took place late in 1850, took charge of the school in accordance with the design of his appointment. Mr. Hoyt was connected with the institution for ten years as professor and president, or from 1850 to 1860, his reappointment from the conference having been annually requested by the Board of Trustees. During the long period of Mr. Hoyt's service as the principal and president of the institution there was, with the exception of the president, but little permanency in the Board of Instruction. While he had the direction of the school the assistants that were employed under him were numerous, and a particular account of them all would extend this chapter to an undue length. It will be sufficient simply to insert their names as nearly in the order in which they served the institution as the data which we have in our possession will admit. In connection with the Primary Department the following names appear: Miss Belle Walker, now Mrs. Cook; Mrs. Dillon; Miss Mary Leslie, since Mrs. Jones, now deceased; Miss Julia Bryant, now Mrs. Terry; Miss Mary Waller, now Mrs. Hall; Miss Sarelia Pringle, now Mrs. Northrup; Mrs. Wilson, Mrs. S. B. Wilber, Miss Jordan, Miss Draper, now Mrs. Arthur Nicklen, and Miss S. A. Cornell.

In the Academic or Preparatory Department during the same period we find the names of the following persons: Mr. J. Dillon, Mrs. Hoyt, Mr. C. Hall as Professor of Exact Sciences, Mr. Newcomb, Mr.

D. L. Spaulding, Mr. S. B. Wilber, Miss Lucia A. N. Jordan, Miss L. Boise, Miss Mary Miller, now Mrs. Col. Kelley, Mr. I. L. Powell, Mr. F. D. Hodgson, Mr. Barnard, Mr. Stinson, Edwin Cartwright, Mrs. Joseph Wilson, Mr. F. Grubbs, and Mrs. Thurston, now Mrs. Wm. Odell.

Doubtless there were other persons that taught in the school during the administration of Mr. Hoyt, but the above-named were the principal. Through their assistance the Oregon Institute, under the superintendence of Mr. Hoyt, moved on slowly but surely in the path of improvement, from the character of a primary to that of a well-developed academical and preparatory school, and had already begun to assume many of the airs of even a collegiate institution. At the session of the Oregon Annual Conference, held at Albany in August, 1859, President Hoyt was elected a delegate to the General Conference of the Methodist Episcopal Church, which was to be held the following May in the city of Buffalo, in the state of New York. Consequently I find in the records of the Board under date of October 19, 1859, this action: "On motion, it was voted that Mr. Hoyt be allowed leave of absence to visit the Eastern States, and that his salary be continued without intermission during his absence."

This action of the Board was with the expectation that Mr. Hoyt, after having discharged his obligations as a delegate to the General Conference, and availed himself, by visiting colleges and other institutions of learning, of the more recent improvements and facilities for the conduct and management of such institutions, would return again to Oregon and resume his position as president of the Willamette University. In this, however, the Board was doomed to disappointment. Mr. Waller, who was the colleague of Mr. Hoyt to the General Conference, had returned, and in a meeting of the Board, held at Salem, August 18, 1860, gave the information that President Hoyt had made application for a situation in the Ohio Wesleyan University; but as no official communication had been received from him by the Board no action was taken at this time. At a meeting, however, held Sept. 26, 1860, the president of the Board of Trustees, Rev. David Leslie, presented a letter from Rev. F. S. Hoyt, resigning his situation as president of the Willamette University, which was read, and, on motion, the resignation was accepted.

The following preamble and resolutions were then read and adopted:

Whereas the Rev. F. S. Hoyt has resigned his position as president of the Willamette University in order to return with his family to the Atlantic States; therefore,

Resolved, That after an intercourse of nearly ten years, during which time he has had charge of this institution, we have learned very highly to appreciate the capabilities of Rev. F. S. Hoyt as an instructor of youth, a Christian gentleman, and fellow-laborer in the cause of education.

Resolved, That while we part with himself and family with regret, we learn with pleasure that he has become connected with an eminent institution of learning in Ohio, and that we follow him with our most ardent wishes for success.

Resolved, That we cherish a most grateful recollection of the peace and harmony with which our mutual labors with our beloved brother have been characterized, and shall richly enjoy such correspondence in the future as the duties of his new relation may permit.

Thus terminated the long and onerous term of service of Rev. F. S. Hoyt, as principal of the Oregon Institute, and president of the Willamette University. Before taking leave of him after having so faithfully conducted the growing institution in the midst of many discouragements, arising as well from its poverty as from the heterogeneous character of its patrons and students, for ten long years, it will be proper here to accord to him the meed of praise which is justly his due. As a teacher, inside the walls of the Institute, he was decidedly popular and efficient, gaining not only the good-will and affection of the students generally, but also their highest respect. With the Board of Trustees his course was characterized by kindness, affability, a high respect for their judgment and authority, and a manifest disposition to carry out faithfully the instructions which from time to time they thought proper to communicate. This rendered him popular with the Board of Trustees, while his character as a gentleman, a Christian, and a minister was such as to entitle him to the high consideration of the public generally where he was known. Before entering upon his labors in connection with the Ohio Wesleyan University, he returned to Oregon, disposed of his property, took leave of his friends, of whom he had many, and bade adieu to the scenes of his early toil on the Pacific shores, and returned to the East, where it is hoped that his labor will be vastly lighter, his usefulness more extended, and his emoluments and honors much greater than any that he could have secured in the Western world. He now, 1867, occupies the chair of theology in the Ohio Wesleyan University, having been connected with that institution since he left Oregon.

On the 3d of August, 1860, the Board received information through Hon. J. S. Smith that Professor T. M. Gatch, who had been teaching in Washington Territory, and who was previously connected with a college in California, had, in answer to a proposition made to him some time before, indicated to him his willingness to be employed as a professor in the University, and consequently the Board proceeded at once to elect T. M. Gatch Professor of Ancient Languages and Moral Science. This was before word was received that Mr. Hoyt had severed his connection with the institution. So soon as this information was given, at a special meeting of the Board held Sept. 26, 1860, it was resolved that Professor T. M. Gatch be constituted the acting president of the institution until a president shall be duly elected. Measures were taken also to hold correspondence with various persons on the subject of the presidency, preparatory to an election at the next meeting. This was held October 3, 1860, and the correspondence reported that they had had the subject under careful consideration, and recommended the immediate election of a president. Whereupon the Board proceeded to ballot, and the Rev. Wm. J. Maclay was unanimously elected president of the Willamette University. The secretary of the Board, Rev. Wm. Roberts, was instructed to inform Mr. Maclay of his election, which accordingly he did, and on Dec. 5, 1860, the Board was informed that Mr. Maclay declined to accept of the presidency of the institution. Immediately upon this, Professor T. M. Gatch was placed upon nomination, and having received the vote of every member present, twenty-two in all, he was declared duly elected president of the Willamette University. Mr. Hoyt, who had not left the country, was appointed a committee to wait on Mr. Gatch and inform him of his election, and ask him to signify his acceptance. Being assured that the election was unanimous, Mr. Gatch signified his acceptance, and Mr. Hoyt had the pleasure of placing one well qualified to fill it in the chair which he had vacated by a voluntary resignation.

Various changes had occurred from year to year in the membership of the Board of Trustees, but it is not necessary to speak of these particularly. At the time, however, of the election of Mr. Gatch to the presidency of the institution the classes stood as follows:

The officers of the Board elected at the previous
annual meeting were as follows: DAVID LESLIE,
president; JOHN H. MOORES, vice-president; WM.
ROBERTS, secretary; GEO. H. JONES, treasurer.

L. F. Grover, C. N. Terry, A. F. Waller, J. H.
Moores, J. S. Smith, F. S. Hoyt, and Gustavus Hines,
executive committee; J. R. Moors, C. N. Terry,
and J. S. Smith, auditing committee.

Sustained by this array of ability on the part of
the Board, every member of which seemed to feel a
deep interest for the advancement of the institution,
Mr. Gatch applied himself to his responsible task

with great tact and energy, which seemed to extend into every department of the school, giving it, as it were, new life and vigor, and causing it to exhibit satisfactory evidences of real prosperity.

At a meeting of the Board held February 20, 1861, Mr. Gatch made a statement in regard to the school, in which it appeared that it was more full than ever known at any corresponding season of the year. Mr. Gatch himself, during the quarter, had taught twelve classes, and the necessity of assistance in the Board of Instruction was obvious, and measures were taken to procure such assistance.

The Board of Instruction at this time consisted of the following persons: T. M. Gatch, L. S. Dyer, F. H. Grubbs, Mary Millar, Lucia A. N. Jordan. During the year William E. Barnard was added to the list of teachers, by an election to the chair of mathematics, and also Mrs. J. G. Wilson was employed for one term. Mr. L. J. Powell was elected teacher in the school, November 20, 1861, to perform such duties as might be assigned him by the president, and being informed of his election, he at once came forward and entered upon his work. There were other teachers employed during this collegiate year, so that at the close in July, 1862, the following persons were found to have rendered service some portion of the year: T. M. Gatch, William E. Barnard, L. J. Powell, F. H. Grubbs, T. H. Crawford, Mary Millar, Lizzie Boise, L. Draper.

By a vote of the Board, August 19, 1862, Mr. L. J. Powell was promoted to the chair of mathematics, heretofore occupied by W. E. Barnard, who had resigned his place, and J. A. B. Stinson was elected a teacher under the direction of the president. With these changes in the Board of Instruction, the first three years of Mr. Gatch's administration passed away harmoniously and prosperously; but at a meeting of the Board, which was held at the chapel January 17, 1863, the president presented the following paper:

"REV. DAVID LESLIE, PRESIDENT OF THE BOARD OF TRUSTEES OF WILLAMETTE UNIVERSITY.

"DEAR SIR: I hereby resign the presidency of the Willamette University. Permit me through you to return my sincere thanks to the honorable Board of Trustees, for their hearty co-operation in everything that has pertained to the successful management of the school, and let me express the hope that the confidence reposed in me has not been entirely misplaced. With the assurance that I earnestly desire the prosperity of the university, I subscribe myself.

Yours, respectfully,   T. M. GATCH."

The Board received this announcement with deep regret, and proceeded at once to pass the following preamble and resolutions:

"Whereas President Gatch has tendered to this Board his resignation of the office of president; and whereas his administration has been entirely successful, having the respect and confidence of the community, the affection of the students, and the unqualified approbation of the Board of Trustees; therefore,

" *Resolved*, 1. That the Trustees have received the communication of President Gatch with feelings of profound regret. That during his continuance in office he has showed himself eminently fitted for the trust reposed in him at his election by the unanimous vote of this Board.

"2. That it would be very gratifying to the members of this Board, and in their judgment highly promotive of the best interests of the university, if he would consent to withdraw his resignation, and continue his past relation to the school.

"3. That if he cannot, consistently with his interests or views of duty, consent to remain permanently at the head of the university, he be requested to continue to perform the duties of president thereof as long as he conveniently can, and, if possible, until the close of the collegiate year."

A copy of the above resolutions was put into the hands of President Gatch, and resulted much to the gratification of all the friends of the institution, in his withdrawal of the act of resignation, and continuing the president of the school.

Favored with the supervision of an excellent president, and a corps of teachers that were disposed to labor with him in perfect unison, the school progressed satisfactorily to all concerned through the collegiate year, terminating July 14, 1863, with but little change in the *personnel* employed, save the addition of a few new names to the list of teachers.

In the third quarter of this year, May 20, 1863, the name of Lucy A. M. Lee, still a student in the school, first appears among the teachers for half time. Miss Samantha Cornell was also employed to enter the Primary Department at a future time. Mr. John W. Johnson was elected as a teacher, but never connected himself with the institution.

The faculty at this date stood as follows: T. M. GATCH, president; L. J. POWELL, professor; W. E. BARNARD, academical department; MARY B. MILLAR, preparatory and French; LUCY A. M. LEE, assistant; MRS. BELLE COOK, primary department.

At the close of the year, July 16, a slight change appears in the list of teachers, but no names that have not already been mentioned. Thomas H. Crawford is added to the list, and Samantha A. Cornell takes the place of Mrs. Belle Cook.

The annual meeting of the Board, the twenty-first since the school was founded, and the thirteenth since it became a chartered university, was held in the chapel of the Institute, July 14, 1863.

The officers of the Board elected for the ensuing year were: DAVID LESLIE, president; CHESTER N. TERRY, secretary; E. N. COOK, treasurer; JOHN H. MOORES, J. S. SMITH, A. F. WALLER, THOMAS CROSS, T. M. GATCH, GUSTAVUS HINES, J. L. PARRISH, executive committee; J. C. PEEBLES, ELISHA STRONG, J. R. ROBB, auditing committee.

The faculty underwent a slight change, as will appear from the following action of the Board of Trustees:

" *Resolved*, That the Board of Instruction for the ensuing year consist of the following persons, and that we agree to pay them the following rates of salary : T. M. Gatch, $1,200; Lucy A. M. Lee, $500; L. J. Powell, $1,000; Samantha A. Cornell, $500.

And it was also ordered that the Executive Committee be empowered to employ any additional teachers that might be needed.

The Board of Trustees at this meeting, which was well attended, there being some twenty members present, was very highly gratified and encouraged by the evidences of the growing prosperity of the institution which appeared before them. A number of the old trustees who witnessed the struggles of the school for existence in its earliest infancy, and had watched it with the most earnest solicitude at every step of its history, were present, and what they were now permitted to behold was to them exceedingly satisfactory and cheering. Previously to this, though there had many persons left the school who had received a thorough education in English science and literature, yet there had but two persons regularly graduated, after having entitled themselves to the honors of the institution by completing the whole course of study.

The first graduate was Emily J. York, in 1859, who, having finished the course prescribed for young ladies, was constituted Mistress of English Literature.

The second was Addie B. Locey, who received similar honors in 1862.*

* Deceased.

At the present meeting of the Board, however, the president of the university, T. M. Gatch, made a communication which showed that the harvest time of the institution had already come, when the laborers were to reap the fruits of their exertions.

The communication was as follows:

"To the Honorable Board of Trustees of Willamette University.

"Gentlemen: The following young men have completed the full classical course of study in the university: Thomas H. Crawford, Francis H. Grubbs, and J. C. Grubbs, and the same are hereby recommended as entitled to the degree of Bachelor of Arts, and Latin diplomas certifying to their attainments.

"Emily N. Belt, Margaretta Grubbs, Lucy A. M. Lee, Mary M'Ghee, Angeline Robb, and Nelly Stipp have completed the course prescribed for young ladies, and Colon T. Finlayson, Alva M'Wharter, and John B. Waldo have completed the English branches laid down in the course, and it is recommended that a suitable diploma be furnished each.

"Respectfully submitted,   T. M. Gatch,
          "*President Willamette University.*
"*July 14, 1863.*"

The Board carried out the recommendation of the president, and the appropriate degrees were conferred upon this interesting class of twelve young persons, the legitimate fruits of our toils in sustaining the now rising institution. On the following day after this action of the Board the large Methodist Episcopal Church in Salem, beautifully and appropriately decorated with festoons and mottoes of evergreens, and hung with the national banner, the red, white, and blue, was filled to its utmost capacity with the population of the town and visitors from the surrounding country to witness what was never seen before on the Pacific shores, but what is doubtless hereafter often to be witnessed—a large, respectable, and thoroughly educated class of young gentlemen and ladies publicly receiving the honors to which they had entitled themselves by their industry and perseverance, and then to take their affectionate leave of each other, of their long cherished friends and teachers, and of their young alma mater, and go forth to take upon themselves the responsibilities of life for which, by long years of faithful study and training, they had endeavored to qualify themselves. The orations of the young men, and the essays of the young ladies on this occasion were truly of an elevated character, and did great credit to their respective authors, reflecting much honor also upon the faculty of instruction. Indeed all present to witness these commencement exercises, the Board of Trustees, the patrons and spectators, were all impressed with the great importance and immense value of the institution which was now beginning fully to develop its capabilities of meeting the educational demands of the community, and thereby of becoming of incalculable benefit to the rising country.

The Board of Instruction for the collegiate year

commencing September, 1863, was changed only by the addition, by the election by the trustees, of Francis H. Grubbs, to take charge of the Academical Department. The faculty stood as follows:

T. M. GATCH, President of Faculty, and Teacher of Ancient Languages; L. J. POWELL, Teacher of Mathematics and Natural Science; LUCY A. LEE, Teacher of French and English Composition; FRANCIS H. GRUBBS, Academical Department; SAMANTHA A. CORNELL, Primary Department; LOUISA BRAYMAN, Music Teacher.

The Board of Teachers during this year assumed a little more permanency than formerly, there being fewer changes called for on account of the transient character of the material employed. This is in part accounted for from the fact that the school itself, through its thoroughly trained graduates, was now providing for its own wants as well as those of the country at large. This corps of teachers operated in great harmony, as a general rule, both in their teaching and in the discipline which they exercised over their respective departments. There was, however, during the third quarter of this year a matter of discipline which it may be proper and useful to relate. A meeting of the Board was called, at the instance of Mr. Gatch, to decide a case of discipline in relation to one of the students, concerning which there was a difference of opinion between him and Professor Powell. It appears that Professor Powell had dismissed a student from his department for some misdemeanor, and that President Gatch had received him back, so far as his department was concerned, to recite Latin and French, which were not taught in Professor Powell's department. Professor Powell thought that the president ought not to have received him back to those classes until he had made the satisfaction required. The matter elicited considerable discussion, and, as a result, a resolution was presented which embodied the views entertained by the Board : that we consider the discipline of Professor Powell in the case of the student in question to have been correct, and therefore should be sustained ; and that as neither he nor President Gatch understood that his dismission from Professor Powell's department was an expulsion from the school, that therefore the act of President Gatch in allowing the student to recite Latin and French in other departments was also correct. Entertaining these views, the Board passed a resolution sustaining the course of President Gatch.

Mrs. C. A. Wilson, during the first part of this year, made arrangements for the accommodation in her commodious house of a number of young ladies both with rooms and board for the benefit of the school. This arrangement was advertised in the papers, and resulted in the collection of several young ladies at Mrs. Wilson's. To enable her to exercise a proper discipline and control over these young ladies she was, at Mr. Gatch's instance, at the close of the third quarter, appointed governess of the Ladies' Department of the university.

The school moved on without anything occurring

of special interest in its internal character, except that it was characterized by general prosperity, until the close of the collegiate year, when, at the annual meeting, held July 19, 1864, President Gatch presented the following communication:

"To the Honorable Board of Trustees of Willamette University.

"Gentlemen: Charles W. Parrish and Sylvester C. Simpson have completed the full classical course of the university; Eliza A. Cross, Anna R. Robb, Clara A. Watt, and Pauline Whitson have completed the course prescribed for young ladies. Joseph P. Jones has completed the English studies of the institution. As all these have passed satisfactory examinations, it is recommended that the degree of Bachelor Artium be conferred on Mr. Parrish and Mr. Simpson, and that suitable diplomas be granted to all herein mentioned.

"Respectfully submitted,   T. M. Gatch,
    "*Pres. of Faculty, and Teacher of Anc. Lang.*
                "L. J. Powell,
    "*Teacher of Mathematics and Natural Science.*
                "Lucy A. M. Lee,
    "*Teacher of French and English Composition.*"

Diplomas were awarded to each of the persons recommended by the president, and on the day of public commencement they acquitted themselves in their orations and essays with equal honor with the class of the previous year, and with corresponding credit to the institution that had nurtured them. The Faculty of Instruction for the collegiate year commencing September, 1864, was the same as the previous year. Prosperity crowned the efforts of both the faculty and trustees during the year, and at its close, July 18, 1865, the Board were gratified to receive from the Faculty of Instruction the following communication :

"GENTLEMEN : Presley M. Denny and Parrish L. Willis have completed the full classical course of study, and are hereby recommended to the Board as qualified to receive the degree of Bachelor of Arts. Charles W. Kahlor has completed the English course, Janette M'Calley and Frances Wilson have completed the course prescribed for young ladies. All these, having passed satisfactory examinations, are recommended as entitled to the honors of graduation."

Accordingly the Board conferred the degree of A. B. upon Presley M. Denny and Parrish L. Willis, and of B. S. upon Charles W. Kahlor, and of M. E. L. upon Janette M'Calley and Frances A. Wilson.

At the annual meeting of the Board, which was held July 26, 1865, Mr. Gatch, after five years of most acceptable and efficient service as president of the university, resigned his position, and as it was evident that he could not be prevailed upon to recall his act, as in the former instance, his resignation was accepted, with many thanks for the services which he had rendered the institution, and regrets that we were losing the same. After Mr. Gatch had taken leave of the school, at a meeting of the Board, held August 25, 1865, a motion, presented by Rev. I. Dillon, was carried, that L. J. Powell, F. H. Grubbs, and Lucy A. M. Grubbs constitute the Board of Instruction for the ensuing year, and that L. J. Powell act as president until otherwise ordered. Mrs. C. A. Wilson was continued also as governess.

At the same time J. S. Smith, G. Hines, and A. F. Waller were appointed a committee to correspond in relation to procuring a president for the university. Bishop Kingsley was present at this meeting of the Board, and by the committee of correspondence was respectfully requested to aid the Board and committtee in procuring a suitable person to take charge of the institution as president. He was then on his way to California.

The academical year opened September 10 more promisingly than any preceding year, there being in the senior class nine young gentlemen and nine young ladies at the beginning of the year. The other departments were correspondingly full, and the faculty addressed themselves to their work with courage and unanimity.

On the twentieth of September a special meeting of the Board was called, when a telegram from Bishop Kingsley from California was read, recommending the election of Rev. J. H. Wythe, A. M., M. D., to the presidency of the institution. The secretary was instructed to write to Dr. Wythe, giving him information of his election. October 31, 1865, Dr. Wythe had arrived in the country, and, pursuant to a call from the president of the Board, Rev. David Leslie, a meeting was held at the chapel of the Institute, and Dr. Wythe was introduced to the meeting. He made some remarks indicating his views and feelings in " assuming charge of the institution."

During the collegiate year there were some changes introduced by the president of the faculty in regard to the course of study and the plan of graduation, which were approved, except as to the course of study. As there appeared to be a necessity for another revision of the course of study, the paper introduced by Dr. Wythe was referred to a committee of five, to wit: H. K. Hines, J. S. Smith, J. C. Peebles, D. Rutledge, and C. N. Terry. The committee was requested to invite Dr. Wythe and the rest of the faculty to participate in their action. The report of this committee made at an adjourned meeting, after some amendments by the Board, was adopted, and fixed the price of tuition in all the different branches, and provided that the academical year should be divided into three terms of fourteen weeks each. The course of study which was adopted may be found in the published catalogue of the institution.

During the year, though the records do not specify the precise time, a change was made in the Board of Instruction by the connection of Miss Frances A. Wilson with the Intermediate Department.

Some time during the first part of the year the

senior class of young gentlemen was enlarged by the addition of two from California, who, because of their attainments, were allowed to enter the university three years in advance in the college course, and take position in the graduating class.

On the eighteenth of July, 1866, the names of the following persons were reported by President Wythe as having finished the prescribed course of studies and passed creditable examinations in the same, and were entitled to appropriate diplomas setting forth their attainments: In the Collegiate Department, classical and scientific course, Nehemiah L. Butler, Henry H. Gilfrey, Edward E. Dodge, J. M. Garrison, Joseph Hannan, James R. N. Sellwood, Jos. A. Sellwood, Samuel L. Simpson, and William T. Wythe.

In the scientific course, John M. Bewley.

In the young ladies' course, Fannie S. Case, Elizabeth Harrison, Frances M. M'Farland, Ellen E. Starkey, Irene H. Strattan, Helen L. Williams, Jane E. Miller, Mary E. Robinson, and Maria E. Smith.

The degree of Bachelor of Arts was conferred upon the nine first named; John M. Bewley received the degree of Bachelor of Science, and each of the young ladies was constituted Mistress of English Literature. This was the largest class that had as yet graduated from the institution, and the manner in which they acquitted themselves in their examination, orations, and essays was peculiarly gratifying to the Board of Trustees, the crowd of spectators that witnessed them, but especially to those teachers present who had conducted most of them along the paths of science from the primary branches up through all the grades of study, until they had the happiness of beholding them upon the platform, standing, with palpitating hearts, to receive the honors of graduation. The commencement exercises that closed this year were held in what is to be the chapel of the new building when finished, and though large was filled to overflowing. Increasing maturity characterized the exercises, and the impression was made that our work was indeed growing upon our hands. During the annual meeting of the Board, which, from the amount of business to be transacted, was adjourned from time to time, a very warm discussion arose in relation to matters affecting the Board of Instruction, a detailed account of which would neither be interesting nor profitable. I therefore simply allude to it and pass it by. The results of this discussion were such, that the changes which were sought to be made by some in the Board of Instruction were not secured, but most of the members of the last year's Board were still retained. There was, however, a reorganization of the faculty as follows:

Rev. J. H. WYTHE, A. M., M. D., still retained the presidency, and was elected to the chair of Mental and Moral Science; Rev. L. J. POWELL, A. M., was elected professor of Mathematics and Natural Science; Mr. S. C. SIMPSON, professor of Ancient Languages; Mrs. LUCY A. M. GRUBBS, preceptress. and teacher of French and English Composition; Mr. F. H. GRUBBS, principal of the Academic Department; Miss JANETTE M'CALLEY, Primary Department; Mrs. G. BERRY, teacher of Instrumental Music; Miss MARY HOLMAN, teacher of Painting and Drawing.

With the different departments thus provided for, the school entered upon the twenty-fourth year of its history since it was first originated, with great encouragement as to its future advancement.

At a quarterly meeting of the Board, held November 14, 1866, measures were taken to organize a medical department under the charter of the university. Some two years previously, by the solicitation of a number of medical gentlemen at Portland, the Board had organized a medical department of the university, to be located at that place, but as it never went into operation it has been hitherto passed over without any particular notice. But it became fully apparent, from the number of gentlemen in the country desiring an education that should qualify them for the practice of medicine, that the time had now come to put into successful operation a medical department. Consequently, at the meeting of the Board alluded to G. Hines presented the following resolution, which was adopted by the Board:

Resolved, That, whereas the gentlemen heretofore elected professors in the Medical Department of the Willamette University, which was established at Portland, have failed to organize, so as to perform the duties imposed upon them by their election, and have also resigned their positions and discontinued their relations to the university, the said Medical Department be, and the same is hereby, established and located at Salem. That it shall consist of seven or more professorships, so arranged and conducted as to afford a full course of instruction by lectures and studies, conforming to the latest and most approved practice of the best medical institutions, and of such a grade and character as to thoroughly qualify its graduates for the responsible duties of a professional life.

The Board proceeded to designate the various professorships, and to elect professors to the same, as follows:

H. CARPENTER, M. D., professor of Civil and Military Surgery ; E. R. FISKE, A. M., M. D., professor of Pathology and Practice of Medicine; JOHN BOSWELL, M. D., professor of Obstetrics and Diseases of Women and Children; J. H. WYTHE, A. M., M. D., professor of Physiology, Hygiene, and Microscopy; D. PEYTON, M. D., professor of Materia Medica and Therapeutics ; J. W. M'AFEE, M. D., professor of Chemistry and Toxicology; W. C. WARRINER, M.D., demonstrator of Anatomy; Hon. J. S. SMITH, professor of Medical Jurisprudence.

A. F. Waller, G. Hines, and John H. Moores were appointed a committee to confer with the members of the Medical Faculty, and report to the next meeting of the Board a set of rules for the regulation of the Medical Department.

The result of the conference of this committee with the Medical Faculty was the report of the fol lowing articles for the regulation and government of said Medical Department, which were adopted by the Board.

"1. All vacancies which may occur in the Medical Faculty shall be filled by the Board of Trustees, but said faculty shall have the right to nominate candidates for election, and no person not nominated shall ever be elected a member thereof, unless said Medical Faculty shall neglect for six months to make such nomination.

"2. The financial obligations and disbursements shall be limited to the actual receipts from tuitions and donations. Any unusual expense that may be deemed necessary shall be first authorized by the Board of Trustees before it is incurred.

"3. The Medical Faculty shall have the control of all property and means donated, or devised to the university for the use of the Medical Department; but no use shall be made of the same for any purpose but the promotion of medical science and education.

"4. All moneys ensuing from tuition in the Medical Department shall belong exclusively to the Medical Faculty, except that all graduation fees shall go into a fund, to be called the Medical Educational Fund, the proceeds of which shall be applied exclusively to the purchase of appliances to facilitate medical instruction and payment for diplomas.

"5. Charges of incapacity, neglect of duty, ungentlemanly conduct, or other unfitness for the position, made against any member of the Medical Faculty, shall be first investigated by the Medical Faculty, and in case of disagreement among the members thereof in reference to excluding the one against whom the charges are made, they shall be referred to the Board of Trustees for final action.

"6. The Trustees of the university shall at all times have the right to examine into the condition and management of the Medical Department, and advise with regard to its interests, and the dean of the faculty shall annually submit a report of its financial and educational condition, which, with its list of graduates, shall be embodied in the annual catalogue.

"7. The degree of Doctor of Medicine shall be granted by the Board of Trustees on the recommendation of the Medical Faculty, and shall be conferred in the customary manner at the annual commencement of the university.

"8. The Medical Faculty shall have power to elect their own officers, at such times and in such manner as they may choose, and to make all needful rules, regulations, and by-laws for the management and control of the Medical Department not inconsistent with the charter of the university."

Doctor Warriner subsequently resigned his position in the faculty, and M. B. Lingo, M.D., was elected to fill his place. Hon. J. S. Smith resigned his position as professor of Medical Jurisprudence, and at a subsequent meeting the Medical Faculty placed in nomination Hon. J. H. Mitchell, who was elected to fill the place.

Thus organized, the Medical Department of the Willamette University opened on the first day of April, 1867, under very favorable auspices, with twenty students in attendance.

The collegiate year closed with appropriate commencement exercises on the 25th of July, 1867. In the Collegiate Department there were no graduates this year; but in the Young Ladies' Department a class of five, who did great credit to themselves in their examination and essays, received the honors of the institution. The following are the names of the members of the class: Susan Harrison, Louisa A. Simpson, Eliza Witten, Sarah J. Wythe, Mary L. Wythe. These all received the degree of M. E. L., and diplomas setting forth their attainments. There were three gentlemen in the Medical Department who entered the institution so far advanced in their studies as that one course of lectures entitled them to the honors of graduation. Accordingly, they received the degree of Doctor of Medicine in accordance with the rules of the institution. These were John L. Martin, of Sio, Linn County, William A. Cusick, of Waconda, Marion County, and Daniel M. Jones, of Sublimity, Marion County. At the same time that the above-named persons received the honors of the institution, the honorary degree of LL.D. was conferred upon three very worthy and distinguished citizens of the state of Oregon, namely, Hon. George H. Williams, United States Senator,

Hon. M. P. Deady, United States District Judge, and Hon. Addison C. Gibbs, ex-Governor of the state of Oregon. These were the first honorary titles which the university had ever conferred. Twenty-five years had now passed since the Board of Trustees was first organized, and fourteen since the institution was chartered as a university by the legislature of Oregon. True, the school had experienced some severe reverses, but it had survived them, and was assuming a permanency of character which not only commended it to the confidence of the community, but which gave satisfactory promise that, whatever changes might occur, the future success of the school was secured beyond a peradventure. At the annual meeting of the Board, held on the evening of the 23th of July of the present year, (1867,) Dr. J. H. Wythe, for reasons which need not be stated here, but which were doubtless satisfactory to himself, resigned his position as president of the university, and the resignation was accepted by the Board of Trustees. The Board then proceeded to the election of a new president, and also to fill the various chairs. Dr. Benson, of the *Pacific Christian Advocate*, was elected president, T. M. Gatch, A.M., and Mr. O. S. Frambes, A. M., were elected professors. Doubtless the prosperity of the institution would have been greatly promoted if these gentlemen had found it convenient to accept of the positions offered them; but the obligations resting upon them, growing out of their present positions, were such, that in their judgment they could not consistently do so, and, con-

sequently, they respectfully declined. The Board of
Trustees was thrown upon the necessity of calling
another meeting for the election of a Faculty of
Instruction. This they did on the evening of the 3d
day of September, and the Board went into the
election of a faculty with the following results:
Rev. L. T. Woodward, A.M., was elected professor
of Ancient Languages and Moral Science, and constituted the acting president of the institution.
Rev. L. J. Powell, A.M., professor of Mathematics
and Natural Science. F. H. Grubbs, A.M., principal of Academical Department. Lucy A. M.
Grubbs, M.E.L., preceptress and teacher of French
and English Composition. Elizabeth H. Woodward,
Primary Department. Almira Holman, teacher of
Instrumental Music.

Of the members of this faculty who now (October
23, 1867) constitute the Board of Instruction in the
Willamette University, three, Rev. L. J. Powell,
A. M., F. H. Grubbs, A. M., and Mrs. L. A. M.
Grubbs, have been connected with the school as
teachers for six years; the other members of the
faculty have been newly elected.

The present academical year opened very flatter-
ingly on the sixteenth of September in the old building, with upward of one hundred students in attendance on the first day of the session, and with the
prospect of soon occupying the new building, the
second and third stories of which were being prepared for the reception of the school. And now,
while the school is retained for a few weeks only in

the old dilapidated frame house, which has buffeted the severe winter storms of Oregon for twenty-five years, as we have only casually alluded to the fact that efforts were being made to provide more comfortable quarters, we will leave the newly-organized faculty to prosecute their work under serious disadvantages, and proceed to give an account of the efforts of the Board of Trustees to erect a new college edifice.

WILLAMETTE UNIVERSITY.

CHAPTER XI.

HISTORY OF THE NEW COLLEGE BUILDING.

FOR some years previous to 1860 the trustees and friends of the institution generally had felt the need of a more commodious building for the accommodation of the school. The old building had been constructed with a view to its occupancy for other purposes than that of a college edifice, and though it answered a very good purpose for many years, yet the rooms were low and uncomfortable, and the building was becoming dilapidated, the roof being scarcely a protection from the storm, as the shingles in many places were worn literally through to the sheeting, and the whole building had become so weakened by age and decay that the winter winds would shake it from the cupola to the foundation. Besides this the old building was becoming too small for the school, the number of which varied from year to year from one hundred and seventy-five to three hundred and twenty students. The inability of the community to meet the expenses of such an undertaking restrained the Board for some time from making the attempt to erect a new college edifice; but the increasingly dilapidated condition of the old building and the increase of students rendered it absolutely necessary for them either to build or abandon the whole enterprise. The latter idea, however, did not belong to their vocabulary. A new and commodious building had become an absolute necessity for the interests and perpetuity of the institution, and as Providence had smiled upon our efforts thus far, and conducted us safely through every trying emergency, guiding our bark at times in the midst of storms and breakers on every hand, we decided to venture out upon another sea of uncertainty, so far as human view could determine results, not doubting but that the same good Providence that had sustained and prospered us thus far on our voyage would bring us safe to land. Consequently, influenced by these considerations, at a meeting, held October 3, 1860, the Board resolved to take immediate measures to prepare for the erection of a new college building, and the agent, Rev. A. F. Waller, was instructed to raise subscriptions for that purpose. The necessities of the case prompted to this action of the Board at this time more than the prospect of immediate success. The action was found to be a little premature. Consequently two years passed and little progress was made, except that the subject of building during that time was thoroughly canvassed by the agent and others, and the necessity for a new building became more and more apparent. Again, November 19, 1862, the question of a new college edifice was introduced before the Board by the secretary, Rev. William Roberts, and, on motion of J. L. Parrish, it was again resolved that the Board now proceed to take measures for the erection of a new college building some time during the ensuing year. Pursuant to this, for the purpose of setting the wheels in motion, a committee, consisting of J H. Moores, J. Lamson, G. Hines, A. F. Waller, and J. L. Parrish, was appointed to prepare and submit plans of college buildings to the Board at the next meeting.

The committee thus appointed reported a number of plans at a meeting held December 2, 1862, and on motion of Gustavus Hines the Board instructed the agent to solicit subscriptions for, and appointed a committee to call a public meeting at the Methodist Episcopal church for the purpose of raising funds to aid in the erection of the building. The agent was further instructed to obtain subscriptions, to the amount of twenty thousand dollars or more, for this purpose, and the subscribers were made liable for their respective subscriptions when the amount of fifteen thousand dollars was subscribed, the money to be paid in gold or silver coin, or its equivalent. To bring the matter properly before the public the substance of the above resolutions was published in the *Oregon Statesman* and the *Pacific Christian Advocate*. The agent, Rev. A. F. Waller, thus backed by the Board of Trustees, entered upon his work of soliciting subscriptions, but found it to be a slow and tedious process; for, five months after commencing, at a meeting of the Board, held May 20, 1863, he reported that twelve thousand eight hundred dollars only had been subscribed. Such, however, were the encouragements for an increase of subscriptions that the Board proceeded to appoint a building committee, consisting of J. H. Moores, A. F. Waller, and E. N. Cook, to which was added subsequently the names of T. M. Gatch and G. Hines.

As yet no particular plan of building had been adopted by the Board, and a somewhat warm and lengthened discussion arose in the Board in regard to the kind of building which should be erected. Two or three plans were adopted at different times, and subsequently set aside. Finally, at a meeting of the Board held February 22, 1864, a settlement of the plan was effected by a vote of sixteen to one, a number of the members being absent, and the action was thought sufficiently harmonious to warrant the breaking of ground for the foundation of the building. It had previously been decided to build of brick, and by examination it was found that the earth to be removed to make room for the basement, and for the foundation of the building, was as good a material for the manufacture of the brick as any that could be found; hence it was decided to make the brick upon the ground. The earth was broken the last part of the month of February, 1864, and a professional brick-maker was employed to superintend the manufacture of five hundred thousand brick, Rev. A. F. Waller having the general oversight of the whole matter as agent of the Board. This plan succeeded to admiration, for in due time the workmen employed presented us with a most magnificent kiln of brick of the very first quality, which seemed waiting to be employed to elevate the walls of our college edifice.

Stone of the most durable quality was procured to lay the foundation three feet high. This precaution was entered into to protect the brick from the dampness of the earth. While these things were moving forward Mr. Waller was enlarging the subscription for the building, so that when the bricks were ready, and the stone-masons were laying the foundation, and the time approached to lay the corner-stone of our college, the subscription amounted to about twenty-five thousand dollars. The corner-stone of the university was laid July 24, 1864, with somewhat imposing ceremonies. Governor Gibbs delivered an address on the occasion, and a historical sketch of the institution was read before a very large assembly of the citizens of Salem and vicinity by Gustavus Hines. Rev. David Leslie, the venerable president of the Board of Trustees, performed the ceremony of laying the corner-stone, various other gentlemen assisting in the services. The historical sketch, Bible, Hymn Book, Methodist Discipline, and the names of many of the old pioneers, with various other documents and trinkets, were deposited in an excavation in the corner-stone, according to the usual custom in such cases, and then the blessing of Almighty God, without whose aid

> "The best concerted schemes are vain,
> And never can succeed,"

was devoutly invoked upon the enterprise by the Rev. William Roberts, that it might be carried forward to a triumphant and glorious success. And now the walls begin to assume shape and form, and gradually to rise from their foundation. At length the last brick is laid, the timbers are all adjusted to their places, the roof covers the beautiful superstructure, the symmetrical dome crowns the pile, and the whole stands forth in its beauty and grandeur as a monument of the indomitable perseverance and energy of the few men who were the active members of the Board of Trustees, whose plans and policies and instructions were faithfully carried out by Rev. A. F. Waller, perhaps the most indefatigable agent with whom an institution of learning was ever favored.

The plan of the building is that of a Greek cross, and was recommended to the agent by Bishop Janes when he last visited the Oregon Conference. The two parts of the cross are each eighty-four feet long and forty-four feet wide. These cross each other exactly in the center, so that the building presents about the same appearance from which ever side you take your observation. The height of the building from the base to the top of the dome is one hundred feet, and from the base to the eaves fifty feet. The basement story is twelve feet, the first story above is sixteen feet, the second twelve feet, and the third twelve feet. There are three entrances to the building, the main entrance into the chapel being in the end of the north wing, and the other entrances being in the east and west wings. These wings are mainly occupied by a broad and commodious winding stairway which lead to the school rooms above, so that the members of the school on entering are not obliged to pass through the chapel. The chapel is very commodious, occupying the entire story of the cross above the basement, running north and south. That is, the chapel is forty-four by eighty-four feet, with the walls taken out. It is nicely finished, with a broad platform at the south end, and finely and comfortably seated throughout. At each side there is a door which passes into the east and west wings to the stair-ways. One of these doors is designed for the ingress and egress of the ladies, and the other for the gentlemen of the school. The school rooms in the second and third stories are large and very neatly finished, and furnished with seats of the latest improvement. They are of sufficient capacity to accommodate about four hundred pupils. The house is judiciously arranged for the accommodation of the different departments, together with the literary societies, of which there are three connected with the institution. Until other arrangements can be made by the Medical Faculty, the Medical Department will occupy one room in the third story.

The faculty and students of the institution had often, during the last year, been flattered with the idea that they would soon be able to remove from their uncomfortable quarters in the old building into the new building; but up to this period (October 14,) the progress of the building toward completion was so retarded by circumstances that the Board of Trustees seemed unable to control, that the rooms remained in so unfinished a condition that no one of them could consistently be occupied. At this time, however, it was announced that on Monday, the 21st of October, the removal could be made.

Accordingly, at 9 o'clock of the 21st day of October, 1867, the school was marched, by the acting president, to the sound of martial music, from the old house to the new, where some of the members of the Board of Trustees, and friends of the institution, were assembled to receive them. There was no formal dedication of the house, as is usual on such occasions; but the venerable president of the Board of Trustees, Rev. David Leslie, by an appropriate address to the faculty and students, opened so much of the house as had been finished for their occupancy, and, with other members of the Board present, gave the school a most cordial and hearty welcome and greeting to the neat and commodious halls of the new college edifice.

The financial condition of the building which we have thus described, according to a close estimate, is as follows:

Cost of the building thus far	$40,000
Subscriptions collected "	30,000
Subscriptions on hand "	8,000
Liabilities "	10,000
Finishing the building will cost	7,000

Besides this, we need to furnish the building with additional apparatus, a library, a good piano, warming apparatus, and other things necessary, say ten thousand dollars.

This showing, and the figures are very moderate,

presents the fact that the university needs for present use to set it fully in working order twenty thousand dollars.

The question here arises, How is this twenty thousand dollars to be obtained? The people of the city of Salem, and the community generally where the institution is located, have contributed already to the extent of their ability.

The lands that have been donated with a view to the permanent endowment of the institution cannot be used for building purposes, neither would it be wise to so use them, even if the Board had the right to do it. The Board indulged the hope that considerable material aid might be afforded them from the Centenary collections within the bounds of the Oregon Conference; but the territory embraced within the limits of the conference was new and thinly settled, and each community had its own Church and educational interests to promote, and, consequently, most of the offerings made were designed to promote interests of a local character, and hence the assistance from this quarter will be very limited.

Sometimes the Board has looked with hope toward the East, when they have heard of the millions of money that have been placed as Centenary offerings upon the altar of the Church, and have wondered whether, in the general distribution of Centenary gifts, a struggling, feeble people on the Pacific coast might not be remembered. We have also thought of those wealthy members of the Church who are always ready to every good work, and have most ardently desired an opportunity to set clearly before them our necessities, believing that if we could do so they would extend their generosity even to us. If it be the object of wealthy men in the bestowment of money to do good, surely there never was a better opportunity than to relieve the Willamette University in its present needs, and place it upon a proper basis, by bestowing upon it a suitable endowment.

CHAPTER XII.

MISCELLANEOUS MATTERS CONNECTED WITH OUR HISTORY.

IN a previous chapter we have spoken of the establishment of a Medical Department in connection with the Willamette University; but as a few changes have occurred in that department since its first organization, it will be proper to refer to it again. The first session opened, in the spring of 1867, with twenty students in attendance, a very encouraging number for so young an institution. We have already stated that three of the students received the honors of the institution.

The second session was to open on the fifth of November, with the prospect of an increase of one third in the number of students in attendance. The announcement for the session of 1867–8, sets forth the following as the Medical Faculty for the present year :

DEPARTMENT OF MEDICINE AND SURGERY.

J. H. WYTHE, A. M., M. D., President.

MEDICAL FACULTY.

H. CARPENTER, M. D., professor of Civil and Military Surgery; E. R. FISKE, A. M., M. D., professor of Pathology and Practice of Medicine; J. BOSWELL,

M. D., professor of Obstetrics and Diseases of Women and Children; J. H. WYTHE, A. M., M. D., professor of Physiology, Hygiene, and Microscopy; D. PEYTON, M. D., professor of Materia Medica and Therapeutics; J. W. M'AFEE, M.D., professor of Chemistry and Toxicology; A. SHARPLES, A. B., M. D., professor of Descriptive and Surgical Anatomy; M. B. LINGO, M. D., demonstrator of Anatomy; Hon. J. H. MITCHELL, professor of Medical Jurisprudence.

The gentlemen composing the above faculty are mostly persons of long practical experience in the medical profession, and are well qualified to sustain the department, and to carry it forward until it shall be placed in the highest rank of schools for the promotion of sound medical learning and practical acquirements.

The requirements for graduation are as follows:

The candidate must be twenty-one years of age, and must present proper testimonials of a good moral character, and satisfactory evidence of having studied medicine three years, lectures included, with a reputable practitioner of medicine. He must have attended two full courses of lectures, the last of which must have been in the Medical Department of the Willamette University. He must pass a satisfactory examination, and submit to the faculty an acceptable thesis on some medical subject in his own handwriting.

For an *ad eundem* degree, a diploma from a regular medical college and a satisfactory examination in the practical branches, and the payment of the usual fee.

Though this medical department is in its infancy, yet from the manner in which it has been conducted thus far, and the confidence reposed in the faculty by the profession and the public generally, it has doubtless become a fixed fact in connection with our university, and its future history will run parallel with that of the parent institution so long as the healing art shall be needed among men.

In the progress of our history we have had occasion to record the deaths of but very few who have been connected with our institution either as trustees or as teachers; and here we will take occasion to mention some in this regard whose names have been omitted. In the list of teachers the name of S. B. Wilber should not be forgotten. Mr. Wilber was a very efficient and successful teacher in the Academical Department of the university, and could have retained his position to an indefinite period, but resigned his place, and returned to his home in the state of New York, where he soon after passed from the labors of earth to the rewards of eternity. He was a relative of the Rev. James H. Wilber, who was the founder of the Umpqua Academy, the principal agent in the establishment of the Portland Seminary, and at the present writing is the laborious and successful missionary and Indian agent in the Yakima nation.

Mrs. Jones, formerly Mary Leslie, the amiable and excellent daughter of "Father Leslie," the venerable president of the Board of Trustees, who received her education mainly in connection with the university, and for some time was employed as a teacher, and was very successful in her department, has also gone to her reward.

Miss Lucia A. N. Jordan is another who should not be passed in connection with this history simply with the mention of her name. She left a large circle of friends and acquaintances in Newbury, Vermont, where she had received her education, and took passage in a steamer for Oregon by the way of Panama and San Francisco. At the latter place she went on board the ill-fated Northerner, bound for Portland, which was wrecked on the Pacific coast midway between the two ports. She endured all the horrors and perils of that most fearful disaster, and witnessed hundreds of her fellow-passengers sink to their watery graves. Calmly and quietly she addressed herself to one effort to save herself from the terrible fate of most of her comrades, clasped a life-preserver around her, and knowing that it was the only chance, committed herself to the angry billows. Her life-preserver buoyed her up, though the rolling surges often broke with violence over her. She neared the shore, retaining her consciousness until within a few yards of land. Having been so often submerged by the breaking waves, she received so much of the briny element as to experience all the sensations of drowning, and losing herself, she sunk as into the arms of death. At length a friendly wave bore her to the shore, and she was snatched from the under-current by the persons who had been so fortunate as to reach the shore in safety, and borne away to the dry land. The usual resuscitating means in cases of drowning were resorted to, and at length, to the great joy of all, signs of life appeared. She survived the terrible ordeal, and after partially recovering from the shock which her sensitive nature had received, she proceeded on to Washington Territory, where she engaged in teaching for a season, and then, in answer to a call from the Board of Trustees of the university, she came to Oregon and became associated with the faculty as a teacher of the ornamental branches, occasionally assisting in other departments. But it is thought that she never entirely recovered from the injury received from her shipwreck. After a few months of very acceptable and efficient service as a teacher, her Master called and found her ready to obey the summons. Though mysteriously removed, in the vigor of youth and amid scenes of great usefulness, from the associations of earth to the realities of eternity, she did not fail to leave the impression of her many excellences upon the minds of the youth she taught, as upon all who knew her.

The present Board of Trustees is very large, and will compare well in every respect with any similar board in any portion of the country. For the information of all interested, both east and west, where their friends reside, I would here append their names.

Rev. David Leslie, President; Hon. S. E. May, Secretary; J. H. Moores, Esq., Treasurer; Rev. Wm. Roberts, Hon. A. C. Gibbs, Rev. A. F. Waller, Hon. L. F. Grover, A. M., Rev. G. Hines, Hon. J. C. Peebles, Rev. J. H. Wilber, Hon. J. R. Moores, Rev. J. Dillon, A. M., F. R. Smith, Esq., Rev. C. S. Kingsley, A. M., Rev. J. L. Parrish, Rev. H. K. Hines, A. A. M'Cully, Esq., L. Heath, Esq., Rev. D. Rutledge, J. N. Gilbert, Esq., Jos. Waldo, Esq., T. M. Gatch, A. M., Hon. E. N. Cook, Hon. J. S. Smith, J. H. Nicklin, Esq., Thos. Cross, Esq., L. S. Dyer, Esq., W. R. Patty, Esq., E. Strong, Esq., Jos. Holman, Esq., Hon. C. N. Terry, D. Waldo, Esq., C. Craft, Esq., Hon. R. Mallory, Hon. J. Lamson, Hon. J. H. Harrison, Hon. J. H. Mitchell, E. R. Fiske, A. M., M. D., Rev. N. Doane, Rev. L. T. Woodward, A. M., Rev. C. G. Belknap, Hon. Wm. Watkins, M. D., W. S. Ladd, Esq., Hon. E. D. Shattuck, Hon. G. H. Williams, W. Hauxhurst, Esq., Hon. G. Abernethy, J. R. Robb, Esq., Dr. A. M. Belt, Rev. T. H. Pearne, Rev. J. H. Wythe, A. M., M. D., W. B. Gray, Esq., Rev. J. F. Devore, Rev. J. B. Calloway, Rev. C. S. Strattan.

Four only of the present Board of Trustees were members of the original Board elected in 1842 when the Oregon Institute received its birth, namely, Rev. David Leslie, Hon. George Abernethy, Rev. J. L. Parrish, and Rev. Gustavus Hines. With the exception of the latter name these have been members of the Board from the beginning, and he also, with the exception of a few years, during which he was absent from the country. Three of the original nine members of the first Board have died, Rev. Jason Lee and Alanson Beers, whose departure has already been noticed, and Rev. Hamilton Campbell. It should be observed in reference to Mr. Campbell that he was for many years an efficient and active member of the Board, and a liberal patron of the institution. His children he mainly educated in the institute, and his girls, most of whom are now in the care of families of their own, are all of them adorning society in the city of Portland.

Mr. Campbell unfortunately failed in business, and in his efforts to raise himself from his shattered condition he went to the silver mines of Northern Mexico, and while in the act of washing out the shining dust he met with a violent death at the hands of a treacherous peon.

While speaking of those members of the Board who have taken their departure, we should not be doing justice to the memory of one who, though not among the original nine, was early connected with the Board, and contributed much to promote the interests of the institution without naming John Force, a relative of Rev. Manning Force, of the New Jersey Conference. For years he was among the most active, efficient, and stirring members of the Board. He also has passed away, but his name is recorded in the list of the true friends and patrons of the school.

With this record of the dead, it may not be improper to refer to some who are yet among the living, who have been cognizant not only of everything connected with the history of the school from its first incipiency, but also with the growth and progress of the entire country. I now refer to Rev. J. L. Parrish, Rev. A. F. Waller, and Rev. David Leslie. The first mentioned was one of the original nine, and has ever taken a very prominent part in every enterprise involving the interests of the university. He was one of the large reinforcement to the Oregon Mission of 1840, and from that period until the present has never left the Pacific coast. He has occupied prominent positions in the country, and has been identified with many extensive business operations, and Providence has greatly smiled upon him in the bestowment of wealth; but whether in want or abundance he has remained the unchangeable friend and supporter of the Oregon Institute and Willamette University. Rev. A. F. Waller was elected a member of the Board of Trustees in 1843, one year from the time of its organization. He also arrived in Oregon in 1840, and has always taken an active part in all the moral, religious, and educational enterprises which have promised success since that period. For many years he has been the indefatigable and successful agent of the university, and besides being a liberal contributor to its needs from time to time, he performed some three years of laborious service as agent of the school without fee or reward.

Rev. David Leslie arrived in Oregon in 1837, and constituted one of about a dozen Americans at that

time on the Pacific coast. Perhaps the incipient
measures which led to the establishment of an institution of learning are attributable more to him than
to any other individual now living. Identified with
all the interests of the country from its infancy, and
especially with those connected with our rising seminary, and consecrating all of his energies in the promotion of those interests, he has ever been rightfully
esteemed as the father, the patriarch of the institution. With the exception of one year, when he performed a voyage to the Sandwich Islands on account
of the health of his family, he has occupied the very
responsible position of president of the Board of
Trustees from the beginning to the present time.
Ready always to relinquish personal and family
interests and make great sacrifices for the benefit
of the institution, he has proved himself worthy of
the honor that has been conferred upon him by an
annual election to the presidency of the Board for
twenty-three years.

Being cognizant of all the trials and reverses
through which the institution has passed, and sym-
pathizing with it in all the struggles connected with
its rise and progress, the needle is no truer to the
pole than these persons have been to all the interests
of the Willamette University. And, though it would
not be proper to speak of them while living as we
would feel at liberty to do if they had entered into
rest, yet we will take the responsibility of saying as
it is, that they are closing up a record in regard to
the Willamette University, and education in general

in Oregon, of which their descendants to all generations will have occasion to be proud.

There are many other gentlemen who have become connected with the Board since 1850, who, by their counsel, their liberality, and their untiring devotion to all the interests of the institution, are engraving their names upon this educational monument so deeply that all the revolutions of time itself, that great obliterator of human record, will not be able to erase them. Identified with this noble enterprise, and consecrated to the truly patriotic and Christian work of promoting the educational interests of Oregon, and filling it with a true Christian civilization while living, when they shall have filled up their earthly record, and shall have passed from the labors of time to the rewards of eternity, their names will be cherished in the grateful recollection of posterity, so long as virtue is lovely, and patriotism, philanthropy, and sanctified learning are appreciated among men.

The alumni of our institution would be creditable to one even of higher pretensions. Twenty-two young gentlemen and twenty-eight young ladies have already graduated from our young university, having completed the regular course. They have now gone forth from their alma mater into the various departments of active life, and, with scarcely an exception, are now doing honor to themselves and to the institution that nourished them. They are to be found in the different professions, and wherever found they occupy enviable positions. As aspirants after military and naval honors, they stand an equal chance with those who boast a higher parentage. As ministers of the Gospel, some of them are winning golden opinions from their contemporaries, and others, having shone brightly amid the dark scenes of earth for a season, have passed from those scenes to the glories of an eternal day. Of them it may be said,

"Nor fade those stars in empty night;
They hide themselves in heaven's own light."

The university is under the patronage of the Oregon Conference of the Methodist Episcopal Church, and though denominational, is not strictly sectarian. Great care is taken to exert within its walls a most wholesome and controlling moral and religious influence, yet efforts to give a sectarian bias are carefully avoided. The result is, that there may be found within the walls of the institution students from almost all the Christian Churches in the land, and already young men have graduated from our college who were trained in other communions, and who designed to enter the ministry in other Churches so soon as they received the honors of our institution. Three excellent young men, sons of an Episcopalian clergyman, claim our institution as their alma mater.

As a result of the religious influence exerted among the students, there are occasional seasons of revival, in which awakenings and conversions often occur. In the winter of 1866-67, under the labors of Dr. J. H. Wythe, there was a very gracious revival, in which nearly thirty of the students professed religion, and united with the Methodist Episcopal

Church. An incident this, truly worthy of note in the history of our rising institution.

The university is furnished with an ordinary set of philosophical apparatus, which cost $1,500. The library, however, is very deficient. It contains but six hundred volumes, and these mostly composed of a very indifferent collection of books. We have also in the institution a cabinet of natural history, composed of specimens of minerals, fossils, and conchology, furnished by the Smithsonian Institute at Washington. Contributions to all these departments are needed and solicited.

We have now brought up the history of our university to the present period of time, and have endeavored to present it so minutely that the reader cannot fail to understand and appreciate the difficulties under which we have labored, and the persevering efforts which we have been obliged to put forth to bring it forward to its present state. We have not been dealing in fiction, but in sober facts, while we have been presenting the struggles of a people, poor as to money and few in numbers, to build an institution to meet the demands of teeming humanity on the shores of the great Pacific. We have shown that we have not been laboring in vain, nor spending our strength for naught, but that every inch that we have gained in our enterprise we have been able to maintain. We have shown that our institution has become a fixed fact, that its permanence is without doubt secured. We have shown that it occupies a most commanding and eligible position in the city of Salem, the established capital of the state of Oregon, and near the center of one of the most beautiful valleys upon which the sun ever shone, and commanding scenery as delightful as ever greeted the eye of man. And we have done this for the purpose of eliciting the attention of patriots, philanthropists, and Christians, and especially the Methodist Episcopal Church of the Atlantic states, whose offspring we are, again to a most important though neglected portion of the world, and to the necessities of an infant people, who, from a disposition to do all they possibly can to help themselves, are entitled to the sympathies of all those who are abundantly able to afford them the necessary aid. By the memory of a Lee, who died for Oregon's advancement, blessing his adopted country with his latest breath; and of a Shepherd, who fell a sacrifice in the same work; and a Whitman and his wife, whose love for Oregon could not be quenched but with their life's blood; and by all the former benevolence of the Church, when for Oregon she poured out her money like water, and by a thousand considerations which might be pressed, allow me, dear brethren in the ministry and in the membership of the Church throughout the land, to commend to your serious consideration, to your benevolence, and to your prayers, the interests of the Willamette University. Lay a portion of your offerings on the altar of religious education erected on the Pacific shores, and millions hereafter will rise up and call you blessed.

CHAPTER XIII.

A BRIEF SUMMARY OF FACTS.

THE attention of the reader is called expressly to the summary of facts in relation to the state of Oregon which is presented in this chapter of our volume. The surface and beautiful scenery of the country have been sufficiently dwelt upon in the earlier chapters of the book; we wish now to present another view of its resources, its present condition, its future prospects, and the present state of the Methodist Episcopal Church within its bounds.

We have seen that its area embraces one hundred and one thousand four hundred square miles. This multiplied by six hundred and forty, the number of acres in a square mile, would give the astonishing amount of sixty-four million eight hundred and ninety-six thousand acres of land. Of this vast number of acres we have, according to a very careful estimate, but three hundred and thirty-seven thousand and fifty-eight acres under cultivation. It is estimated that at least ten million acres of land are susceptible of cultivation. The amount of land now cultivated produced in 1864 one million two hundred and nineteen thousand and thirty-four bushels of wheat, eighty-seven thousand six hundred and ninety-one bushels of barley, one million six hundred and thirty-one thousand nine hundred and sixty-two bushels of oats, fifty-four thousand three hundred and eighty bushels of corn, two thousand seven hundred and thirty-seven bushels of rye, seventy thousand and forty-five pounds of tobacco, thirty-eight thousand and thirty tons of hay, two hundred and sixty thousand one hundred and four bushels of potatoes, three hundred and eighteen thousand seven hundred and eighteen bushels of apples, seven hundred and seventy-nine thousand four hundred and forty-six pounds of wool. The aggregate of that year of wheat, barley, and oats was nearly three million bushels. Since then every year it has been much larger, and in 1867 it was probably not less than five million bushels. Now, with the ten million acres of arable land, it would be perfectly practicable, with the requisite amount of labor, to so develop the agricultural resources of the state as to raise twenty times as much annually as has ever been produced in a single year.

The kinds of grain, etc., named above are the staple products of the country, and can be raised in any quantities.

The adaptation of Oregon to the culture of fruits is worthy of special notice. There can be no question but that Oregon, taken as a whole, is decidedly the best fruit-growing state in the Union. It may in truth be said that in no part of the world do fruit trees grow so rapidly, bear so early, so regularly, and so abundantly, and produce fruit of so large size and of so delicious a flavor. This is true not only with respect to apples, but also with a great variety of fruits; pears, plums, cherries, currants, gooseberries, raspberries, strawberries, peaches, and grapes. The last two mentioned flourish better in California than in Oregon, but with respect to every other kind mentioned Oregon is every way superior to her southern sister. Fruit trees are generally as large at three years old in Oregon, and bear as abundantly, as they do in New York or Ohio at six or eight years old. Oregon has realized from her fruit considerable revenue. She has shipped annually to San Francisco, Victoria, and other places, more than one hundred thousand boxes of apples. This fruit has become so abundant all through the state that it can be generally had for the gathering.

Experiments also in the culture of flax, hemp, tobacco, and hops have settled the question fully that the soil and climate are most admirably adapted to their cultivation and growth. The amount of flax seed produced from the acre averages about twenty-five bushels, and already extensive works for the manufacture of oil have been established at Salem, ·under the direction of Edwin Cartwright, Esq., which promises to be a source of income to its projectors, and a great saving to the state.

The stock-growing qualities of the state deserve separate mention. Perhaps there are few portions of the world where there are so many cattle and horses and mules and hogs and sheep in proportion to the population as roam over the extended pastures of the state of Oregon. They increase more rapidly, and are kept with less expense, than in any other state of which we have any knowledge. During one half of the winter they do not require to be fed at all, and the other half not more than from three to six weeks. This renders stock raising one of the most profitable employments in which men can engage, as the extensive mining population south and east and north, together with the cities and the shipping that visit the country, constitute an abundant market for all such supplies as can be produced.

The timber of the country demands a separate paragraph. Though it is not of a great variety, yet it is of a most magnificent growth and of a good quality. The forests are composed of fir, cedar, spruce, hemlock, balm, ash, oak, and in the lower valleys of Southern Oregon myrtle, maple, and chick-opin. Some of the kinds grow to an incredible size. It is no uncommon thing to find fir and cedar, pine and spruce trees measuring from twenty-four to thirty-six feet in circumference, and three hundred feet high. In various portions of the country there may also be found cotton-wood, alder, sumach, willow, and dogwood; and the laurel is also indigenous to the country, and in many places abounds. These vast forests of the finest of timber constitute one of the most extensive and inexhaustible sources of revenue with which the country is favored.

The mineral resources of the state are varied, and of paramount importance. Mines of various kinds have been developed in almost every part of the state, and have been productive of vast amounts of money. Placer gold diggings have been extensively worked for years past in the southern, northern, and eastern portions; and in Jackson County alone, in Southern Oregon, the mines which have been worked since 1850 have produced annually one million dollars. There are numerous quartz veins of silver in Southern and Eastern Oregon, permanent and enduring as the mountains, which need only the requisite capital for advantageous working to produce rich returns. It has been estimated that the amount of gold taken from the mines of Oregon in 1866 was eight million dollars, and from the whole Pacific slope belonging to the United States one hundred and six million dollars the same year. With these facts before the mind it will not be regarded as visionary if we say that there is no portion of the Union that combines within the same space, to an equal extent, all the varied and reliable elements of wealth, and a steadily increasing prosperity.

The great necessity for the development of the capabilities of this interesting state is an increase of population. The present population of the state, as near as can be estimated from the census of former years, is about eighty thousand, and she needs and could set to profitable employment one million of people, and is capable of sustaining ten times that number. Possessing the capabilities which we have delineated, and offering the strong inducements of a bland and wholesome climate, and of inexhaustible stores of natural wealth, together with the fact that she must ultimately command a large share of the trade of Northern Russia, China, and the islands of the Pacific Ocean, and that the time is not distant when the neighing of the iron horse will be heard, as with lightning swiftness he comes rushing down from the gorges of the Cascade Mountains, and darting along the valleys—and when we consider also that the God of providence never could have intended that a country of such unrivaled beauty, such amazing fertility, such salubrity of climate, and with such exhaustless stores of wealth standing in her forests, and embedded in her mountains, should remain forever in the possession of the Cayote and the besotted savage, undeveloped and unblessed, but that it should become the home of civilization, intelligence, and refinement, a place of schools, academies, and colleges, of towns and cities, and courts of justice and temples of worship, and manufactures, and institutions of charity and benevolence, and teem with every excellence that the religion of the meek and lowly Jesus can confer upon such a land—there can be no question but that in the order of events there must be, and that speedily, a vast increase of population not only in Oregon, but in Washington Territory, and in every other eligible portion of this extended coast. The increased population may be what the present is, and what it has been from the beginning, a mixed multitude from many lands; but the Christianity of the Bible, wielded by heaven's appointed instrumentalities, shall mold the moral masses until they shall be prepared to receive the impress of true religion. The Churches in the land have a fearful responsibility resting upon them. They should lay broad

and deep the foundations of righteousness and god-
liness and peace and love. They should lay aside
all party spirit and party strife and non-essentials,
and under the power of the spirit of Christian unity
and unreserved consecration to a course of self-denying, prayerful, vigorous, and persevering labor for
God and salvation, prepare the country for the on-
coming multitudes which, with the certainty of the
rush of the majestic Columbia westward to ocean's
bed, will fill every valley, line every river, adorn
every hill side, and spread over every extended plain
of this heaven-appointed land. God has ordained it,
and he will surely bring it to pass.

Many persons may read this volume who will
desire more information in regard to the summer
and winter seasons of Oregon; and for the benefit of
such attention is called to the following remarks,
which were penned by the author more than twenty
years ago, and which, by so many years of subsequent
observation and experience, have been confirmed as
correct:

"An Oregon winter is vastly different from a winter in the Eastern States occupying the same degrees
of latitude, mainly for the reason that in the Eastern
States the prevailing winds are from the north and
west, and on the Pacific coast they are from the south.
There is no definite period when these winter winds
in Oregon commence blowing, but the different seasons vary much in this respect. As a general rule
the commencement may be considered as about the
middle of November. When they do come they

bring with them continued falls of rain, and hence the period of their continuance is properly called the rainy season. They generally continue, with occasionally a short interval, for two or three months, and sometimes four, after which there is usually a month of warm, pleasant weather. This sometimes comes in February, sometimes in March, but is generally followed by three or four weeks of chilly, rainy weather from the southwest.

"Though the winters are disagreeable on account of the humidity of the atmosphere, yet the cold is very moderate, the mercury seldom falling as low as the freezing point. As a matter of course, the ground is seldom frozen; and as to skating privileges, there is so little ice in the country that it is seldom that skates can be found in the market, and plowing is often done during a great portion of the winter. Occasionally, however, there is an exception to this.

"At one time the mercury fell in the Willamette Valley to five degrees below zero, and at the Dalles on the east side of the Cascade Mountains to fifteen degrees below zero. This intense cold lasted at that time for several days, and the lakes were all frozen over, and the Columbia River was bridged with ice as far down as the mouth of the Willamette. It will be correctly inferred from what has been said, that, as in the Eastern States, there is a great difference in the winters of Oregon. Some are vastly more rainy than others; but one half of the winters on the Pacific coast are not characterized by as much falling weather as is frequently experienced in the state of

New York, and are, in consequence of their warmness, decidedly pleasant.

" If the winters of Oregon are rather stormy and unpleasant, the summers are sufficiently delightful amply to compensate for the wintry blasts. In the months of March and April the weather usually becomes sufficiently warm to start vegetation, so that thus early the prairies become beautifully verdant, and many of Flora's choicest gifts appear, to herald the approach of summer. Now the summer winds, which are from the west and north, begin to prevail; the howl of the winter storm, and the roar of the southern winds, are hushed to silence; the hills and valleys are gently fanned by the western zephyr from the bosom of the Pacific; and the sun, pouring his floods of light and heat from a cloudless sky, causes nature, as by enchantment, to enrobe herself in all the glories of summer. The delightful weather thus ushered in continues with but little variation throughout the entire summer, with occasional showers; but these are much ' like angels' visits, few and far between.'

" Generally, in the months of July, August, and September the ground becomes exceedingly dry; but the rains that fall in April, May, and June, with the moisture which is deposited in the heavy dews of the valleys, serve to insure the crops by bringing the grains and vegetables to maturity.

"The temperature of the summer ranges from sixty-five to eighty degrees at noon in the shade, but the evenings are much cooler. There is no such thing as sultry weather on this part of the Pacific coast. The nights in this respect are admirable for rest and sleep."

From a personal experience and observation extending through a period of twenty-nine years, we are fully prepared to express the opinion that the climate of Oregon is decidedly favorable to the promotion of health. And why should it not be? The temperature is remarkably uniform, particularly in the western half of the country. Oregon is not subject to the evils resulting from the sudden changes from extreme heat to extreme cold, as are most of the states east of the Rocky Mountains.

The exhilarating ocean breeze, which fans the country almost every day during the summer, contributes greatly to purify the atmosphere; and this circumstance, in connection with the facts that there is little decaying vegetable matter, and but few dead swamps and marshes to exhale their poisonous miasma to infect the surrounding regions, are sufficient to show that this country must be the abode of health, and that human life is as likely to be protracted, and men and women as likely to die of old age here, as in almost any other portion of the world.

But every country has its defects, and this is not free from them. It is neither the garden of Eden, nor is it a barren waste. That it is a land of valleys and mountains, of rivers and streamlets, of mighty forests and extended prairies, of a salubrious and healthy climate, a rich and productive soil, of abundant deposits of mineral wealth, and of boundless lumbering agricultural, pastoral, mechanical, and manufacturing resources, the foregoing remarks will fully show.

Such are the main characteristics of the field of our operations as a Church within the limits of the Oregon Conference. It is not assuming too much to say, that, for the moral, intellectual, and religious culture of the present population, and of the multitudes who are destined in the future to crowd every part of that extended country, there rests upon the Methodist Episcopal Church a very great responsibility. Her system in every respect is fully adapted to the condition of the country, and no other system extant can compete with hers. Her spiritual Christianity, her itinerant and extemporaneous preaching, her songs of praise, her high religious experience, and all her ancient modes of worship, and especially her camp-meetings, to which the bright, clear summers of the country are peculiarly adapted, cannot fail, if properly brought to bear upon the masses by a consecrated ministry in connection with a sanctified literature, to check the progress of error and vice, to counterbalance the influence of Skepticism and Popery, to roll back defiant Mormonism and Deism and Spiritism to their native hell, to quicken dead souls into spiritual life, and to preserve the country to a pure religion, a true patriotism, substantial happiness, and a perpetuated prosperity.

The Methodist Episcopal Church has the right to lead on the sacramental hosts of God's elect on the Pacific coast, arising from priority of occupancy and organization. She was the first established; and the locality of the first class, which was organized by Rev. Jason Lee, in the fall of 1834, was at a point ten miles below the city of Salem; but subsequently the class removed to that place, so that really, the Salem Church was the first Christian organization in the Oregon Territory, and first Protestant Church west of the Rocky Mountains.

The history of the rise and progress of the Methodist Episcopal Church within the limits of the Oregon Conference would be replete with interest; but it must constitute the subject of a future volume, our present plan not permitting us even to introduce an outline. All that we have space to furnish is a simple statement of the present condition of the Church in the wide-spread field which is covered by the Oregon Conference.

Within this field, the boundaries of which have been given in the first part of this volume, there are six presiding elders' districts, three of which are entirely within the state of Oregon, and one, the Walla Walla District, is divided by the line between Oregon and Washington Territory, and the other two lie within the limits of said Territory. Each one of these districts, if we except the Yakima Indian Mission, is much larger in extent of country than many of the conferences of the Atlantic states.

In the whole conference there are upward of fifty appointments, besides the districts, the institutions of learning, and the *Pacific Advocate*. There were but fifty-five preachers to supply this vast field of labor, and, consequently, many portions of it will fail to be reached by the ministry of the Methodist Episcopal Church during the present year. Besides the fifty-five effective men there are five who are returned superannuated, and two supernumerary, making in all sixty-two preachers, embracing those who are yet on trial. There are sixty-eight local preachers, four thousand two hundred and eighteen members and probationers, forty-three houses of worship, estimated at seventy-five thousand dollars, twenty-seven parsonages, worth thirty thousand dollars, sixty-two Sabbath-schools, five hundred and thirty-four officers and teachers, three thousand two hundred and ninety-nine scholars, and thirteen thousand nine hundred and eighty-two volumes in libraries.

When compared with the numerical strength of the Church in many other conferences, the Oregon Conference looks indeed very small; but considered in proportion to the population of the state, it will compare favorably even with the conferences embracing New York.

CHAPTER XIV.

REMINISCENCES OF MISSIONARY LIFE.

It was on the 18th day of August, 1840, that Rev. Jason Lee, Dr. Elijah White, myself, and an Indian guide, whom we designated by the name of Captain, started from the old mission premises on the Willamette to perform a missionary tour to the Umpqua Valley, then to white men but little known. Our specific object was to explore the country watered by the Umpqua River, with a view to the establishment of a missionary station somewhere within its limits. Report had made the number of Indians in the country so great that it was thought to be a very eligible position for the establishment of missionary operations. But before deciding in reference to a mission, we resolved to examine the country and satisfy ourselves. The mode of traveling we adopted was on horseback, and in addition to our riding horses, we had three for carrying our baggage, and four spare ones, that in case of the loss or failure of any we might not be left destitute. This was a precaution in those days indispensably necessary to be taken by all who would secure their ultimate safety in traversing the extended plains of this wild country. As this was the first prairie expedition with which I had ever been connected, it was necessary for me at the outset to learn the peculiarities of horseback traveling on the Pacific coast. Mr. Lee had performed two journeys across the Rocky Mountains, and was well qualified to be my instructor. Watching him closely while he was packing our bedding, provisions, and cooking utensils on the backs of the horses, I soon observed that it required considerable skill and practice to wind the lash-rope around the pack and the body of the horse, so as to secure the burden to the back of the animal in case of fright, stumbling, or running against any obstruction, all of which, in the process of binding the packs, it was necessary to guard against with the utmost precaution.

Mr. Lee magnified his office as our instructor by packing the three horses himself; then we all mounted, each man with his gun athwart the pommel of his saddle, and our little cavalcade put off on a moderate gallop across the beautiful and fertile plain lying in the rear and south of the mission premises. Traveling ten miles to the south, at noon we reached the place where the city of Salem now stands, then known by the Indian name of Chemekete. Here the Oregon Mission had broken ground preparatory to the erection of a saw and grist mill, and here it was in contemplation to establish the Mission Manual Labor School. This locality, though almost a perfect solitude so far as the existence of humanity was concerned, appeared to us to be one of the most delightful that we had ever seen. The extensive and fertile plains surrounding it, the enchanting nature of its scenery, and the fine water privilege, afforded by the beautiful rivulet meandering through it, rendered it, in our judgment, a place of great future importance. Surveying this beautiful locality, and indulging in many conjectures in regard to the probable time that would elapse before its then silent and broad area would become the theater of busy life, and a flourishing city with its din and noise occupy the fields of solitude by which we were surrounded, we proceeded on our course through a country beautifully diversified with rising grounds, varying from the gentle undulation to the majestic hill, and fertile valleys, variegated with here and there a grove of yellow and white oak, and now and then a stately fir which had braved the fury of a thousand storms, and at nightfall we encamped near one of the tributaries of the Willamette River, called "Santiam's Fork." We reposed for the night under the wide-spread branches of a majestic fir, and our trusty horses cropped the wild grass of the prairie around us while we slept. Six o'clock the next morning found us prepared to resume our journey, and at twelve we had traveled twenty miles over a beautiful prairie country now densely populated, then without an inhabitant, when we stopped for dinner on the bank of the Callapooia Creek. Repacking our animals after resting two hours, we traveled in the evening about ten miles, and encamped for the night by the side of a small pool of water in the center of a large prairie. The country through which we passed was flat, low, and subject to inundations. The prairies had been all overrun with fire a short time previous, and it was with difficulty that we could find sufficient feed for our horses. However, around the pool the grass was so green that the fire had passed it by, and this rendered it a suitable place to spend the night, particularly for our animals. There was something very peculiar about this pool. It embraced a superficial area of some ten rods of ground, with no visible inlet or outlet, and it was several miles from any other water, though the water of the pool was nearly upon a level with the surrounding land. It was also literally filled with frogs, there being at least five to every square foot.

We spread down our bed of blankets where the grass was abundant, but soon after lying down we were disturbed by a somewhat novel circumstance. I began to feel a gentle stir directly under my back, though for some time I made no mention of it, not yet deciding what it might be. But as the effort beneath me continued, as though some living being was thrown into convulsions through suffocation, I at length cried out that there was some living creature under my blanket. The "captain," understanding, exclaimed, "A snake! a snake!" and knowing that rattlesnakes were no uncommon thing on these prairies, and not fancying one as my bedfellow, I sprang to my feet, seized my blankets, and scattered my bed around the prairie, when, to the amusement of our party, out jumped a large bullfrog, who made his best way back to the pool.

After the excitement occasioned by this little episode passed away we again composed ourselves to sleep, and on the morning of the twentieth arose invigorated, and were moving on at an early hour; and traveling twenty-five miles, we found ourselves at one o'clock on the bank of the Willamette River, at the place where we designed to cross that stream, our trail having been thus far on the east side of the river. Examining the ford we found the river too deep and the current too strong to admit of our crossing our pack-horses in safety, and discovering an Indian below us in his canoe, we beckoned him to come up to us, which he accordingly did. He appeared very shy at first, was entirely naked, not having so much clothing as an apron of fig-leaves; but after a while we induced him to take our things into his canoe and carry them across the river. Dr. White accompanied him, while Mr. Lee, myself, and the captain crossed over the horses. The water was up to the animals' backs, and the current so strong that we feared it would bear us down; but with the exception of getting thoroughly wet, we gained the opposite shore without difficulty. Here the most luxurious grass covered the prairie, and we allowed our horses an hour to avail themselves of its benefits, while at the same time we refreshed ourselves from our diminishing stock of viands, and then continued our way over a delightful plain known as the Grand Prairie for fifteen miles, and at night stopped on the California trail at a place which, by the numerous fires which had been built around, and other signs which we discovered, we judged had been recently occupied by a band of Indians. None, however, had the temerity to show themselves. Friday, 21, we resumed our march, and traveling about twenty miles over a rolling country, presenting almost every variety of scenery, we halted for dinner on a stream called "Bridge River," on account of a log bridge having been thrown across it by some California party. This stream runs in a deep cut, and but for the bridge would have been difficult to cross. It is now known as Siuselaw.

In the afternoon we crossed the Callapooia Mountains, which consist of a vast assemblage of overgrown hills thrown together in wild confusion, and covered with a heavy forest of fir and cedar trees. The latter is the most stately and majestic timber of the kind which I had ever seen. On beholding it one is reminded of the Scripture account of the cedars of Lebanon. It required three hours to cross this mountain, and as we were descending it to the south the fire was making sad havoc with the fine timber with which its sides were adorned. In some places it raged so fiercely along the trail as to render it quite difficult for us to pass; but urging our way along, we succeeded at sundown in reaching Elk River, at the foot of the mountain, and crossing over, we camped for the night on a beautiful plain on its south bank.

Saturday, 22, leaving the California trail, we took a path that bore further to the west, following the direction of the Elk River. During the day we passed over an exceedingly mountainous country. Some of the mountains were rocky and precipitous, and it was with great difficulty that we were able to keep our balance on the narrow path among the rocks that in its zigzag course marked our way up and down their almost perpendicular sides; but urging our way along, now plunging into the deep ravine, now scaling the high ledge of rocks, now climbing the precipitous mountains, now descending into the dark valley, and fording Elk River over the slippery rocks, where the water came to our saddle seats not less than five times, at two P. M. we found ourselves on the bank of the Umpqua River, directly opposite a trading fort owned by the Hudson's Bay Company. We stripped our horses of their packs and saddles, and turned them loose to roam at large on the north side of the river until we performed a voyage to the coast, and crossing over in a canoe, we were kindly received at the fort by an old Frenchman having charge of it by the name of Gonea. We were made welcome to all the comforts the place afforded, and a king could not have done better. This Frenchman lived with an Indian woman, whom he called his wife, and who belonged to a tribe that resided on the Pacific coast, near the mouth of the Umpqua River.

A liberal supply of boiled pork and potatoes, furnished us by our Indian hostess, and a good night's rest on a bed of Mackinaw blankets, wonderfully recruited us after the excessive fatigues of our journey. We found no Indians around the fort, except a small band of twenty-five Callapooias from the Willamette Valley. These, on Sunday, the 23d, we collected in one of the huts within the stockades of the fort, and held religious service with them, Mr. Lee addressing them concerning the things that belonged to their peace ; and the chief, who understood the jargon, interpreted it to his people. As we expected to return by the way of his country, we engaged to meet him and his people on a certain day and give them another talk.

On Monday morning, the 24th, Dr. White and the captain left us and returned to the Willamette, and Mr. Lee and myself went about making preparations to visit the Indians at the mouth of the Umpqua River. We had been informed by Mr. Gonea that there would be great danger in our going among them alone, and indeed he seemed to stand in the utmost fear of them. Of their hostility to the whites, and especially the Americans, we were ourselves aware, as they had in more than one instance attacked them, and only a few years before they had cut off an entire party of fourteen men who were coming through from California to Oregon, except three persons, who fortunately escaped to tell the story of the massacre of their companions. But Providence seemed to favor our design of going among them. On Sunday afternoon a brother of the Frenchman's wife, with a small party of Indians from the coast, arrived at the fort, having come up the river in a canoe. After having an interview with them, we proposed to the Frenchman that his wife, who, we learned, was a relative of the principal chiefs of the tribe, should take us under her protection, and with her brother and his party conduct us to her people. To this the Frenchman consented, saying, "Now I think the danger small, before it was great." According to arrangements which were mainly superintended by the Indian woman, under whose protection we had placed ourselves, at ten o'clock on Monday, the 24th, we put out with our light canoe into the dashing current of the Umpqua. We ran a number of narrow shoots where the current was at least twelve knots an hour, and in some instances shot past the rocks which projected into the stream with the velocity of an arrow; but our Indians, of whom there were seven, showed themselves to be in their proper element by the astonishing dexterity with which they ran the dangerous rapids with which the river abounds. Fifteen miles below the fort the river rushes over a ledge of rocks in a number of narrow channels, and falling about twenty-five feet in so many rods, forms a fine salmon fishery. Here we found, crowded into four small lodges, about one hundred Indians, exceedingly squalid in their appearance, and subsisting entirely on fish. We remained here but a few moments, and, passing on, nine of them, five men and four women, jumped into a large canoe for the purpose of accompanying us down the river.

Having thus increased our company more than half we proceeded on our voyage, contemplating the barbarous appearance of both animate and inanimate nature around us until the gathering shadows reminded us that night approached, and running our canoes in along the right hand shore. we at length found a place sufficiently broad from the river to the base of the mountain to admit of our encamping, and here we pitched our tent for the night.

Our Indians soon struck up two good fires, one for themselves, and one for us. Mr. Lee and myself prepared our supper, our female friend providing us with a choice piece of salmon, which she had broiled, and which, with bread, butter, and tea, constituted our humble repast. Never did we partake of a supper with a better relish.

While we were enjoying it, our newly-made neophytes prepared supper for themselves, and it was not a little interesting, to one who was not familiar with such scenes, to see them prepare their food. Their supper consisted of fresh salmon and a species of hazel-nut, which is found in the country in great abundance. Having made a suitable fire, they commenced the operation of cooking their salmon. This was performed in the following manner. They all provided themselves with sticks about three feet long, pointed at one end and split at the other. They then apportioned the salmon, each one receiving a large piece, and filling it with splinters to prevent its falling to pieces when cooking, placed it with great care into the forked end of the stick, and fastened the forks together with a small withe. Then placing themselves around the fire so as to describe a circle, they stuck the pointed end of the sticks into the ground a short distance from the fire, inclining the top toward the flames so as to bring the salmon in contact with the heat, thus forming a kind of pyramid of salmon over the whole fire. One side being cooked the other was turned to the heat, and speedily the whole was prepared for eating. Stones were then provided for the purpose of cracking nuts, and all being seated on the ground the eating process commenced. The extreme novelty of their appearance, the nut cracking, the general merriment, the apparent jokes, ready repartees, and bursts of laughter were sufficient to have excited the risibilities of even a Romish priest, however phlegmatic. And certainly a more jovial set of fellows than these sons of nature I have never seen. They were as untamed as the elk they chase over their mountains, but they feasted upon their fish and nuts with as much of a zest, and with as much seeming satisfaction to themselves, as the most fashionable and refined party that ever graced the gay saloon ever enjoyed while regaling themselves with the most costly viands. Supper being over, we called the attention of the Indians while we engaged in our evening devotions. I sang a hymn, and then we both engaged in prayer, the Indians all kneeling with us, and evidently manifesting a peculiar interest in what was passing before them. And thought I, Why should they not feel interested? Never before had the death-like silence which reigned along this valley been broken by the voice of prayer and praise. The somber shades of moral darkness, which had ever cast a melancholy gloom upon the people, had never before been penetrated by the rays of Gospel light. The heralds of mercy, who bring glad tidings of good things to those who wander upon the dark mountains, had never before set their feet upon these hostile shores. After prayer Mr. Lee addressed the Indians through our interpreter in relation to the objects of our visit, and they listened as to a story calculated to excite the utmost wonder, but expressed great satisfaction at what they had heard. At ten o'clock we lay down upon our bed of blankets in quietness, slept in peace, arose in the morning in safety, and breaking our fast on bread and salmon, proceeded on our way along the widening Umpqua toward the great Pacific, and at noon arrived among the Indians at the mouth of the river.

We found the Indians living in three small villages, the larger being on the south, and the other two on the north side of the river. The whole number, including some that were absent, as near as we could ascertain, amounted to about three hundred men, women, and children. About one third of the tribe had gone into the mountains for the purpose of gathering berries. It was thought best by our guardian and adviser to pitch our tent some half a mile distant from the larger village, on the south side of the river, near which, she told us, the chiefs and their people would meet us to hold a talk.

Though the news of our arrival quickly flew to all the lodges, none of the people came near us until we sent them a message that we had come and desired to see them at our tent. Complying with our invitation, three chiefs and fifty-five of their people, mostly men, came out to see us. Seating themselves in the sand in the form of a crescent in front of our tent, the chiefs very ceremoniously informed us through our interpreter that "they were ready to hear what we had to say." Mr. Lee then addressed them on the objects of our visit. He told them whence we came; how long it took us to perform our voyage from our native land to their country; that we had many friends at home who desired us not to leave them; that a sense of duty had brought us to their country to tell them about Jesus Christ; that in coming to them we had been exposed to a thousand dangers, but had been preserved in the midst of them all by the "Great Chief above;" that we had heard much about them and the Indians generally in the country, and that we were glad now to be permitted to see them for ourselves, and become acquainted with them. He then inquired of them whether they approved of our visit, and whether they desired to be instructed?

After a few moments' consultation among themselves, the chiefs, one after another, arose, and advancing to within six feet of Mr. Lee, addressed him in substance as follows, there being but little difference in their speeches: "Great Chief, we are very much pleased with our lands. We love this world. We wish to live a great while. We very much desire to become old men before we die. It is true we have killed many people, but we have never killed any but bad people. Many lies have been told about us. We have been called a bad people, and we are glad that you have come to see us for yourselves. We have seen some white people before, but they came to get our beaver. None ever came before to instruct us. We are glad to see you; we want to learn; we wish to throw away all our bad things and become good." They spoke very loud, and their gestures were remarkably violent. Sometimes in the course of their speeches they would rise upon tiptoe, with both hands stretched high above their heads, and then throw themselves forward until their faces almost touched the ground. After they concluded their speeches they returned to their places in the sand, and told us that they would then hear us more particularly on the subject of our mission.

At the request of Mr. Lee, who was no singer himself, I stepped out into an open space and struck into Heber's Missionary Hymn,

" From Greenland's icy mountains," etc.,

and while singing the first verse the Indians all seated themselves on the sand, forming three fourths of a circle around us, and then with the most fixed attention listened to the remaining part of the hymn. We then both engaged in prayer, all the Indians kneeling with us, and invoked upon our enterprise the blessing of Almighty God. Though our congregation was totally ignorant of the true nature of worship, yet the scene to us was deeply affecting. Never before had they thus bowed; never before had they heard the voice of prayer. We then preached to them the Gospel as well as we could through the jargon of the country. giving them an account of the creation of the world, the fall of man, the advent, sufferings, death, resurrection, ascension, and intercession of Christ to save mankind from sin, death, and hell, all of which was interpreted to her people by our female friend. We cherished the fond belief that, for the first time in their history, a few rays from the Sun of Righteousness had pierced the gloom of the long and dismal night which had hung around them. The chiefs expressed their approbation of what they had heard, saying "it was all very good," and that "they had never heard such things before." They then all dispersed and went to their lodges, and Mr. Lee and myself prepared and took our supper of salmon and bread, the last of which our wives had prepared for us ten days before. After the shades of the evening had gathered around us, the Indians all returned to our tent, for the purpose, as they told us, of "hearing us talk to God" previous to our lying down for the night. They collected wood and built a large fire, and then seated themselves around it. I then sang another hymn, after which we again engaged in prayer. As they still lingered around, Mr. Lee gave them another lesson from the word of the Lord, after which they reluctantly scattered away to their wigwams, leaving us to repose ourselves on our bed of blankets spread upon the sand.

Mr. Lee having been accustomed to such experience slept soundly during the night; but the strange scenes of the preceding day, the circumstances attending the night, and the remembrance that we were lying at the mercy of those who had proved themselves among the most treacherous of savages, produced such an effect upon my nerves as to destroy all inclination to close my eyes. From hearing noises outside, I frequently drew aside the tent cloth and cast a look around, and in every instance observed that our protectress and her brother and another Indian, who had lived among the whites but had returned to his people, were keeping up a large fire in front of our tent, which threw its light back into the dense forest which lay in our rear. Sometimes they were in earnest conversation; then they would pile on the dry sticks until the flames would ascend to the height of ten feet, and enabled them to distinguish every object within a circle of twenty rods. This they continued during the whole night, neither of them for a moment attempting to sleep. That night of anxiety wore away and the morning dawned, and none of the Indians, to our knowledge, had shown any disposition to molest us during the night. After our breakfast was over, they all collected again, and seating themselves on the sand, expressed a wish once more to witness our devotions before parting with us. Accordingly we again offered up our fervent prayers to the Desire of nations in their behalf. After prayers we addressed to them a few parting words, and were preparing to leave them, when one of the chiefs, standing on his knees, began to speak. He said he was very glad that we had come to see them; that their hearts toward us were like our hearts toward them; that he wanted us to continue with them another day, and tell them more about God; that they had heard about us, and had been told we were a bad people; that they were glad to see us for themselves, and were convinced that what they had heard was a lie; that they now believed us to be a good people, and that they meant to be good also. When they were informed that probably the next summer one of us would come and visit them again they were exceedingly well pleased, and said, "It is very good, we will be glad to see you."

Having fully satisfied ourselves with regard to the number, disposition, and accessibility of the Indians in this solitary region, we told the chiefs that we must go, and the people all came out to witness our departure. Distributing among them a few presents, on Wednesday morning at nine o'clock, driven forward by the strokes of the Indian paddle, we were rounding a high bluff situated on the south side of the mouth of Umpqua River, and forming one side of a small bay in the bosom of which the Indian village we had just left was situated, and which was fast disappearing behind the point of the projecting cliff. Crossing the mouth of the river, which is about one mile wide, we stopped a few moments on the north side to lay in a little provision, and give ourselves an opportunity to take some observations of the surrounding country.

Contemplating the probable period when the barbarism of both animate and inanimate nature along this river shall give place to civilization and Christianity, we turned our backs upon the great

Pacific, and by the combined assistance of the Indian paddle and the flood tide passed rapidly up the river, and at nightfall encamped again at the salmon fishery. We here ascertained that the Indians at the falls are not of the same tribe of those on the coast, though they speak a similar language.

Spreading our blankets down upon the rocks, we slept without molestation though surrounded by treacherous savages. The next day we started at an early hour, and though we had but fifteen miles to travel, yet on account of the numerous strong rapids we had to ascend, and the portages we had to make, we were till sunset in reaching the fort. We were again welcomed by the Frenchman, and refreshed with a supper of bread made of the flour of wheat pounded in a mortar, and roasted elk beef. During the evening Mr. Gonca came to us very much excited, and congratulated us on the safe guardianship his wife had exercised over us in our absence. He told us that in all probability we should have been robbed of all that we had, if we had not lost our lives, had it not been for the faithfulness of his wife and her brother. He said that one of the chiefs of the clan we had visited was at the fort on our first arrival, and saw us as we came in. Learning that we designed to visit his people on the coast, and excited with the utmost fear, he hastened down the river and reported many evil things about us, intending thereby to instigate the Indians to prevent our going among them. Mr. Lee had brought with him a fowling piece, and had in his possession a patent shot-pouch. This was the thing that had alarmed the chief. One story he told was that we had brought medicine in a bag that Mr. Lee wore on his neck for the purpose of killing them all off, and that if we were permitted to come among them the fatal bag would be opened and they would all be destroyed. This story exasperated many of them, especially the younger men of the tribe, and Gonea's wife told him that we were in the greatest danger the night we slept on the coast. She said that the Indians were lurking about us during that whole night, seeking an opportunity to attack when it was dark around our tent; but that she and her brother kept a constant watch over us until morning. This explained to me the exciting circumstances of that anxious night already described. The young men of the tribe had resolved to attack us in the night, and but for the wise precaution of our protectress in first erecting our tent in an open space midway between the ocean and the forest, and second, in keeping up a bright fire during the whole night and watching over us, we doubtless had fallen victims to savage barbarity, and our mission there would have ended, and this story had never been told. But be this as it may, at the time we were not sensible that we were particularly exposed, and, indeed, we felt ourselves safe under the protection of our heavenly Father.

On Friday morning we prepared to continue our exploring tour further into the interior and up the valley of the Umpqua River. Through the kind assistance of Mr. Gonea we procured an Indian guide of the Umpqua tribe, whom the French had designated by the name of "We We," who well understood the jargon of the country and could officiate as our interpreter. The forenoon was spent mostly in finding our horses and preparing our pack. All being ready, between twelve and one o'clock we moved up the river, our guide in advance, and passing over a number of high hills and fording the Umpqua three times where the bottom was very rocky and the water was up to our horses' backs, we camped at night on the bank of a small rivulet and under the shelter of a grove of fir. We had traveled twenty miles.

Saturday, 29, continued our toilsome way over mountains and through valleys, and at noon arrived at the head-quarters of that portion of the Indians of this valley distinguished by the name of the river. Here the head chief of the Umpquas had fixed a temporary abode, and here one of those circumstances had recently transpired which, though of common occurrence in heathen countries, where the vicious propensities of human nature are permitted to revel uncontrolled, are sufficient to freeze the heart's blood even to contemplate at a distance. A report had reached the ears of the chief of the Umpquas that his wife had been guilty of infidelity toward her husband. This so enraged him that, without knowing whether the report was true or false, he seized his musket and went directly to the lodge where his wife was sitting and deliberately shot her through the heart.

Soon after our arrival on the side of the river opposite to the village, this chief with the few men that were with him came over to see us. He made us a long speech, which was interpreted to us by We We, in making which one of his first objects seemed to be to justify the murder of his wife, and then to express his gratitude that Christian teachers had come among them. While he was haranguing us, my attention was caught away from his speech by a terrible burst of heathen passions which took place on the other side of the river among the lodges. In the absence of the men the women had a regular fight, scratching and biting each other, and tearing one another's hair, and squalling most frightfully. So tremendous was the explosion that even the chief paused in the midst of his address and significantly remarked, "Our women are *hias masicha* (very bad.)"

Such were the indications here that we came to the conclusion that the sooner we were out of the place the better it would be for us, and so soon as we had taken a little refreshment from our scanty stores, we told our guide that we were ready to proceed; but he positively refused to go any further that day, saying that it would be using his people very ill, and that the chief would be very angry with us if we did not stop and sleep with them one night. The contention became quite warm, and we began to consider ourselves in rather critical circumstances. If abandoned by our guide it was extremely doubtful, as we had traveled much of the distance without the sign of a trail, whether we could find our way back to the fort, or forward to the valley we were seeking.

But with all these difficulties we showed that we were fixed in our resolutions to leave this suspicious horde of savages before darkness should favor them in the execution of any treacherous designs which they might entertain toward us. Discovering that we were ready to mount our horses, We We became more pliable, and said that he would proceed with us on condition that we would pay him an extra shirt, having at first given him one shirt and a pair of pantaloons. Mr. Lee told him that he would give him no more, but to get rid of the difficulty I told We We that if he would go I would give him the additional shirt so soon as we should reach the California trail leading through the great valley. Turning to his people he addressed them a few words in the Umpqua language, and then told us he was ready to go. Accordingly we left this group of wretched beings about three o'clock P. M., and galloped swiftly over a little plain toward a high mountain. Three hours of hard labor in ascending and descending brought us to the foot of the mountain on the opposite side, and passing through a dense thicket we found ourselves again on the bank of the river. We We brought out a well-known Indian "whoop," and was answered by another Indian just below us on the river. Immediately four Indians came in sight with a canoe, and We We told us we had better unpack our horses, and put all our things in the canoe to be taken up the river a few miles beyond a place where the pass by the way of the trail was very rocky, narrow, and dangerous.

But the strange conduct of the Indians we had just left had excited our suspicions, and supposing that those in the canoe were some of the same party whom We We had perhaps caused to come up the river for no good purpose, we resolved to keep what we had under our own eye as long as we could. We therefore told the guide that we should keep our things on our horses' backs. We We hung his head, and told us we would be sorry for it before we got through.

We proceeded, but found it as We We had fore-warned us. Our trail lay along a frightful precipice which towered far above us, and extended far below us, and in some places was so narrow and broken that a misstep would have precipitated us headlong on the rocks below, or into the rushing waters of the Umpqua. In one instance my own horse, which I happened to be leading at the time instead of riding, fell fifteen feet down the rocks, but catching upon a kind of shelf on the side of the precipice, at length succeeded in gaining the trail without receiving much injury.

But we were not destined to make the pass without receiving a proof that the caution of We We was well founded. We were attempting to pass the last dangerous point when " Old Pomp," our pack-horse, lost his footing, and rolling down a rocky steep of some thirty feet, went backward into the Umpqua

River. We had fastened around his neck a lasso some forty feet long, and the loose end of the lasso remaining on shore, we succeeded, by drawing it around a tree, in raising and keeping the head of the animal above the water until We We had relieved him of his pack. While We We dashed in among the rocks, where the water was up to his neck, and was exerting himself to his utmost to relieve the horse of his burden and save him from drowning, he tauntingly told us that we might have saved ourselves that difficulty if we had trusted to the honesty of an Indian, and we ourselves began to suspect that our fears had been quite groundless. It required our utmost efforts to keep the horse from drowning ; but after we had relieved him of his pack he managed himself a little better, and finding a place which was not quite so steep as the one where he entered the river, we succeeded at that point in getting him up on the rocky shore. All our bedding, provisions, etc., were thoroughly soaked; but gathering up what was not spoiled, putting some on the horses, and carrying some on our own shoulders, we started on, being informed by our guide that it was not far to a fine prairie.

Night began to set in, and as we left the scene of our disaster we entered a dense forest of fir, and the gloom continued to thicken around us until we were enveloped in total darkness. We were leading our animals by the bridle, and feeling our way among the trees in the midst of darkness so dense that it was impossible to see a white horse though within a foot of one's face, when we became so entangled among the logs, ravines, and brush that we found it was impossible to go either forward or backward, to the right or to the left, and colloquizing a little through the darkness, we came to the conclusion to tie our horses to the trees and make the best of the night we could. Having a few matches in my pocket that I had preserved from getting wet, and the leaves and limbs under my feet being perfectly dry, I soon had the forest illuminated, and then was disclosed to our view a most horrible place. We sought for a spot on which to sleep, but could find none level and large enough to stretch ourselves upon. We must either bend over the top of a knoll, or double up in a ravine, or we must remain in a standing or sitting posture. We preferred the second; so wrapping ourselves in our blankets which we had taken time to dry, and rolling into a hollow, we tried to compose ourselves to sleep; but the crackling of limbs by the tramp of our horses, the howling of wolves, and the screech of an owl above our heads, frequently disturbed our repose. The morning sun, however, enabled us so to adjust our rather disarranged affairs that we could quite comfortably prosecute our journey.

The next day was Sabbath, but we could not remain where we were, and we resolved to keep the day in the best manner we could under the circumstances. Learning from We We that a band of the Umpquas was a few miles away we resolved to visit them. We found about thirty, with whom we tarried for several hours, and preached to them "Jesus and the resurrection." They behaved themselves quite orderly, and were anxious to render us all the assistance in their power; and they told us they very much wanted a missionary to come and live among them. Not desiring to sleep in the vicinity of their camp we made signs of wishing to leave, and the old men came around us, of whom there were several, and patting us on the shoulders professed to have conceived for us a strong attachment. But we concluded that their love for us was not so ardent as to render it desirable on our part to stop with them over night; and as our provisions were nearly exhausted, we decided to set our faces toward the Willamette Valley. Gathering up the wreck of our pack we again mounted, and fording the Umpqua for the last time, traveled about twelve miles, and encamped on the bank of a beautiful rivulet known as the Callapooia Creek. We had traveled during the day about twenty-five miles over as fine a country as can be found in any part of the world. An agreeable variety of hills, plains, and groves of pine, fir, and oak, constituted scenery of the most picturesque beauty, and the eye was never weary in gazing upon the ever-varying picture. Though the country was destitute of inhabitants, except the wild beasts and savages as wild as they, yet we could not but contemplate the time as not far distant when it would be teeming with all the activities and associations of a civilized and Christian people.

The Indians inhabiting the Umpqua Valley from

the Pacific Ocean one hundred miles into the interior were very few. All that we could find, or get any satisfactory evidence as then in existence, did not exceed three hundred and seventy-five souls. These lived in several different clans, were hostile to each other, and spoke two distinct languages. They were favorable toward the establishment of a mission in their country, but seemed to think that the greatest benefit it would confer upon them would be to enable them to sell their beaver and deer skins for a higher price. The most of them, residing as they did on the coast, were almost inaccessible, and the establishment and support of a mission among them would have been attended with immense expense.

The best information we could obtain from the Indians and others, led us to the conclusion that the time doubtless had been when the Indians of the valley had been vastly more numerous, but by disease and family wars their numbers had been greatly reduced, and were still rapidly diminishing. Under the solemn impression that the doom of extinction was suspended over this wretched race, and that the hand of Providence was removing it to give place to a people more worthy of this beautiful and fertile country, we committed ourselves to quietness and repose for the night.

Having fulfilled his engagement in bringing us to this point, our guide took leave of us and returned to his people; and on Monday morning, September 1, having the California trail as our guide, we quickened our pace northwardly, and at noon stopped for dinner on Elk River, at the place where, on going out, we left the trail. In the afternoon we again passed over the Callapooia Mountains, and found that the fire was still raging with increased violence. A vast quantity of the large fir and cedar timber had been burned down, and in some places the trail was so blockaded with fallen trees that it was almost impossible to proceed; while now and then we passed a giant cedar or mammoth fir, through whose trunks the fire had made a passage, and was still flaming like an oven. Every few moments these majestic spars would come crashing, crackling, and thundering to the ground.

But while the fire was thus robbing the mountain of its glory, we pushed on over its desolated ridges, and at sundown arrived on a little prairie at its northern base, where we made our camp; but we were often awakened during the night by the crash of falling timber.

Tuesday, 2, proceeded, and at noon arrived in the southern part of the Willamette Valley, where, according to engagement, we met the Callapooia chief. He had collected about sixty of his people, and said he had about forty more. We remained with them four hours, and, as best we could, preached to them "the unsearchable riches of Christ." Many of them were sick, and they appeared wretched beyond description. Our bowels of compassion yearned over them, but it was not in our power to help them.

Commending them to God, at four P. M. we pursued our way, but finding no water, we did not camp till eleven o'clock at night. Though it was very dark, our Spanish horses kept the narrow trail winding along down the valley, while ever and anon the stillness of the evening would be broken by the dismal howling of the wolves that prowled around us. Finding no water yet, fearing that our horses would fail, we stripped them on the open prairie, and turned them loose to shirk for themselves, and lay ourselves down upon our blankets without supper, and with our lips parched with thirst. Next morning, however, like Hagar in the desert, we found ourselves within a short distance of good water. Here I roasted a small duck for our breakfast, which the Callapooia chief had given us, and which we ate with neither bread nor sauce; but a cup of coffee, that *sine qua non* for prairie traveling, washed it down, and on the strength of it we traveled forty miles during the day over a country of surpassing loveliness. Surely, thought I, infinite skill has here been employed in fitting up a country which requires nothing more than a population under the influence of the religion of Christ to render it a perfect paradise. The last night we encamped within fifteen miles of our families and friends, and, picking the bones of our duck, which we had the precaution to carry with us, we rested upon our blankets until morning.

Thursday, the 4th, weary and hungry, about two o'clock P. M. we reached our home in safety, but found that our families in our absence had been invaded by disease; but having been constantly in a healthy exercise ourselves we returned in the enjoyment of excellent health, and the temporary weakness resulting from excessive labor and the want of food for the previous three days was soon remedied by an appropriation of "nature's sweet restorer" and the ample viands spread before us by our companions.

Twenty-eight years have passed since this, to me, memorable tour of observation was performed. The country then, from Salem to Mexico, the distance of seven hundred miles, so far as civilized humanity was concerned, was one vast solitude, now the whole extent is occupied by Anglo-Saxons, and everywhere appear the signs of an advancing civilization and Christianity. The same country which twenty-eight years ago was so desolate and dreary, for four years past has constituted a presiding elder's district, where the writer has been preaching the Gospel to thousands upon thousands in every part of the land. Let it never be forgotten that the missionary of the cross was not only the pioneer, but the instrument of establishing a Christian civilization on the shores of the great Pacific. Surely the wilderness and the solitary places have been made glad for them, and the desert has rejoiced and blossomed as the rose.

THE END.